D'accord! 1

Langue et culture du monde francophone

Cahier de l'élève

ISBN: 978-1-62680-201-8

11 BB 20

Printed in the United States of America.

Table of Contents

Nom ______________________ Date ______________________

Unité 1

Leçon 1A

CONTEXTES

1 **Salutations** For each statement or question, write an appropriate response from the box.

Au revoir!	Il n'y a pas de quoi.	Comme ci, comme ça.
Enchanté.	Je vais bien, merci.	Je m'appelle Sylvie, et toi?
À tout à l'heure.	Monsieur Morel.	

1. Comment t'appelles-tu? ______________________
2. Merci. ______________________
3. Comment ça va? ______________________
4. Je vous présente Anne. ______________________
5. Comment allez-vous? ______________________
6. À plus tard. ______________________
7. Comment vous appelez-vous, Monsieur? ______________________
8. Bonne journée! ______________________

2 **Complétez** Complete these expressions with the missing words.

1. ____________ ça va?
2. Au ____________!
3. À plus ____________!
4. ____________ journée!
5. Excusez-____________.
6. Il n'y a pas de ____________.
7. Comment ____________-tu?
8. Je vous ____________ Martin.
9. ____________ rien.
10. Je ____________ bien, merci.

3 **Officielle ou informelle?** Indicate whether these expressions are used in formal or informal situations. If an expression may be used in either situation, check both columns.

	Situations officielles	Situations informelles
1. Pardon, Madame.	❍	❍
2. Il n'y a pas de quoi.	❍	❍
3. Ça va?	❍	❍
4. Bonsoir!	❍	❍
5. Je te présente…	❍	❍
6. Comment vous appelez-vous?	❍	❍
7. S'il te plaît.	❍	❍
8. Je vous en prie.	❍	❍
9. Et toi, comment vas-tu?	❍	❍
10. Bonsoir, Monsieur.	❍	❍
11. Salut, Caroline!	❍	❍
12. À bientôt!	❍	❍

Nom ______________________ Date ______________________

4 **Choisissez** Indicate whether the expressions in each pair have similar or opposite meanings.

	Similaire	Opposé
1. ici : là-bas	❍	❍
2. À tout à l'heure! : Au revoir!	❍	❍
3. Comment allez-vous? : Comment ça va?	❍	❍
4. Je vous en prie. : De rien.	❍	❍
5. S'il vous plaît. : Merci.	❍	❍
6. Je vais bien. : Je vais mal.	❍	❍
7. À bientôt! : À plus tard!	❍	❍
8. Salut! : Bonjour!	❍	❍
9. Madame : Monsieur	❍	❍
10. Comme ci, comme ça. : Pas mal.	❍	❍

5 **Conversation** Number the lines of this conversation in a logical order.

_______ À demain, Anne.
_______ Bonjour, Madame. Je m'appelle Anne.
_______ Moi aussi, je vais bien. Au revoir, Madame.
_______ Je vais très bien, merci. Et vous?
_______ Enchantée. Je m'appelle Madame Prévot.
_______ Comment allez-vous?

6 **Mini-dialogues** Write four brief conversations based on the illustration. Be sure to use appropriate forms of address.

1. **MME MONTREUIL** ______________________________

   PATRICIA ______________________________

2. **ANTOINE** ______________________________

   IRÈNE ______________________________

3. **PAULINE** ______________________________

   MARIE ______________________________

4. **XAVIER** ______________________________

   JEAN-MARC ______________________________

   FLORENT ______________________________

Nom ______________________ Date ______________________

CONTEXTES: AUDIO ACTIVITIES

1 **Identifiez** You will hear six short exchanges. For each one, decide whether it is a greeting, an introduction, or a leave-taking. Mark the appropriate column with an **X**.

Modèle

You hear: **AUDREY** Bonjour, Laura!
LAURA Salut, Audrey. Ça va?
AUDREY Ça va bien, merci. Et toi?
LAURA Pas mal.
You mark: an **X** under *Greeting*

	Greeting	Introduction	Leave-taking
Modèle	______	______	______
1.	______	______	______
2.	______	______	______
3.	______	______	______
4.	______	______	______
5.	______	______	______
6.	______	______	______

2 **Questions** Listen to each question or statement and respond with an answer from the list. Repeat the correct response after the speaker.

a. Enchanté(e).
b. À demain.
c. Je m'appelle Marie.
d. Il n'y a pas de quoi.
e. Comme ci, comme ça. Et toi?
f. Très bien, merci. Et vous?

3 **Associez** You will hear three conversations. Look at the drawings and write the number of the conversation under the appropriate group of people.

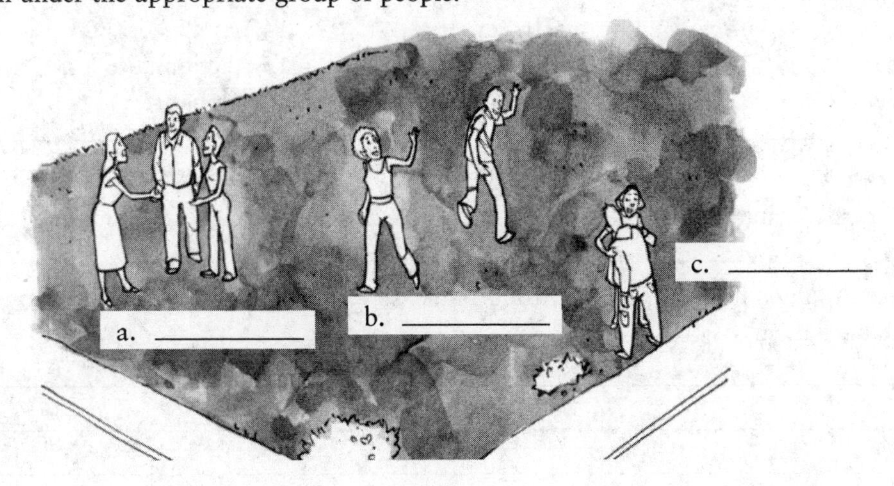

Nom ______________________ Date ______________________

LES SONS ET LES LETTRES

The French alphabet

The French alphabet is made up of the same 26 letters as the English alphabet. While they look the same, some letters are pronounced differently. They also sound different when you spell.

lettre	exemple	lettre	exemple	lettre	exemple
a (a)	adresse	j (ji)	justice	s (esse)	spécial
b (bé)	banane	k (ka)	kilomètre	t (té)	table
c (cé)	carotte	l (elle)	lion	u (u)	unique
d (dé)	dessert	m (emme)	mariage	v (vé)	vidéo
e (e)	rebelle	n (enne)	nature	w (double vé)	wagon
f (effe)	fragile	o (o)	olive	x (iks)	xylophone
g (gé)	genre	p (pé)	personne	y (i grec)	yoga
h (hache)	héritage	q (ku)	quiche	z (zède)	zéro
i (i)	innocent	r (erre)	radio		

Notice that some letters in French words have accents. You'll learn how they influence pronunciation in later lessons. Whenever you spell a word in French, include the name of the accent after the letter. For double letters, use **deux** (**deux** s).

accent	nom	exemple	orthographe
´	*accent aigu*	identité	*I-D-E-N-T-I-T-E-accent aigu*
`	*accent grave*	problème	*P-R-O-B-L-E-accent grave-M-E*
^	*accent circonflexe*	hôpital	*H-O-accent circonflexe-P-I-T-A-L*
¨	*tréma*	naïve	*N-A-I-tréma-V-E*
¸	*cédille*	ça	*C-cédille-A*

1 **L'alphabet** Practice saying the French alphabet and example words aloud.

2 **Ça s'écrit comment?** Spell these words aloud in French.

1. judo
2. yacht
3. forêt
4. zèbre
5. existe
6. clown
7. numéro
8. français
9. musique
10. favorite
11. kangourou
12. parachute
13. différence
14. intelligent
15. dictionnaire
16. alphabet

3 **Dictons** Practice reading these sayings aloud.

1. Grande invitation, petites portions.
2. Tout est bien qui finit bien.

4 **Dictée** You will hear six people introduce themselves. Listen carefully and write the people's names as they spell them.

1. ______________________
2. ______________________
3. ______________________
4. ______________________
5. ______________________
6. ______________________

Nom ______________________________ Date ______________________________

Roman-photo

AU CAFÉ

Avant de regarder

1 **Qu'est-ce qui se passe?** Look at the photo and guess what these people might be saying to one another.

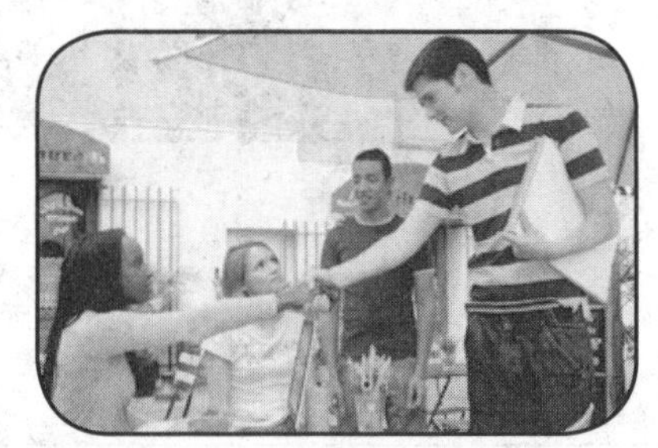

____

____

____

____

____

En regardant la vidéo

2 **Identifiez-les!** Match these characters with their names.

1. ______

5. ______

2. ______

6. ______

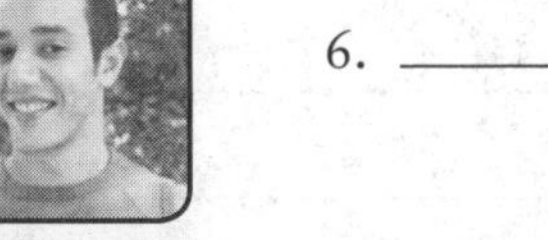

3. ______

7. ______

4. ______

a. Amina
b. David
c. Sandrine
d. Stéphane
e. Rachid
f. Michèle
g. Madame Forestier

3 **Qui...?** Watch the scene on the terrace and indicate which character says each of these lines. Write **R** for Rachid, **A** for Amina, **S** for Sandrine, or **D** for David.

______ 1. Ben... ça va. Et toi?

______ 2. Je vous présente un ami.

______ 3. Enchanté.

______ 4. Bienvenue à Aix-en-Provence.

______ 5. Bon... à tout à l'heure.

______ 6. À bientôt, David.

Nom ______________________ Date ______________________

4 **Complétez** Watch as Valérie takes a phone call from her son's school, and complete the conversation with the missing words from the list.

au revoir	bonjour	problème
beaucoup	Madame	

1. Allô. Oui. ______________, Madame Richard.
2. Il y a un ______________ au lycée?
3. Oui, merci, merci ______________ Richard.
4. Merci ______________!
5. De rien, ______________!

Après la vidéo

5 **Vrai ou faux?** Indicate whether these statements are vrai or faux.

	Vrai	Faux
1. David is a university student.	❍	❍
2. David is Canadian.	❍	❍
3. Madame Richard is a political science teacher.	❍	❍
4. Stéphane is a college student.	❍	❍
5. Rachid rushes off to his French class.	❍	❍

6 **Expliquez** In English, explain what is happening in this photo.

____
____
____
____
____

7 **À vous!** Imagine that Rachid is introducing you to one of his friends. Write a short dialogue in French in which you greet one another, exchange names, and talk briefly before saying good-bye.

____
____
____
____
____
____
____
____

Nom ____________________ Date ____________________

Flash culture

SALUT!

Avant de regarder

1

Les salutations In this video, you're going to learn about French greetings and introductions. In preparation for watching the video, make a list of things you do...

1. when you say hello:

____

____

2. when you say good-bye:

____

____

3. when you are introduced to a person your age:

____

____

4. when you meet a friend's parents for the first time:

____

____

En regardant la vidéo

2

Dans quel ordre? Number these images as they appear on-screen.

_______ a. two young men shaking hands
_______ b. two older family members kissing on cheeks
_______ c. two couples saying good-bye to each other
_______ d. two women shaking hands
_______ e. four friends (three young men and one young woman) meet
_______ f. a young man introducing a young woman to two friends
_______ g. a wide shot of two girls kissing on the cheek
_______ h. a woman and a small child kissing on the cheek

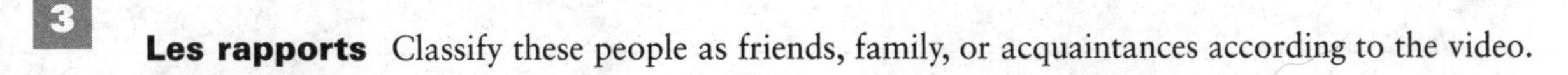

3

Les rapports Classify these people as friends, family, or acquaintances according to the video.

1. ____________________

3. ____________________

2. ____________________

4. ____________________

Nom ______________________ Date ______________________

Après la vidéo

4

Vrai ou faux? Indicate whether these statements are **vrai** or **faux**.

	Vrai	Faux
1. When female friends greet one another, they usually kiss on the cheek.	❍	❍
2. When male friends greet one another, they usually shake hands.	❍	❍
3. When mutual friends are introduced for the first time, they always shake hands instead of kiss on the cheek.	❍	❍
4. When formal acquaintances greet one another, they usually shake hands.	❍	❍
5. Women usually just shake hands when they say good-bye.	❍	❍
6. Handshaking is not very common in France.	❍	❍

5

À vous! Imagine that you are in France. In English, write what you should do in each of these situations according to French custom.

1. A classmate introduces you to his father.

____

2. You greet a girl you met in one of your classes.

____

3. You are introduced to a friend's girlfriend.

____

4. You arrive for a job interview and meet your potential new boss.

____

6

Vive la différence! In English, compare greetings and introductions in France and where you live. In what ways are they similar? How do they differ?

____

Nom ______________________ Date ______________________

STRUCTURES

1A.1 Nouns and articles

1 **Masculin ou féminin?** Write the correct definite article before each noun. Then list each article and noun under the appropriate heading.

1. ____________ amie
2. ____________ littérature
3. ____________ différence
4. ____________ problème
5. ____________ objet
6. ____________ café
7. ____________ télévision
8. ____________ étudiant
9. ____________ bureau

Masculin

____

____

____

____

____

Féminin

____

____

____

____

2 **Le, la, l' ou les?** Write the correct definite article before each noun.

1. ____________ bibliothèque
2. ____________ chanteur
3. ____________ amis
4. ____________ sociologie
5. ____________ examen
6. ____________ ordinateurs
7. ____________ chose
8. ____________ café
9. ____________ bureaux
10. ____________ petit ami
11. ____________ faculté
12. ____________ objets

3 **Singulier ou pluriel?** Give the plural form of each singular noun and article, and the singular form of each plural noun and article. Use definite articles in the first column and indefinite articles in the second.

Modèle

un ordinateur: *des ordinateurs*

1. l'étudiant: ____________________
2. les amies: ____________________
3. la librairie: ____________________
4. les cafés: ____________________
5. le bureau: ____________________
6. les examens: ____________________
7. des étudiantes: ____________________
8. un lycée: ____________________
9. une chanteuse: ____________________
10. des choses: ____________________
11. un animal: ____________________
12. un instrument: ____________________

Nom ______________________ Date ______________________

4 **Les articles** Change the definite articles to indefinite articles and vice-versa.

1. un ami: __________ ami
2. des instruments: __________ instruments
3. la table: __________ table
4. un ordinateur: __________ ordinateur
5. les étudiantes: __________ étudiantes
6. l'examen: __________ examen
7. une télévision: __________ télévision
8. le café: __________ café
9. des professeurs: __________ professeurs
10. la personne: __________ personne

5 **Transformez** Write the feminine forms of masculine nouns and articles, and the masculine forms of feminine nouns and articles.

Modèle

une chanteuse: **un chanteur**

1. l'acteur: __________
2. un ami: __________
3. une étudiante: __________
4. une actrice: __________
5. le chanteur: __________
6. la petite amie: __________

6 **Identifiez** For each illustration, write the noun and its corresponding definite and indefinite articles.

Modèle

la librairie: ***C'est une librairie.***

1. __________: __________
2. __________: __________
3. __________: __________
4. __________: __________
5. __________: __________
6. __________: __________

Nom ______________________ Date ______________________

1A.1 Nouns and articles (audio activities)

1 **Identifiez** You will hear a series of words. Decide whether the word is masculine or feminine, and mark the appropriate column with an **X**.

Modèle

You hear: librairie
You mark: an **X** under **Féminin**

	Masculin	Féminin
Modèle	______	X
1.	______	______
2.	______	______
3.	______	______
4.	______	______
5.	______	______
6.	______	______
7.	______	______
8.	______	______

2 **Changez** Change each word from the masculine to the feminine, or vice versa. Repeat the correct answer after the speaker. (*6 items*)

Modèle

un ami
une amie

3 **Transformez** Change each word from the singular to the plural. Repeat the correct answer after the speaker. (*8 items*)

Modèle

un stylo
des stylos

4 **La classe** What does Sophie see in Professor Martin's French class? Listen to what she says and write the missing words.

1. ______ bureaux
2. ______ professeur
3. ______ étudiants en ______
4. des ______
5. le ______
6. les ______
7. ______ télévision
8. des ______

Nom ______________________ Date ______________________

1A.2 Numbers 0–60

1 **Les mots croisés** Solve the math problems to complete the crossword puzzle. Include hyphens as needed.

Across:

3. neuf + quinze =
7. trois + dix =
9. quatre + douze =
10. vingt-trois - neuf =
11. treize + cinq =

Down:

1. cinq + six =
2. trente - vingt-huit =
3. douze + quinze =
4. trente - vingt-neuf =
5. six + six =
6. huit + neuf =
8. vingt et un - seize =

2 **Combien?** Write questions to ask how many items or people there are. Then write the responses. Be sure to write out the numbers.

Modèle

2 élèves

Il y a *combien d'élèves?* Il y a *deux élèves.*

1. 3 bureaux ______________________
2. 21 examens ______________________
3. 5 professeurs de littérature ______________________
4. 18 amis ______________________
5. 33 acteurs ______________________
6. 12 problèmes ______________________
7. 52 tableaux ______________________
8. 9 cafés ______________________
9. 60 choses ______________________
10. 44 tables ______________________

3 **Répondez** Ask and answer questions according to the illustration. Write out the numbers. Ask and indicate...

Modèle

how many chairs **(chaises)** there are.
Il y a combien de chaises?
Il y a deux chaises.

1. how many people there are.
   ______________________?
   ______________________.
2. how many computers there are.
   ______________________?
   ______________________.
3. how many televisions there are.
   ______________________?
   ______________________.
4. how many girls (**filles**) there are.
   ______________________?
   ______________________.

4 **Comptez** Figure out the logic of each sequence. Then write out the missing numbers in each one.

1. un, trois, ____________, sept, neuf, ____________
2. ____________, quatre, huit, ____________, trente-deux
3. soixante, ____________, quarante, trente, vingt, dix, ____________
4. vingt-deux, vingt-quatre, ____________, vingt-huit, ____________
5. onze, ____________, trente-trois, ____________, cinquante-cinq

5 **Quel chiffre?** Write out the number you associate with each of these items.

1. seasons in a year ____________
2. days in a week ____________
3. number of days in September ____________
4. number of pets you have ____________
5. your age ____________
6. number of classes you are taking ____________

6 **Dans la salle de classe** Answer these questions using complete sentences. Write out numbers.
Dans votre (*your*) salle de classe, il y a combien...

1. de tableaux? ______________________
2. de garçons (*boys*)? ______________________
3. de filles (*girls*)? ______________________
4. de bureaux? ______________________
5. d'ordinateurs? ______________________
6. de professeurs? ______________________

Nom ________________________ Date ________________________

1A.2 Numbers 0–60 (audio activities)

1 **Bingo** You are going to play two games (**jeux**) of bingo. As you hear each number, mark it with an X on your bingo card.

Jeu 1		
2	17	35
26	52	3
15	8	29
7	44	13

Jeu 2		
18	12	16
34	9	25
0	56	41
27	31	58

2 **Numéros** You want to know everything about your friend Marc's new university. Write down his answers to your questions.

Modèle

You see: professeurs de littérature
You say: Il y a des professeurs de littérature?
You hear: Oui, il y a dix-huit professeurs de littérature.
You write: 18

1. étudiants américains ____________
2. ordinateurs dans la bibliothèque ____________
3. télévision dans la classe de littérature ____________
4. bureaux dans la classe de sociologie ____________
5. tables dans le café ____________
6. tableaux dans le bureau du professeur de français ____________

3 **Les maths** You will hear a series of math problems. Write the missing numbers and solve the problems.

Modèle

Combien font deux plus trois?
2 + 3 = 5

plus = *plus* **moins** = *minus* **font** = *equals (makes)*

1. ______ + ______ = ____________
2. ______ – ______ = ____________
3. ______ + ______ = ____________
4. ______ – ______ = ____________
5. ______ – ______ = ____________
6. ______ + ______ = ____________
7. ______ + ______ = ____________
8. ______ – ______ = ____________

4 **Questions** Look at the drawing and answer each question you hear. Repeat the correct response after the speaker. (*5 items*)

Nom ______________________ Date ______________________

Unité 1

Leçon 1B

CONTEXTES

1

Cherchez Find and circle the twelve school-related words, looking backwards, forwards, vertically, horizontally, and diagonally.

calculatrice	dictionnaire
carte	livre
chaise	professeur
copine	porte
corbeille	stylo
crayon	tableau

E	E	R	V	I	L	P	L	S	R	O
C	R	O	B	I	O	D	R	T	R	O
I	I	U	S	E	E	R	C	A	T	E
R	A	I	E	E	S	E	T	R	A	C
T	N	F	T	S	E	T	E	C	H	A
A	N	O	R	L	S	N	Y	A	I	B
L	O	C	O	R	B	E	I	L	L	E
U	I	R	P	A	E	S	F	P	O	S
C	T	A	B	L	E	A	U	O	O	I
L	C	Y	T	U	N	E	T	F	R	C
A	I	O	C	I	A	R	O	A	E	P
C	D	N	L	A	C	L	L	C	O	L

2

Les associations Match the words in the first column with related words in the second.

_______ 1. un crayon — a. une fille

_______ 2. un homme — b. une feuille de papier

_______ 3. une femme — c. un étudiant

_______ 4. un cahier — d. un stylo

_______ 5. une montre — e. un livre

_______ 6. une porte — f. une fenêtre

_______ 7. un élève — g. une horloge

_______ 8. un dictionnaire — h. un garçon

3

Analogies Complete the analogies with words from the box. Some words will not be used. Do not repeat items.

un cahier	une femme	des livres
une corbeille à papier	une fenêtre	un résultat
un garçon	une fille	un stylo

1. un garçon : une fille / un homme : ______________________
2. un professeur : un étudiant / un parent : ______________________
3. un homme : un garçon / une femme : ______________________
4. un cahier : des feuilles de papier / une bibliothèque : ______________________
5. une montre : une horloge / un crayon : ______________________

4 **En classe** Label these people and things. Include the indefinite article for each noun.

1. ______________
2. ______________
3. ______________
4. ______________
5. ______________
6. ______________
7. ______________
8. ______________
9. ______________
10. ______________
11. ______________
12. ______________
13. ______________
14. ______________
15. ______________

5 **Complétez** Complete these sentences using the words below. Not all words will be used.

cahier	corbeille à papier	dictionnaire	stylo
classe	crayons	fenêtre	tableaux

1. Il y a des ______________________ dans (*in*) le sac à dos.
2. Il y a vingt étudiants dans la ______________________.
3. Il y a des mots de vocabulaire dans le ______________________.
4. Il y a une feuille de papier dans la ______________________.
5. Il y a une ______________________ dans la salle de classe.

Nom ____________________ Date ____________________

CONTEXTES: AUDIO ACTIVITIES

1 **Identifiez** Look at the drawing and listen to the statement. Indicate whether each statement is **vrai** or **faux.**

	Vrai	Faux
1.	❍	❍
2.	❍	❍
3.	❍	❍
4.	❍	❍
5.	❍	❍
6.	❍	❍
7.	❍	❍
8.	❍	❍

2 **Les contraires** You will hear a list of masculine nouns. Write the number of the masculine noun next to its feminine counterpart.

_____ a. la femme

_____ b. une élève

_____ c. une camarade de classe

_____ d. la fille

_____ e. une étudiante

_____ f. madame

_____ g. l'actrice

_____ h. une copine

3 **Professeur** This professor needs to order new items at the bookstore. You will hear a series of questions. Look at the professor's list and answer each question. Then repeat the correct response after the speaker.

Liste

- 49 crayons - 12 dictionnaires
- 55 stylos - 18 cartes
- 35 cahiers - 5 corbeilles à papier
- 31 livres - 54 feuilles

LES SONS ET LES LETTRES

Silent letters

Final consonants of French words are usually silent.

français sport vous salut

An unaccented -e (or -es) at the end of a word is silent, but the preceding consonant is pronounced.

française américaine oranges japonaises

The consonants -c, -r, -f, and -l are usually pronounced at the ends of words. To remember these exceptions, think of the consonants in the word careful.

parc	bonjour	actif	animal
lac	professeur	naïf	mal

1 **Prononcez** Practice saying these words aloud.

1. traditionnel	6. Monsieur	11. timide
2. étudiante	7. journalistes	12. sénégalais
3. généreuse	8. hôtel	13. objet
4. téléphones	9. sac	14. normal
5. chocolat	10. concert	15. importante

2 **Articulez** Practice saying these sentences aloud.

1. Au revoir, Paul. À plus tard!
2. Je vais très bien. Et vous, Monsieur Dubois?
3. Qu'est-ce que c'est? C'est une calculatrice.
4. Il y a un ordinateur, une table et une chaise.
5. Frédéric et Chantal, je vous présente Michel et Éric.
6. Voici un sac à dos, des crayons et des feuilles de papier.

3 **Dictons** Practice reading these sayings aloud.

1. Mieux vaut tard que jamais.
2. Aussitôt dit, aussitôt fait.

4 **Dictée** You will hear a conversation. Listen carefully and write what you hear during the pauses. The entire conversation will then be repeated so you can check your work.

AMÉLIE ______________________

NICOLAS ______________________

AMÉLIE ______________________

NICOLAS ______________________

AMÉLIE ______________________

NICOLAS ______________________

AMÉLIE ______________________

Nom ____________________ Date ____________________

Roman-photo

LES COPAINS

Avant de regarder

1 **Qu'est-ce qui se passe?** In this video module, David asks about the people he has just met. In preparation for watching the video, make a list of adjectives you might hear.

____

____

____

____

____

____

En regardant la vidéo

2 **Mettez-les dans l'ordre!** Watch the first scene and number these nationalities in the order in which they are mentioned.

_______ a. anglais

_______ b. américain

_______ c. canadien

_______ d. français

_______ e. italien

3 **Oui, maman!** Watch the scene between Stéphane and his mother, and complete the paragraph with the missing words.

brillant	classe	filles	livre
cahier	fenêtres	intelligent	professeur

Stéphane! Tu es (1) ____________________, mais tu n'es pas (2) ____________________! En (3) ____________________, on fait attention au (4) ____________________, au (5) ____________________ et au (6) ____________________! Pas aux (7) ____________________. Et pas aux (8) ____________________!

4 **Qui...?** Watch the scene as Amina and David chat on the terrace, and indicate which character says each of these lines. Write **A** for Amina, **D** for David, or **V** for Valérie.

_______ 1. Bon, elle est chanteuse, alors, elle est un peu égoïste.
_______ 2. Et Rachid, mon colocataire? Comment est-il?
_______ 3. Michèle! Un stylo, s'il vous plaît! Vite!
_______ 4. Tu es de quelle origine?
_______ 5. Oh! Rachid! C'est un ange!
_______ 6. D'origine sénégalaise.

Après la vidéo

5 **Identifiez-les!** According to the video, which characters do these statements describe? Each description may fit more than one character.

1. Il/Elle est agréable. ____________________
2. Il/Elle est d'origine sénégalaise. ____________________
3. Il/Elle est sociable. ____________________
4. Il/Elle est patient(e). ____________________
5. Il/Elle est américain(e). ____________________
6. Il/Elle est d'origine algérienne. ____________________
7. Il/Elle est égoïste. ____________________
8. Il/Elle est modeste. ____________________
9. Il/Elle est français(e). ____________________
10. Il/Elle est réservé(e). ____________________

6 **Vrai ou faux?** Indicate whether these statements are **vrai** or **faux**.

	Vrai	Faux
1. Rachid est un excellent camarade de chambre.	❍	❍
2. Stéphane est brillant.	❍	❍
3. Sandrine est chanteuse.	❍	❍
4. Madame Forestier est calme.	❍	❍
5. Michèle est optimiste.	❍	❍
6. Il y a un touriste américain.	❍	❍

7 **À vous!** In this episode, you see the contents of Stéphane's backpack. In French, list as many items as you can that you carry in your backpack.

Dans mon sac à dos, il y a... ____________________

____

____

____

____

____

Nom ______________________ Date ______________________

STRUCTURES

1B.1 The verb être

1 **Les pronoms** In the second column, write the subject pronouns you would use when addressing the people listed. In the third column, write the pronouns you would use when talking about them.

People	Addressing them	Talking about them
1. Madame Martin		
2. Elsa et Caroline		
3. Julien (un ami)		
4. trois femmes et un homme		
5. un professeur		
6. une étudiante		
7. un acteur		
8. trois garçons		

2 **Complétez** Complete these sentences with the correct subject pronouns.

1. ______________ est étudiante.
2. ______________ sommes à l'université
3. ______________ suis un ami.
4. ______________ est professeur.
5. ______________ sont copains.
6. ______________ es acteur.
7. ______________ êtes ici?
8. ______________ sont chanteuses.

3 **Nous sommes...** Rewrite each sentence with the new subject and the correct form of the verb **être**. Make other changes as needed.

Modèle

Il est professeur. Nous *sommes professeurs.*

1. Nous sommes étudiants. Vous ______________________________.
2. Elle est à Paris. Tu ______________________________.
3. Je suis actrice. Il ______________________________.
4. Vous êtes copines. Ils ______________________________.
5. Tu es à la librairie. Je ______________________________.

4 **Bienvenue à Aix-en-Provence!** David has just arrived in Aix-en-Provence. Complete his paragraph with the correct forms of **être**.

Bonjour! Je m'appelle David. Je (1) ______________ étudiant ici, à Aix-en-Provence. Rachid, Sandrine, Amina et Stéphane (2) ______________ des amis. Sandrine, elle (3) ______________ chanteuse. Rachid, Amina et moi, nous (4) ______________ étudiants à l'université. Stéphane (5) ______________ élève au lycée. Et toi, tu (6) ______________ étudiant?

5 **Identifiez** Identify these people or things using **c'est** or **ce sont**.

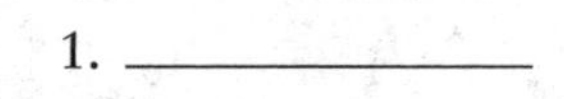

1. ______________ ______________
2. ______________ ______________
3. ______________ ______________
4. ______________ ______________

5. ______________ ______________
6. ______________ ______________
7. ______________ ______________
8. ______________ ______________

6 **Répondez** Answer these questions using complete sentences.

1. La France est-elle en Europe?

   Oui, ____

2. Johnny Depp est-il acteur?

   Oui, ____

3. Céline Dion et Beyoncé sont-elles chanteuses?

   Oui, ____

4. Tu es un(e) élève?

   Oui, ____

5. Tes (*Your*) cours sont-ils intéressants?

   Oui, ____

Nom ______________________ Date ______________________

1B.1 The verb être (audio activities)

1 **Identifiez** For each drawing, you will hear two statements. Choose the one that corresponds to the drawing.

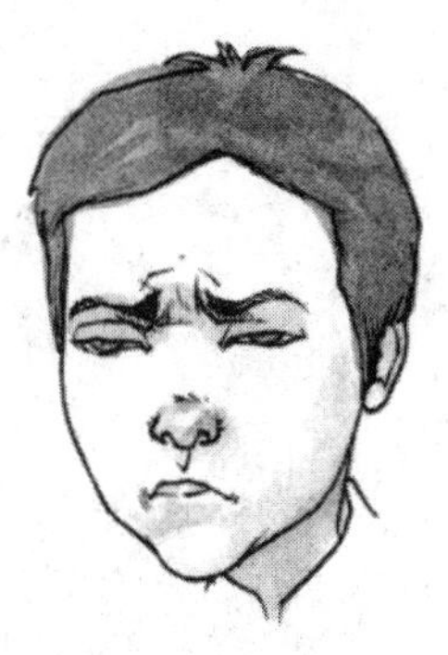

1. a. b. 2. a. b. 3. a. b. 4. a. b.

2 **Complétez** Listen to the following sentences and write the missing verb. Repeat the sentence.

1. Je ______________________ étudiante à Boston.
2. Mon amie Maéva ______________________ suisse.
3. Nous ______________________ des États-Unis.
4. Mes professeurs ______________________ intéressants.
5. Vous ______________________ Madame Dufour?
6. Tu ______________________ en retard (*late*).

3 **Questions** Answer each question you hear. Repeat the correct response after the speaker.

Modèle

You hear: Et toi?
You see: timide
You say: **Je suis timide.**

1. égoïste
2. intelligent
3. sincère
4. difficile
5. sociable

1B.2 Adjective agreement

1 **Les contraires** Match the words in the first column with their opposites in the second. Use a dictionary, if necessary.

______ 1. optimiste	a. désagréable
______ 2. sociable	b. difficile
______ 3. agréable	c. similaire
______ 4. impatient	d. pessimiste
______ 5. facile	e. dépendant
______ 6. différent	f. impoli
______ 7. indépendant	g. patient
______ 8. poli	h. timide

2 **Chassez l'intrus** Circle the adjective that does not belong with the others.

1. difficile, égoïste, agréable
2. poli, pessimiste, sociable
3. sympathique, italien, espagnol
4. intelligent, brillant, impatient
5. américain, sincère, canadien
6. québécois, sincère, sympathique
7. allemand, charmant, suisse
8. occupé, timide, réservé

3 **Nationalités** What nationalities are these people? Write sentences according to the model.

Modèle

Carole / France: *Carole est française.*

1. Bob et Jim / les États-Unis (*U.S.*): ______
2. Amani et Ahmed / le Sénégal: ______
3. Trevor / l'Angleterre (*England*): ______
4. Francine / le Québec: ______
5. Monika / l'Allemagne (*Germany*): ______
6. Maria-Luisa / l'Italie: ______
7. François et Jean-Philippe / la Suisse: ______
8. Gabriela / le Mexique: ______
9. Yoko et Keiko (*f.*) / le Japon (*Japan*): ______
10. Paul / le Canada: ______

Nom ______________________ Date ______________________

4 **Les personnes célèbres** Finish these sentences using the correct forms of **être** and the adjectives in parentheses.

1. Jim Carrey (amusant) ______________________.
2. Catherine Zeta-Jones (élégant) ______________________.
3. Julia Roberts et Renée Zellwegger (sympathique) ______________________.
4. George Clooney et Kelly Ripa (charmant) ______________________.
5. Stephen Hawking (brillant) ______________________.
6. Dr. Phil et Oprah Winfrey (sociable) ______________________.
7. Le prince Charles et la reine (*queen*) Elizabeth II (réservé) ______________________.
8. Donald Trump (intelligent) ______________________.

5 **Décrivez** Look at the illustration and describe each person using as many adjectives as possible. Use your imagination to describe their personalities. Write complete sentences.

1. Charles ______________________
2. Suzanne ______________________
3. Charlotte ______________________
4. Robert ______________________
5. Thomas ______________________
6. Fido ______________________

Nom ______________________ Date ______________________

1B.2 Adjective agreement (audio activities)

1 **Masculin ou féminin?** Change each sentence from the masculine to the feminine or vice versa. Repeat the correct answer after the speaker. (*6 items*)

Modèle

L'homme est français.
La femme est française.

2 **Singulier ou pluriel?** Change each sentence from the singular to the plural and vice versa. Repeat the correct answer after the speaker. (*6 items*)

Modèle

Le garçon est sympathique.
Les garçons sont sympathiques.

3 **Mes camarades de classe** Describe these people using the cues. Repeat the correct response after the speaker.

Modèle

You hear: Anissa
You see: amusant
You say: **Anissa est amusante.**

1. intelligent
2. patient
3. égoïste
4. optimiste
5. élégant
6. sociable
7. poli
8. différent

4 **Complétez** Listen to the following description and write the missing words.

Brigitte (1) ______________ (2) ______________. Elle et Paul, un (3) ______________, (4) ______________ étudiants à (5) ______________ Laval. Ils (6) ______________ (7) ______________. Paul est étudiant en (8) ______________ et Brigitte, en (9) ______________ (10) ______________. Dans le cours de français, il y a des (11) ______________ et des (12) ______________; il y a aussi une (13) ______________ et une (14) ______________. Les étudiants sont très (15) ______________, (16) ______________ et (17) ______________.

Nom ______________________ Date ______________________

Unité 1

Savoir-faire

PANORAMA

1 **Les villes capitales** Match the countries with their capital cities.

_______ 1. Suisse	a. Conakry
_______ 2. Algérie	b. Bamako
_______ 3. Guinée	c. Port-au-Prince
_______ 4. Mali	d. Alger
_______ 5. Cameroun	e. Paris
_______ 6. Haïti	f. Yaoundé
_______ 7. France	g. Victoria
_______ 8. Seychelles	h. Berne

2 **Francophones célèbres** Where do these people come from?

1. Marie-José Pérec ______________________
2. Marie Curie ______________________
3. René Magritte ______________________
4. Ousmane Sembène ______________________
5. Céline Dion ______________________
6. Jean Reno ______________________

3 **Les professions** Match these people with their professions.

_______ 1. Jean Reno	a. écrivain et cinéaste
_______ 2. René Magritte	b. chanteuse
_______ 3. Ousmane Sembène	c. coureuse olympique
_______ 4. Marie Curie	d. acteur
_______ 5. Marie-José Pérec	e. peintre
_______ 6. Céline Dion	f. scientifique

4 **Vrai ou faux?** Indicate whether these statements are **vrai** or **faux**.

	Vrai	Faux
1. Le français est la langue officielle du Québec.	❍	❍
2. L'Algérie est une colonie française.	❍	❍
3. On a vendu la Louisiane pour 15 millions de dollars.	❍	❍
4. 350.000 personnes en Louisiane parlent français.	❍	❍
5. Le rôle de l'O.I.F est la promotion de la langue française.	❍	❍
6. Ousmane Sembène est un chanteur africain.	❍	❍
7. On parle français sur cinq continents.	❍	❍
8. Le français est la deuxième langue enseignée dans le monde.	❍	❍

5 **Où?** What places do these statements describe?

1. Il y a une loi qui oblige l'affichage en français dans les lieux publics. ______________________
2. On y (*there*) mange du jambalaya. ______________________
3. On y parle arabe et français. ______________________
4. On y fête la Journée internationale de la Francophonie. ______________________
5. C'est une région francophone aux États-Unis. ______________________
6. Les employés du gouvernement sont bilingues. ______________________

6 **La francophonie** Identify these French-speaking countries or regions. Look at the maps at the end of your book, if necessary.

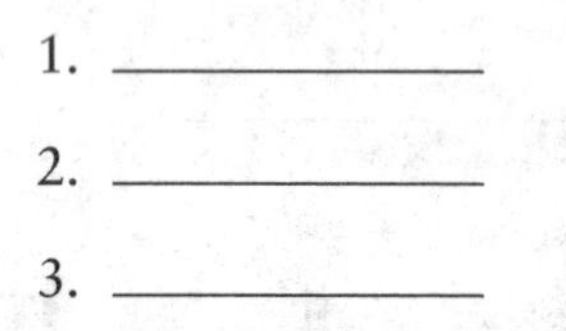

1. ______________
2. ______________
3. ______________
4. ______________
5. ______________
6. ______________

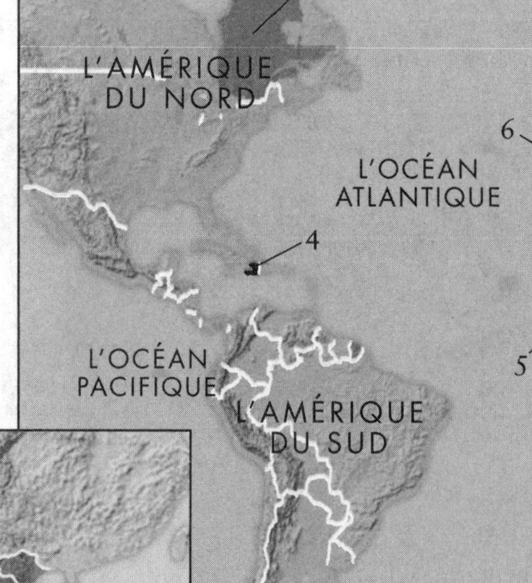

Nom ______________________ Date ______________________

Unité 2

Leçon 2A

CONTEXTES

1 **Cherchez** In the grid, find and circle the fifteen words for courses listed. Look backwards, forwards, vertically, horizontally, and diagonally.

architecture	informatique
art	lettres
chimie	mathématiques
droit	philosophie
espagnol	physique
géographie	psychologie
gestion	sciences
histoire	

M P S Y C H O L O G I E H Ô
S E C N E I C S P S U P G H
P G H H D Y H H T Q T S A P
G É O G R A P H I E O R Y I
H E H S O I U T E I C H R S
S E U Q I T A M É H T A M H
H S R I T M I V I P Î E S A
I P O I R G Q T P O T R E T
S A T O A E E Y E S Q T R T
T G F O S C G S F O S M T C
O N G L T E O F T L U S T U
I O L U E P H Y S I Q U E H
R L R M E T A R R H O R L P
E E I M I H C N P P T N É N

2 **Chassez l'intrus** Circle the word that does not belong in each group.

1. le français, l'anglais, la biologie, l'espagnol
2. un cours, un gymnase, une bourse, un diplôme
3. une note, le droit, un examen, le devoir
4. la physique, la chimie, l'architecture, la biologie
5. les langues étrangères, l'économie, la gestion, le droit
6. l'architecture, l'art, l'informatique, le stylisme

3 **En quel cours?** In what class would you study these people or things?

1. Abraham Lincoln, Winston Churchill ______________________
2. Claude Monet, Léonard de Vinci ______________________
3. Sigmund Freud, Carl Jung ______________________
4. l'Afrique, l'océan Pacifique ______________________
5. la culture française, la grammaire ______________________
6. la mode, les styles modernes ______________________
7. Ernest Hemingway, William Shakespeare ______________________
8. les plantes, les animaux ______________________
9. Jean-Paul Sartre, Emmanuel Kant ______________________
10. Albert Einstein, Stephen Hawking ______________________

Nom ______________________ Date ______________________

4 **C'est pour quel cours?** In which class would you most likely use these objects?

_____ 1. les crayons de couleur — a. les mathématiques

_____ 2. un dictionnaire anglais-français — b. la géographie

_____ 3. une calculatrice — c. la biologie

_____ 4. un ordinateur — d. le français

_____ 5. un microscope — e. l'éducation physique

_____ 6. une carte topographique — f. l'informatique

_____ 7. un ballon (*ball*) — g. le droit

_____ 8. une explication de la constitution — h. l'art

5 **Associations** Choose the word most closely associated with each of these terms.

l'art	un gymnase	les mathématiques
les études supérieures	l'informatique	une note
la gestion	une langue étrangère	les sciences politiques

1. les sports ______________________
2. les ordinateurs ______________________
3. un examen ______________________
4. l'algèbre ______________________
5. l'université ______________________
6. le gouvernement ______________________
7. un poster ______________________
8. la littérature française ______________________

6 **À votre avis** Do you like these subjects? Give your opinion (**votre avis**) on these classes using the words listed below or other adjectives you know. Use a different adjective in each sentence.

Modèle

l'anglais

J'aime bien l'anglais. C'est facile.

agréable	difficile	intéressant
amusant	facile	inutile
différent	important	utile

1. le stylisme ______________________
2. l'éducation physique ______________________
3. le français ______________________
4. la gestion ______________________
5. la philosophie ______________________
6. la psychologie ______________________
7. l'histoire ______________________
8. les mathématiques ______________________

Nom ______________________ Date ______________________

CONTEXTES: AUDIO ACTIVITIES

1 **Classifiez** Indicate whether each word you hear is a person (**personne**), a course (**cours**), an object (**objet**), or a place (**endroit**).

	personne	cours	objet	endroit
1.	______	______	______	______
2.	______	______	______	______
3.	______	______	______	______
4.	______	______	______	______
5.	______	______	______	______
6.	______	______	______	______
7.	______	______	______	______
8.	______	______	______	______

2 **Décrivez** For each drawing you will hear two statements. Choose the one that corresponds to the drawing.

1. a. b. 2. a. b. 3. a. b. 4. a. b.

3 **Les cours** You will hear six people talking about their favorite topics. Decide which classes they attend.

1. ______ a. chimie
2. ______ b. psychologie
3. ______ c. philosophie
4. ______ d. géographie
5. ______ e. stylisme
6. ______ f. histoire

Nom ______________________ Date ______________________

LES SONS ET LES LETTRES

Liaisons

Consonants at the end of French words are generally silent, but are usually pronounced when the word that follows begins with a vowel sound. This linking of sounds is called a liaison.

À tout à l'heure! Comment allez-vous?

An s or an **x** in a liaison sounds like the letter *z*.

les étudiants trois élèves six élèves deux hommes

Always make a liaison between a subject pronoun and a verb that begins with a vowel sound; always make a liaison between an article and a noun that begins with a vowel sound.

nous aimons ils ont un étudiant les ordinateurs

Always make a liaison between **est** (a form of **être**) and a word that begins with a vowel or a vowel sound. Never make a liaison with the final consonant of a proper name.

Robert est anglais. Paris est exceptionnelle.

Never make a liaison with the conjunction **et** (*and*).

Carole et Hélène Jacques et Antoinette

Never make a liaison between a singular noun and an adjective that follows it.

un cours horrible un instrument élégant

1 Prononcez Practice saying these words and expressions aloud.

1. un examen
2. des étudiants
3. les hôtels
4. dix acteurs
5. Paul et Yvette
6. cours important
7. des informations
8. les études
9. deux hommes
10. Bernard aime
11. chocolat italien
12. Louis est

2 Articulez Practice saying these sentences aloud.

1. Nous aimons les arts.
2. Albert habite à Paris.
3. C'est un objet intéressant.
4. Sylvie est avec Anne.
5. Ils adorent les deux universités.

3 Dictons Practice reading these sayings aloud.

1. Les amis de nos amis sont nos amis.
2. Un hôte non invité doit apporter son siège.

4 Dictée You will hear a conversation. Listen carefully and write what you hear during the pauses. The entire conversation will then be repeated so you can check your work.

ANNE ______________________

PATRICK ______________________

ANNE ______________________

PATRICK ______________________

ANNE ______________________

PATRICK ______________________

Nom _______________ Date _______________

Roman-photo

TROP DE DEVOIRS!

Avant de regarder

1 **Qu'est-ce qui se passe?** In this video, the characters talk about their classes and what they think about them. What words and expressions do you think they might say?

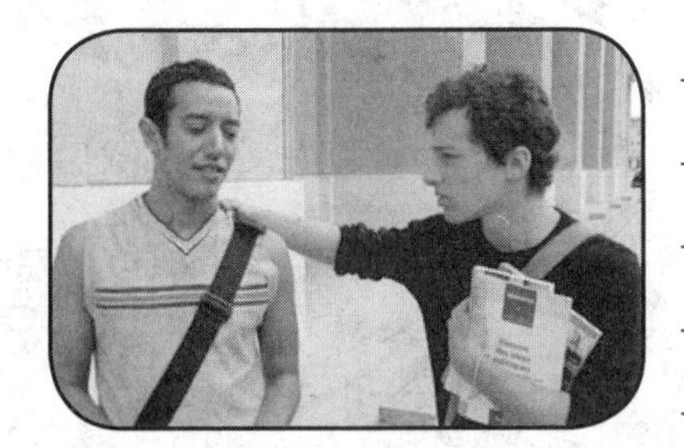

____
____
____
____
____

En regardant la vidéo

2 **Qui...?** Watch the first scene and indicate which character says each of these lines. Write **An** for Antoine, **R** for Rachid, or **D** for David.

_______ 1. Les études, c'est dans la tête.
_______ 2. Est-ce que tu oublies ton coloc?
_______ 3. On a rendez-vous avec Amina et Sandrine.
_______ 4. Je déteste le cours de sciences po.
_______ 5. Le P'tit Bistrot? Sympa.
_______ 6. Je n'aime pas tellement le prof, Monsieur Dupré, mais c'est un cours intéressant et utile.
_______ 7. Ah oui? Bon, ben, salut Antoine!
_______ 8. Moi, je pense que c'est très difficile, et il y a beaucoup de devoirs.

3 **Finissez-les!** Watch the scene as the four friends discuss their day. Match the first half of these sentences with their completions according to what you hear.

_______ 1. Je suis chanteuse, ...
_______ 2. C'est cool, ...
_______ 3. Donne-moi...
_______ 4. Comme j'adore...
_______ 5. C'est différent de l'université américaine, ...
_______ 6. J'aime bien les cours...
_______ 7. Bon, Pascal, ...
_______ 8. Demain, on étudie...

a. j'adore Dumas.
b. au revoir, chéri.
c. *Les Trois Mousquetaires* d'Alexandre Dumas.
d. de littérature et d'histoire françaises.
e. mais c'est intéressant.
f. mais j'adore les classiques de la littérature.
g. penser à toi!
h. le sac à dos, Sandrine.

Nom ______________________ Date ______________________

4 **Les matières** Place check marks next to the subjects Stéphane is studying.

- ❑ 1. les maths
- ❑ 2. la physique
- ❑ 3. l'anglais
- ❑ 4. le droit
- ❑ 5. le français
- ❑ 6. le stylisme
- ❑ 7. l'histoire-géo
- ❑ 8. les sciences politiques
- ❑ 9. la chimie
- ❑ 10. la psychologie

Après la vidéo

5 **Vrai ou faux?** Indicate whether these statements are **vrai** or **faux**.

	Vrai	Faux
1. Rachid déteste le cours de sciences po.	❍	❍
2. Rachid et Antoine partagent un des appartements du P'tit Bistrot.	❍	❍
3. Rachid n'aime pas Monsieur Dupré.	❍	❍
4. Rachid pense que le cours de sciences po est très difficile.	❍	❍
5. Rachid pense que le cours de sciences po est utile.	❍	❍
6. Stéphane n'étudie pas l'anglais.	❍	❍
7. Stéphane déteste les maths.	❍	❍
8. Stéphane pense que Madame Richard donne trop de devoirs.	❍	❍
9. Stéphane adore l'histoire-géo.	❍	❍
10. Stéphane n'aime pas Monsieur Dupré.	❍	❍

6 **Expliquez** What is happening in this photo? In English, describe the events leading up to this moment.

____

____

____

____

____

____

____

____

____

7 **À vous!** Give your opinion about four of your classes. Use a variety of adjectives to describe them.

1. Mon cours de/d'______________________, c'est ______________________.
2. Mon cours de/d'______________________, c'est ______________________.
3. Mon cours de/d'______________________, c'est ______________________.
4. Mon cours de/d'______________________, c'est ______________________.

Nom ______________________ Date ______________________

Flash culture

AU LYCÉE

Avant de regarder

1 **Au lycée français** In this video, you will learn about high schools in France. Make a list of French words related to school life, including places and academic subjects.

______________	______________	______________
______________	______________	______________
______________	______________	______________
______________	______________	______________
______________	______________	______________

2 **Qu'est-ce que c'est?** Check the appropriate column to classify these words as a place (**un endroit**) or a class (**un cours**).

	endroit	cours
1. la librairie	❍	❍
2. la physique	❍	❍
3. la cantine	❍	❍
4. les lettres	❍	❍
5. la bibliothèque	❍	❍
6. la salle de classe	❍	❍
7. le gymnase	❍	❍
8. le bureau	❍	❍
9. les mathématiques	❍	❍
10. l'histoire	❍	❍
11. la chimie	❍	❍
12. la philosophie	❍	❍

En regardant la vidéo

3 **Mettez-les dans l'ordre** Number these places and subjects in the order in which they are mentioned in the video.

_______ a. le lycée Cézanne

_______ b. l'anglais

_______ c. le point de rencontre des élèves

_______ d. la philosophie

_______ e. la physique

_______ f. la salle de cours

_______ g. le cours de français

4 **Choisissez** Watch as Benjamin interviews several students about their classes, and place check marks next to the classes the students mention.

- ❑ 1. biologie
- ❑ 2. anglais
- ❑ 3. français
- ❑ 4. sciences politiques
- ❑ 5. histoire-géo
- ❑ 6. maths
- ❑ 7. informatique
- ❑ 8. physique
- ❑ 9. philosophie
- ❑ 10. psychologie

5 **Qu'est-ce qu'ils disent?** Match these images with their captions.

1. ______________

2. ______________

3. ______________

4. ______________

5. ______________

6. ______________

a. Bof, ça va.
b. C'est ici qu'ils passent le temps entre les cours.
c. Oui, mais c'est difficile.
d. C'est un cours de français.
e. Vous avez quel cours maintenant?
f. Chut! Nous sommes maintenant dans la bibliothèque.

Après la vidéo

6 **Dans mon école** List five different places around your school. Then describe what you usually do at each one.

____

____

____

____

____

____

____

____

Nom ______________________ Date ______________________

STRUCTURES

2A.1 Present tense of regular -er verbs

1 **Les verbes** Write the missing forms of each verb.

Le présent des verbes en -er					
je	tu	il/elle	nous	vous	ils/elles
1. travaille					
2.	oublies				
3.		mange			
4.			aimons		
5.				commencez	
6.					pensent

2 **Complétez** Complete each sentence using the correct form of the verb in parentheses.

1. Les élèves ____________ (manger) à la cantine.
2. Hélène et moi, nous ____________ (parler) français en classe.
3. Corinne ____________ (étudier) les mathématiques.
4. Vous ____________ (adorer) le chocolat.
5. Tu ____________ (travailler) à la bibliothèque.
6. Je ____________ (détester) les examens.
7. Florent et Michèle ____________ (regarder) la télévision.
8. Tu ____________ (aimer) mieux retrouver des amis au lycée.

3 **Phrases** Form sentences using the words provided. Remember to conjugate the verbs and add any necessary words.

1. Je / habiter / à New York

   ____

2. Nous / manger / une pizza

   ____

3. Olivier et Sylvain / aimer / cours de biologie

   ____

4. Le professeur / donner / devoirs

   ____

5. Les élèves / oublier / livres

   ____

6. Tu / rencontrer / amis / à l'école

   ____

Nom ________________________ Date ________________________

4 **Une lettre** Complete this letter with the appropriate forms of the verbs in parentheses.

le 14 septembre

Salut Marie!

Ça va bien à l'université? Moi, j' (1) ____________ (adorer) les cours. Ils sont très intéressants. Les profs sont sympas, mais ils (2) ____________ (donner) beaucoup de devoirs. Mon camarade de chambre s'appelle Jean-Pierre. Il (3) ____________ (étudier) les sciences politiques. Nous (4) ____________ (partager) un appartement. Jean-Pierre est très sociable. Il (5) ____________ (travailler), mais il (6) ____________ (aimer) mieux le sport et il (7) ____________ (parler) beaucoup au téléphone. Le week-end, nous (8) ____________ (retrouver) des amis au café ou nous (9) ____________ (regarder) des films à la télé. Et toi, tu (10) ____________ (rencontrer) des amis sympas? Les filles (11) ____________ (aimer) beaucoup le prof de français. Elles (12) ____________ (penser) qu'il est charmant.

Grosses bises,

Charles

5 **Et vous?** Write sentences giving your opinion of these activities. Use one of the verbs listed in each sentence.

adorer aimer bien aimer mieux détester

1. partager mes vêtements (*my clothes*)

____

____

2. voyager

____

____

3. parler au téléphone

____

____

4. dessiner

____

____

5. manger des sushis

____

____

2A.1 Present tense of regular -er verbs (audio activities)

1

Transformez Describe what you and your friends do using the cues. Repeat the correct response after the speaker.

Modèle

You hear: Édouard
You see: manger à la cantine
You say: **Édouard mange à la cantine.**

1. adorer la mode (*fashion*)
2. détester les examens
3. étudier à la bibliothèque
4. retrouver des amis au café
5. aimer mieux la philosophie
6. penser que la chimie est difficile

2

Changez Listen to the following statements. Using the cues you hear, say that these people do the same activities. Repeat the correct answer after the speaker. (*8 items*)

Modèle

J'étudie l'architecture. (Charles)
Charles étudie l'architecture.

3

Choisissez Listen to each statement and choose the most logical response.

1. a. Nous mangeons. b. Vous mangez.
2. a. Vous travaillez. b. Ils travaillent.
3. a. Nous regardons la télé. b. Nous dessinons la télé.
4. a. Tu habites à Paris. b. J'habite à Paris.
5. a. Elle aime travailler ici. b. Elles aiment travailler ici.
6. a. Tu adores parler. b. Tu détestes parler.

4

Regardez Listen to each statement and write the number of the statement below the drawing it describes.

a. ______

b. ______

c. ______

d. ______

2A.2 Forming questions and expressing negation

1 **Est-ce que...?** Make questions out of these statements using est-ce que.

1. Vous êtes canadien.
______
2. Tu regardes la télévision.
______
3. Ils cherchent un livre à la bibliothèque.
______
4. Nous arrivons à l'école.
______
5. Elle parle chinois (*Chinese*).
______

2 **Les questions** Make questions out of these statements by inverting the word order.

1. Ils sont québécois.
______
2. Elles adorent voyager.
______
3. Tu parles espagnol.
______
4. Il y a vingt-cinq élèves.
______
5. Le professeur donne des devoirs difficiles.
______

3 **Quelle est la question?** Write questions that would prompt these responses. Use the type of question indicated in parentheses.

1. (est-ce que) ______?
Non, les cours ne commencent pas demain.
2. (n'est-ce pas) ______?
Oui, j'aime voyager.
3. (est-ce que) ______?
Non, il n'y a pas de problème.
4. (inversion) ______?
Oui, nous sommes étudiants.
5. (d'accord) ______?
Mais non! Je n'aime pas manger à la cantine.

Nom ______________________ Date ______________________

4 **Mais Robert!** Robert is very negative and contradicts everything. Write his answers to these questions using complete sentences.

Modèle

—Tu partages le chocolat?
—Non, *je ne partage pas le chocolat.*

1. —Études-tu les sciences politiques?
   —Non, ______________________
2. —Cherches-tu le stylo?
   —Non, ______________________
3. —Aimes-tu le chocolat?
   —Non, ______________________
4. —Est-ce que l'examen est facile?
   —Non, ______________________
5. —Tu aimes parler avec des amis, n'est-ce pas?
   —Non, ______________________
6. —Tu n'es pas sociable?
   —Si, ______________________

5 **Et vous?** Write your answers to these questions using complete sentences. Vary your responses by including a variety of words and expressions from the list.

bien sûr	oui	peut-être
mais non	pas du tout	si

1. Vous n'aimez pas voyager?
   ____
2. Aimez-vous les examens?
   ____
3. La physique, c'est facile?
   ____
4. Vous êtes intelligent(e), n'est-ce pas?
   ____
5. Est-ce que vous étudiez avec des copains?
   ____

2A.2 Forming questions and expressing negation (audio activities)

1

Mes camarades de classe You want to know about your classmates, so you ask your friend Simon questions with est-ce **que** using the cues. Repeat the correct question after the speaker.

Modèle

You hear: parler en cours
You see: Bertrand
You say: *Est-ce que Bertrand parle en cours?*

1. Émilie
2. toi
3. Antoine et Ahmed
4. Pierre-Étienne
5. Sophie et toi
6. Sara et Maude

2

Questions You want to know about your classmates, so you ask your friend Guillaume questions with inversion using the cues. Repeat the correct question after the speaker.

Modèle

You hear: chercher un livre
You see: Catherine
You say: *Catherine cherche-t-elle un livre?*

1. toi
2. Marie
3. Michel et toi
4. Martin
5. le professeur
6. vous

3

Répondez Answer each question in the negative. Repeat the correct response after the speaker. (6 *items*)

Modèle

Est-ce que tu habites en France?
Non, je n'habite pas en France.

4

Complétez Listen to the conversation between Mathilde and David. Answer the questions.

1. Est-ce que Mathilde aime les maths?
____

2. Pourquoi est-ce qu'elle déteste la biologie?
____

3. Est-ce qu'il y a des étudiants sympas?
____

4. Est-ce que le professeur de physique est ennuyeux (*boring*)?
____

5. Y a-t-il des étudiants stupides dans la classe de David?
____

Nom ______________________ Date ______________________

Unité 2

Leçon 2B

CONTEXTES

1

Complétez Complete each series with the next logical word.

1. vendredi, samedi, ______________________
2. le matin, midi, ______________________
3. avant-hier (*the day before yesterday*), hier, ______________________
4. lundi, mercredi, ______________________
5. aujourd'hui, demain, ______________________
6. mardi, jeudi, ______________________

2

Choisissez Complete these sentences with a logical word from the list.

année	jours	samedi
dernier	jeudi	semaine
dimanche	lundi	mercredi

1. Il y a sept jours dans une ______________________.
2. Le jour avant (*before*) mardi, c'est ______________________.
3. Il y a douze mois dans une ______________________.
4. Le mois de novembre a trente ______________________.
5. Dimanche, c'est le ______________________ jour du week-end.
6. Le jour avant jeudi, c'est ______________________.

3

Le calendrier Use this calendar to answer the questions below.

octobre

L	M	M	J	V	S	D
		1	2	3	4	5
6	7	8	9	10	11	12
13	14	15	16	17	18	19
20	21	22	23	24	25	26
27	28	29	30	31		

novembre

L	M	M	J	V	S	D
					1	2
3	4	5	6	7	8	9
10	11	12	13	14	15	16
17	18	19	20	21	22	23
24	25	26	27	28	29	30

1. Quel jour de la semaine est le premier octobre? ______________
2. Quel jour de la semaine est le 24 novembre? ______________
3. Quel jour de la semaine est le 19 octobre? ______________
4. Quel jour de la semaine est le 4 novembre? ______________
5. Quel jour de la semaine est le 11 octobre? ______________
6. Quel jour de la semaine est le 2 octobre? ______________
7. Quel jour de la semaine est le 28 novembre? ______________

4 **Décrivez** What are these people doing? Complete each sentence with the correct form of a verb from the list.

Amina arrive chez Sandrine.

arriver	regarder
dîner	rentrer
écouter	téléphoner à
préparer	voyager

1. David ______________ à la maison.

2. Sandrine ______________ des amis.

3. Stéphane ______________ l'examen de maths.

4. David ______________ au café.

5. Amina ______________ de la musique.

6. Stéphane ______________ la télévision.

5 **Complétez** Complete the weekly calendar with activities you plan to do or might like to do next week. Choose from the activities listed or include other activities. List at least eight different activities.

assister au cours de...	passer l'examen de...	regarder	trouver
dîner avec...	préparer l'examen de...	téléphoner à...	visiter
écouter		travailler	

la semaine prochaine							
	lundi	mardi	mercredi	jeudi	vendredi	samedi	dimanche
matin							
midi							
soir							

Nom ______________________ Date ______________________

CONTEXTES: AUDIO ACTIVITIES

1

L'emploi du temps You will hear a series of statements. Look at Élisabeth's schedule and indicate whether the statements are **vrai** or **faux**.

	lundi	mardi	mercredi	jeudi	vendredi	samedi	dimanche
matin	cours de français		téléphoner à Florence		cours de français		
après-midi		examen de maths		cours de danse		visiter Tours avec Carole	
soir	préparer examen de maths		dîner avec Christian			dîner en famille	dîner en famille

	Vrai	Faux		Vrai	Faux
1.	❍	❍	5.	❍	❍
2.	❍	❍	6.	❍	❍
3.	❍	❍	7.	❍	❍
4.	❍	❍	8.	❍	❍

2

Quel jour? Olivier is never sure what day of the week it is. Respond to his questions saying that it is the day before the one he mentions. Then repeat the correct answer after the speaker. (*6 items*)

Modèle

Aujourd'hui, c'est mercredi, n'est-ce pas?

Non, aujourd'hui, c'est mardi.

3

Complétez Listen to this description and write the missing words.

Je (1) ______________________ Nathalie et j' (2) ______________________ en Californie.

J' (3) ______________________ le français et j' (4) ______________________ la grammaire à l'Alliance française. Les étudiants (5) ______________________ un peu. Ils (6) ______________________ des vidéos et ils (7) ______________________ des CD. Ils (8) ______________________ beaucoup mais ils (9) ______________________ la classe amusante.

Après le cours, les étudiants et moi, nous (10) ______________________ dans un restaurant français.

LES SONS ET LES LETTRES

The letter r

The French **r** is very different from the English *r*. The English *r* is pronounced by placing the tongue in the middle and toward the front of the mouth. The French **r** is pronounced in the throat.
You have seen that an **-er** at the end of a word is usually pronounced **-ay**, as in the English word *way*, but without the glide sound.

chant**er** mang**er** expliqu**er** aim**er**

In most other cases, the French **r** has a very different sound. Pronunciation of the French **r** varies according to its position in a word. Note the different ways the **r** is pronounced in these words.

rivière litté**r**atu**r**e o**r**dinateu**r** devoi**r**

If an **r** falls between two vowels or before a vowel, it is pronounced with slightly more friction.

ra**r**e ga**r**age Eu**r**ope **r**ose

An **r** sound before a consonant or at the end of a word is pronounced with slightly less friction.

po**r**te bou**r**se ado**r**e jou**r**

1 **Prononcez** Practice saying the following words aloud.

1. crayon
2. professeur
3. plaisir
4. différent
5. terrible
6. architecture
7. trouver
8. restaurant
9. rentrer
10. regarder
11. lettres
12. réservé
13. être
14. dernière
15. arriver
16. après

2 **Articulez** Practice saying the following sentences aloud.

1. Au revoir, Professeur Colbert!
2. Rose arrive en retard mardi.
3. Mercredi, c'est le dernier jour des cours.
4. Robert et Roger adorent écouter la radio.
5. La corbeille à papier, c'est quarante-quatre euros!
6. Les parents de Richard sont brillants et très agréables.

3 **Dictons** Practice reading these sayings aloud.

1. Qui ne risque rien n'a rien.
2. Quand le renard prêche, gare aux oies.

4 **Dictée** You will hear six sentences. Each will be read twice. Listen carefully and write what you hear.

1. ______
2. ______
3. ______
4. ______
5. ______
6. ______

Nom ______________________ Date ______________________

Roman-photo

ON TROUVE UNE SOLUTION

Avant de regarder

1 **Qu'est-ce qui se passe?** Look at the title of this episode and the photo below. What problem do you think Rachid and Stéphane are discussing? What solution might they find?

____

____

____

____

____

En regardant la vidéo

2 **Qui...?** Indicate which character says each of these lines. Write **R** for Rachid, **As** for Astrid, **S** for Sandrine, **D** for David, or **St** for Stéphane.

_______ 1. Quel jour sommes-nous?

_______ 2. Alors, cette année, tu as des cours difficiles, n'est-ce pas?

_______ 3. C'est un examen très important.

_______ 4. C'est difficile, mais ce n'est pas impossible.

_______ 5. Euh, n'oublie pas, je suis de famille française.

_______ 6. Mais le sport, c'est la dernière des priorités.

_______ 7. Tu as tort, j'ai très peur du bac!

_______ 8. Il n'est pas tard pour commencer à travailler pour être reçu au bac.

3 **Complétez** Watch the conversation between Astrid and Stéphane, and complete the conversation with the missing words.

copains	envie	oublient
d'accord	livres	passer

Je suis (1) ______________________ avec toi, Stéphane! Moi non plus, je n'aime pas (2) ______________________ mes journées et mes week-ends avec des (3) ______________________.
J'ai (4) ______________________ de passer les week-ends avec mes (5) ______________________... des copains qui n'(6) ______________________ pas les rendez-vous!

4 **Mettez-les dans l'ordre!** Number these events in the order in which they occur in the video.

_______ a. Astrid et Rachid parlent du bac.
_______ b. Stéphane parle de ses problèmes.
_______ c. Rachid présente David à Astrid.
_______ d. Rachid propose une solution.
_______ e. Astrid et Rachid trouvent Stéphane au parc.

Après la vidéo

5 **Qui est-ce?** Select the person each statement describes.

_______ 1. Il/Elle a cours de stylisme.
a. Sandrine b. Amina c. Astrid d. Rachid e. Stéphane

_______ 2. Il/Elle ne fait pas ses devoirs.
a. Sandrine b. Amina c. Astrid d. Rachid e. Stéphane

_______ 3. Il/Elle a cours de chant.
a. Sandrine b. Amina c. Astrid d. Rachid e. Stéphane

_______ 4. Il/Elle n'écoute pas les profs.
a. Sandrine b. Amina c. Astrid d. Rachid e. Stéphane

_______ 5. Il/Elle travaille avec Stéphane le mercredi.
a. Sandrine b. Amina c. Astrid d. Rachid e. Stéphane

6 **Vrai ou faux?** Indicate whether these statements are vrai or faux.

	Vrai	Faux
1. Le cours de stylisme est à quatre heures vingt.	❍	❍
2. Aujourd'hui, c'est mercredi.	❍	❍
3. On a rendez-vous avec David demain à cinq heures.	❍	❍
4. Le cours de chant est le mardi et le jeudi.	❍	❍
5. Stéphane n'assiste pas au cours.	❍	❍
6. Stéphane a rendez-vous avec Rachid dimanche.	❍	❍

7 **À vous!** In this episode, you heard the characters discuss their classes and when they have them. Complete these sentences to tell what days you have classes. Use the words listed and any other words you know.

anglais	maths
français	sciences
histoire	

lundi	jeudi
mardi	vendredi
mercredi	samedi

Modèle

J'ai cours de *physique* le *lundi et le mercredi*.

1. J'ai cours de/d' ____________ le ______________________________.
2. J'ai cours de/d' ____________ le ______________________________.
3. J'ai cours de/d' ____________ le ______________________________.
4. J'ai cours de/d' ____________ le ______________________________.

Nom ____________________ Date ____________________

STRUCTURES

2B.1 Present tense of avoir

1 **Assortissez-les** Choose the best completion for each sentence.

ans	des insectes
décembre	le matin
d'étudier	visiter la France

1. J'ai besoin ____________________.
2. Eugène a dix-neuf ____________________.
3. Tu as peur ____________________.
4. Nous avons envie de ____________________.
5. J'ai sommeil ____________________.
6. J'ai froid en ____________________.

2 **Choisissez** Choose the expression that most logically completes each sentence.

1. Tu ____________ des examens.
   a. as chaud b. as peur c. as raison
2. J' ____________ de téléphoner à mon cousin.
   a. ai envie b. ai sommeil c. ai quinze ans
3. Laure ____________ le soir.
   a. a tort b. a envie c. a sommeil
4. Marie et Mireille sont jeunes. Elles ____________.
   a. ont cinq ans b. ont peur c. ont l'air

3 **Les possessions** Use the correct form of the verb **avoir** to tell what these people have or don't have.

1. Je / un ordinateur

   ____
2. Vous / trois cahiers

   ____
3. Nous / un professeur intéressant

   ____
4. Tu / ne… pas / un cours aujourd'hui

   ____
5. Ils / des calculatrices

   ____
6. Jules et Odile / un examen demain

   ____
7. Yves / ne… pas / un problème

   ____
8. Je / ne… pas / les yeux (*eyes*) bleus

   ____

Nom ______________________ Date ______________________

4 **Complétez** Complete these sentences with the most logical expression from the list. Remember to use the correct form of **avoir**.

avoir besoin	avoir envie	avoir peur
avoir de la chance	avoir froid	avoir tort

1. Il y a un examen demain. Nous ______________________ d'étudier.
2. Vous écoutez de la musique. Vous ______________________ de danser.
3. Ils n'ont pas raison. Ils ______________________.
4. Tu trouves 100 euros. Tu ______________________.
5. La température est de 10 degrés. Sophie ______________________.
6. Voilà un monstre! J' ______________________!

5 **Qu'est-ce qu'ils ont?** Describe these illustrations using an expression with **avoir**.

1. Elle ______________________
2. Elle ______________________

3. Ils ______________________
4. Ils ______________________

6 **Et vous?** Answer these questions using complete sentences.

1. Quel âge avez-vous?
____
2. Est-ce que vous avez toujours (*always*) raison?
____
3. Avez-vous sommeil le matin?
____
4. De quoi (*what*) est-ce que vous avez peur?
____
5. De quoi avez-vous besoin?
____
6. Avez-vous un examen la semaine prochaine?
____
7. Est-ce que vous pensez que vous avez de la chance? Pourquoi?
____

Nom ______________________ Date ______________________

2B.1 Present tense of **avoir** (audio activities)

1

Question d'opinion People don't always do what they should. Say what they have to do. Repeat the correct answer after the speaker. (*6 items*)

Modèle

Lucie ne mange pas le matin.
Lucie a besoin de manger le matin.

2

Changez Form a new sentence using the cue you hear. Repeat the correct answer after the speaker. (*6 items*)

Modèle

J'ai sommeil. (nous)
Nous avons sommeil.

3

Répondez Answer each question you hear using the cue. Repeat the correct response after the speaker.

Modèle

Tu as chaud? (non)
Non, je n'ai pas chaud.

1. oui
2. non
3. non
4. oui
5. non
6. non

4

Choisissez Listen to each situation and choose the appropriate expression. Each situation will be read twice.

1. a. Elle a honte. b. Elle a de la chance.
2. a. J'ai tort. b. J'ai raison.
3. a. Il a peur. b. Il a froid.
4. a. Nous avons chaud. b. Nous avons sommeil.
5. a. Vous avez de la chance. b. Vous avez l'air gentil.
6. a. Ils ont envie. b. Ils ont tort.

Nom ______________________ Date ______________________

2B.2 Telling time

1 **L'heure** Give the time shown on each clock. Use complete sentences and write out the times.

1. ______________________

2. ______________________

3. ______________________

4. ______________________

5. ______________________

6. ______________________

2 **Quelle heure est-il?** Convert these times into digits using the 24-hour clock.

Modèle

Il est quatre heures de l'après-midi.
16h00

1. Il est quatre heures moins vingt de l'après-midi. ______________
2. Il est six heures du matin. ______________
3. Il est neuf heures et quart du soir. ______________
4. Il est midi. ______________
5. Il est une heure dix de l'après-midi. ______________
6. Il est onze heures moins le quart du matin. ______________
7. Il est cinq heures cinq du soir. ______________
8. Il est minuit moins dix. ______________
9. Il est une heure et demie du matin. ______________
10. Il est dix heures du soir. ______________

Nom ______ Date ______

3 Transformez

Convert these times into conversational time. Write out the times.

Modèle

13h00: *une heure de l'après-midi*

1. 12h30: ______
2. 13h10: ______
3. 7h45: ______
4. 22h50: ______
5. 9h15: ______
6. 18h40: ______
7. 3h05: ______
8. 15h30: ______

4 Dans cinq minutes

Look at the clocks below and tell what time it will be in five minutes. Write out the times.

1. ______

2. ______

3. ______

4. ______

5. ______

5 À vous!

Answer these questions using complete sentences. Write out the times.

1. À quelle heure est-ce que vous arrivez à l'école?

______

2. Le cours de français commence à quelle heure?

______

3. À quelle heure est-ce que vous rentrez à la maison?

______

4. À quelle heure est-ce que vous dînez?

______

5. À quelle heure est-ce que vous regardez la télévision?

______

6. À quelle heure est-ce que vous étudiez?

______

Nom ______________________ Date ______________________

2B.2 Telling time (audio activities)

1 **L'heure** Look at the clock and listen to the statement. Indicate whether the statement is **vrai** or **faux.**

1. vrai ❍	2. vrai ❍	3. vrai ❍	4. vrai ❍	5. vrai ❍	6. vrai ❍
faux ❍	faux ❍	faux ❍	faux ❍	faux ❍	faux ❍

2 **Quelle heure est-il?** Your friends want to know the time. Answer their questions using the cues. Repeat the correct response after the speaker.

Modèle

You hear: Quelle heure est-il?
You see: 2:15 p.m.
You say: Il est deux heures et quart de l'après-midi.

1. 10:25 a.m.
2. 12:10 a.m.
3. 7:45 p.m.
4. 3:30 p.m.
5. 9:15 a.m.
6. 10:50 p.m.
7. 5:20 p.m.
8. 12:30 p.m.

3 **À quelle heure?** You are trying to plan your class schedule. Ask your counselor what time these classes meet and write the answer.

Modèle

You see: le cours de géographie
You say: À quelle heure est le cours de géographie?
You hear: Il est à neuf heures et demie du matin.
You write: 9:30 a.m.

1. le cours de biologie ______________
2. le cours d'informatique ______________
3. le cours de maths ______________
4. le cours d'allemand ______________
5. le cours de chimie ______________
6. le cours de littérature ______________

4 **Les trains** Your friend is in Paris and plans to go to the Riviera. He wants to know the train schedule. Using the 24-hour clock, answer his questions using the cues. Repeat the correct response after the speaker.

Modèle

You hear: À quelle heure est le dernier train pour Nice?
You see: 7:30 p.m.
You say: Il est à dix-neuf heures trente.

1. 9:05 p.m.
2. 8:15 a.m.
3. 10:30 a.m.
4. 5:25 p.m.
5. 12:23 p.m.
6. 10:27 p.m.

Nom ______________________ Date ______________________

Unité 2

PANORAMA

Savoir-faire

1 **Vrai ou faux?** Indicate whether these statements are **vrai** or **faux**.

	Vrai	Faux
1. La population de la France est de moins de (*less than*) 50.000.000 d'habitants.	❍	❍
2. Paris, Lille et Marseille sont des villes importantes.	❍	❍
3. L'énergie est une des industries principales en France.	❍	❍
4. Il y a plus de 12.000 musées en France.	❍	❍
5. La France a une superficie de moins de 550.000 kilomètres carrés.	❍	❍
6. Auguste Renoir est un écrivain français.	❍	❍
7. Claude Debussy est compositeur et musicien.	❍	❍
8. Les Académiciens défendent le bon usage du français.	❍	❍
9. La France n'est pas une puissance (*power*) industrielle.	❍	❍
10. La France est un pays membre de l'Union européenne.	❍	❍

2 **Choisissez** Choose the correct completion for these sentences.

1. On appelle le cinéma le ______________________.
   a. 5e art
   b. 6e art
   c. 7e art
2. La France est en forme ______________________.
   a. d'hexagone
   b. de triangle
   c. de pentagone
3. Le TGV roule à plus de ______________________ kilomètres à l'heure.
   a. 200
   b. 300
   c. 400
4. François Truffaut et Luc Besson sont des ______________________ français.
   a. cinéastes
   b. acteurs
   c. peintres
5. Peugeot et Citroën sont des ______________________ françaises.
   a. films
   b. voitures
   c. trains
6. La Loire, la Garonne et le Rhône sont des ______________________ de France.
   a. châteaux
   b. fleuves
   c. forêts

Nom ______________________ Date ______________________

3 **Complétez** Complete these statements with words from the list.

actrices	euro	industries
cinéma	femme sculpteur	maritimes
écrivain	héroïne	trains

1. Les produits de luxe et le tourisme sont des ______________________ principales.
2. La monnaie de la France s'appelle l'______________________.
3. Jeanne d'Arc est une ______________________ française.
4. Camille Claudel est une ______________________ française.
5. Émile Zola est un ______________________ français.
6. La mer Méditerranée et la Manche sont des fronts ______________________.
7. La SNCF est le système des ______________________ français.
8. Catherine Deneuve et Audrey Tautou sont des ______________________ françaises.

4 **La France** Label the French cities numbered on the map.

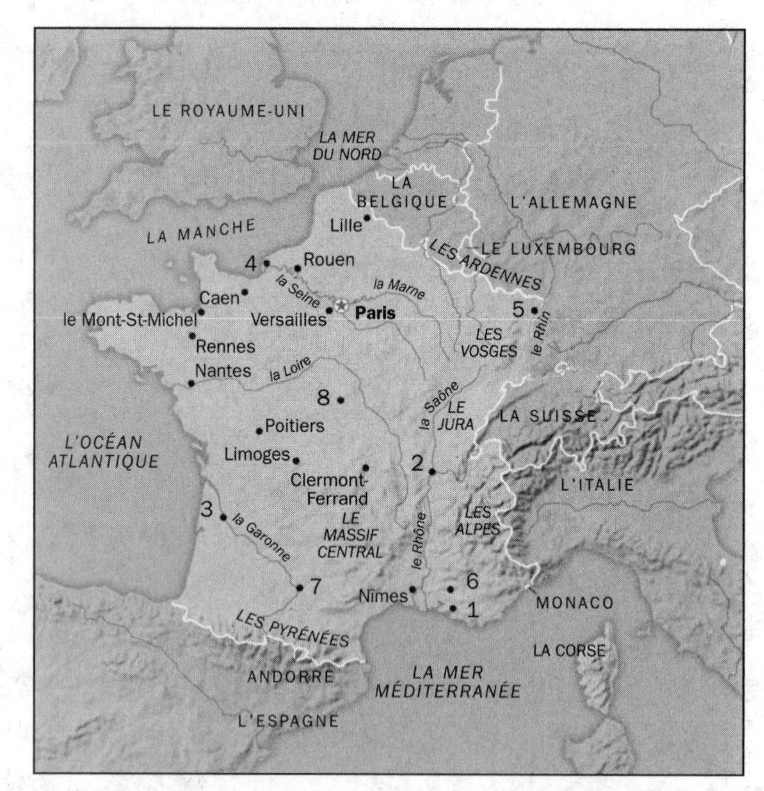

1. ______________________
2. ______________________
3. ______________________
4. ______________________
5. ______________________
6. ______________________
7. ______________________
8. ______________________

Nom ______________________ Date ______________________

Unité 3

Leçon 3A

CONTEXTES

1 **L'arbre généalogique** Use the clues below to complete Amandine's family tree.

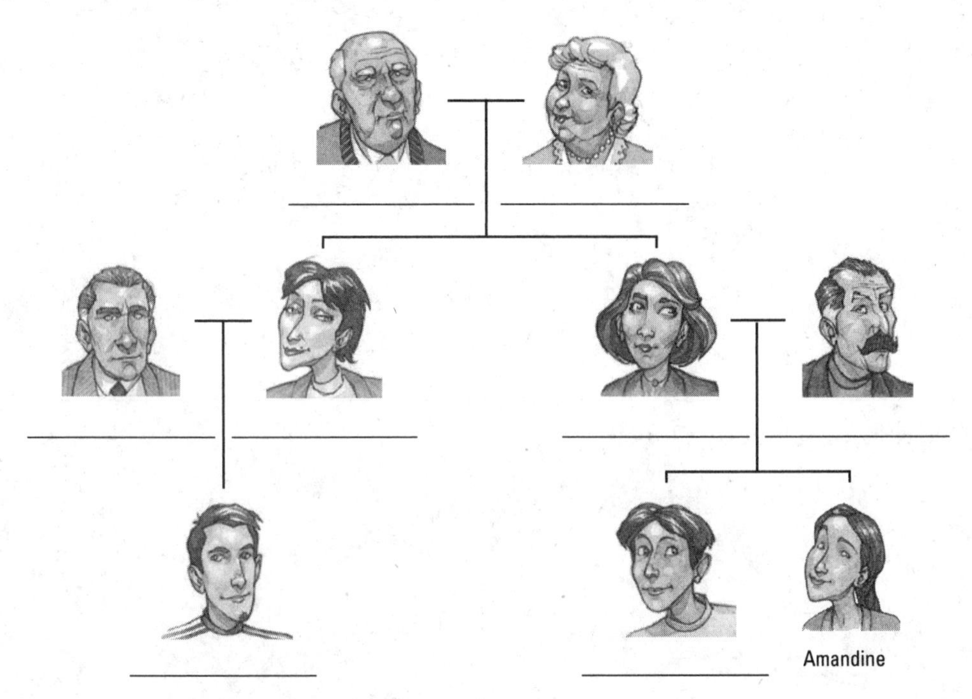

1. Marcelle est la mère d'Amandine.
2. Raymond et Marcelle ont une fille et un fils.
3. Michel est le frère d'Amandine.
4. Aminata et Hassan ont un enfant.
5. Marcelle est la belle-sœur d'Hassan.
6. Aminata a une sœur.
7. Gustave est le petit-fils de Pierre.
8. Hassan est le beau-fils d'Aïcha.

2 **L'album de photos** Decide which picture best corresponds to each description.

_____ 1. C'est mon cousin, Franck, et ma cousine, Séverine. Ils étudient à l'Université de Lyon.

_____ 2. Voici la mère de ma mère. Elle est veuve. Elle s'appelle Anne-Marie.

_____ 3. Voici mes grands-parents. Ils habitent à Aix-en-Provence.

_____ 4. Voici mon oncle, Stéphane, et sa femme, Véronique. Mon cousin, Guillaume, a un chat.

_____ 5. Voici ma sœur aînée. Elle a 21 ans. Elle est avec son petit ami, Frédéric.

_____ 6. Voici mon demi-frère. Il a 2 ans. Il est le cadet de la famille.

Nom ______________________ Date ______________________

3 **Cherchez** Find fifteen more family-related words in the grid. They may appear horizontally, vertically, or diagonally.

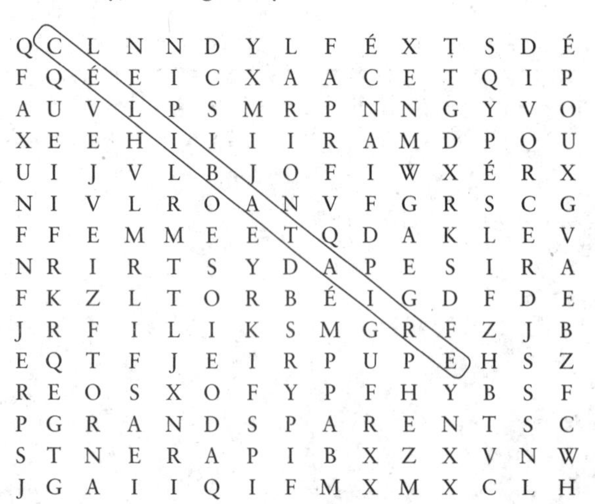

célibataire	grands-parents
divorcer	mari
époux	neveu
famille	parents
femme	petits-enfants
fiancé	séparé
fille	veuf
fils	voisin

4 **Complétez** Complete these analogies according to the model.

Modèle

demi-frère : demi-sœur :: frère : *sœur*

1. cousine : cousin :: sœur : ____________
2. marié : séparé :: épouser : ____________
3. épouse : époux :: femme : ____________
4. neveu : oncle :: nièce : ____________
5. parents : grands-parents :: enfants : ____________
6. mère : fille :: père : ____________

5 **Écrivez** Read this e-mail from your French pen-pal. Then describe your family in your response.

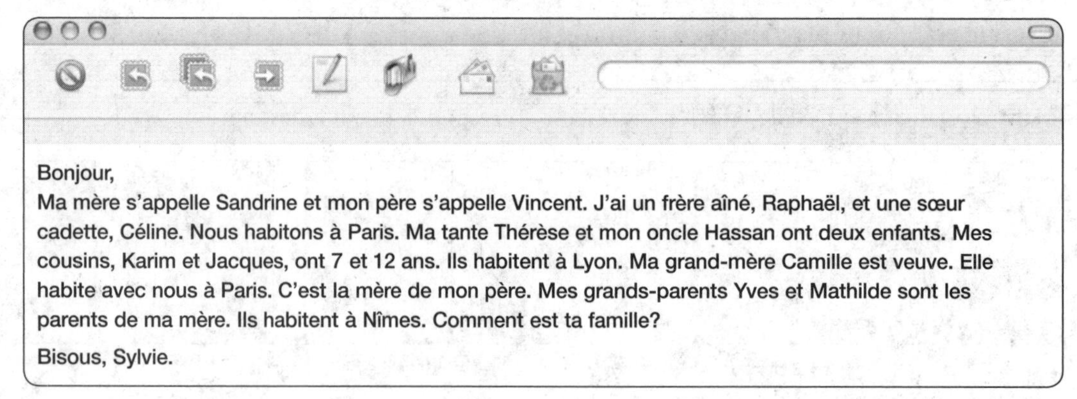
Bonjour,
Ma mère s'appelle Sandrine et mon père s'appelle Vincent. J'ai un frère aîné, Raphaël, et une sœur cadette, Céline. Nous habitons à Paris. Ma tante Thérèse et mon oncle Hassan ont deux enfants. Mes cousins, Karim et Jacques, ont 7 et 12 ans. Ils habitent à Lyon. Ma grand-mère Camille est veuve. Elle habite avec nous à Paris. C'est la mère de mon père. Mes grands-parents Yves et Mathilde sont les parents de ma mère. Ils habitent à Nîmes. Comment est ta famille?
Bisous, Sylvie.

____

____

____

____

____

CONTEXTES: AUDIO ACTIVITIES

1 **Qui est-ce?** You will hear some questions. Look at the family tree and give the correct answer to each question.

1. ______________________
2. ______________________
3. ______________________
4. ______________________
5. ______________________
6. ______________________
7. ______________________
8. ______________________
9. ______________________
10. ______________________

2 **La famille Martin** Lise's new friend just met her family and wants to verify the various relationships. Look at the family tree in **Activité 1,** and answer the questions. Repeat the answer after the speaker. (*6 items*)

Modèle

Paul est le frère de Gérard, n'est-ce pas?

Non, Paul est le beau-père de Gérard.

3 **Complétez** Listen to this story and write the missing words.

Je m'appelle Julien. Mes (1) ______________ sont divorcés. J'habite avec ma (2) ______________ et ma (3) ______________. Nous partageons une maison avec le (4) ______________ de ma (5) ______________. Mon (6) ______________ et ma (7) ______________ ont trois (8) ______________. Mon (9) ______________ s'appelle Simon et mes (10) ______________ s'appellent Coralie et Sixtine. Mon (11) ______________ est marié et ma (12) ______________ s'appelle Sabine. J'ai un (13) ______________ Théophile.

Nom ______________________ Date ______________________

LES SONS ET LES LETTRES

L'accent aigu and l'accent grave

In French, diacritical marks (accents) are an essential part of a word's spelling. They indicate how vowels are pronounced or distinguish between words with similar spellings but different meanings. **L'accent aigu** (´) appears only over the vowel **e**. It indicates that the **e** is pronounced similarly to the vowel *a* in the English word *cake* but shorter and crisper.

étudier	réservé	élégant	téléphone

L'accent aigu also signals some similarities between French and English words. Often, an **e** with **l'accent aigu** at the beginning of a French word marks the place where the letter *s* would appear at the beginning of the English equivalent.

éponge	épouse	état	étudiante
sponge	*spouse*	*state*	*student*

L'accent grave (`) appears only over the vowels **a**, **e**, and **u**. Over the vowel **e**, it indicates that the **e** is pronounced like the vowel *e* in the English word *pet*.

très	après	mère	nièce

Although **l'accent grave** does not change the pronunciation of the vowels *a* or *u*, it distinguishes words that have a similar spelling but different meanings.

la	là	ou	où
the	*there*	*or*	*where*

1 **Prononcez** Practice saying these words aloud.

1. agréable
2. sincère
3. voilà
4. faculté
5. frère
6. à
7. déjà
8. éléphant
9. lycée
10. poème
11. là
12. élève

2 **Articulez** Practice saying these sentences aloud.

1. À tout à l'heure!
2. Thérèse, je te présente Michèle.
3. Hélène est très sérieuse et réservée.
4. Voilà mon père, Frédéric, et ma mère, Ségolène.
5. Tu préfères étudier à la fac demain après-midi?

3 **Dictons** Practice saying these sayings aloud.

1. Tel père, tel fils.
2. À vieille mule, frein doré.

4 **Dictée** You will hear eight sentences. Each will be said twice. Listen carefully and write what you hear.

1. ______________________
2. ______________________
3. ______________________
4. ______________________
5. ______________________
6. ______________________
7. ______________________
8. ______________________

Nom ____________________ Date ____________________

Roman-photo

L'ALBUM DE PHOTOS

Avant de regarder

1 **Examinez le titre** Look at the title of the video module. Based on the title and the video still below, what do you think you will see in this episode? Use your imagination and answer in French.

____
____
____
____
____

En regardant la vidéo

2 **Les photos de tante Françoise** As the characters look at the family photos, check off each family member you see or hear described.

❑ 1. Stéphane's younger cousin, Bernard
❑ 2. Valérie's older brother, Henri
❑ 3. Valérie's sister-in-law
❑ 4. Valérie's sister
❑ 5. Stéphane's least favorite cousin, Charles
❑ 6. Stéphane's dog, Socrates
❑ 7. Charles' dog, Socrates
❑ 8. Françoise's daughter, Sophie
❑ 9. Sophie's brother, Bernard
❑ 10. Henri's oldest son, Charles

3 **Associez** Match each person with the adjective(s) used to describe them in this video segment. Some adjectives may be used for more than one person.

a. heureux/heureuse
b. sérieux/sérieuse
c. brillant(e)
d. intelligent(e)
e. timide
f. sociable
g. joli(e)
h. curieux/curieuse

______ 1. Amina
______ 2. Michèle
______ 3. Henri
______ 4. Charles
______ 5. Sophie
______ 6. Françoise
______ 7. Rachid
______ 8. Stéphane

4 **Vrai ou faux?** Indicate whether each statement is **vrai** or **faux**.

	Vrai	Faux
1. Amina connaît (*knows*) bien Cyberhomme.	❍	❍
2. Michèle et Amina sont amies.	❍	❍
3. Valérie pense que Stéphane doit (*should*) étudier davantage (*more*).	❍	❍
4. Stéphane pense qu'il étudie beaucoup.	❍	❍
5. Stéphane ne comprend (*understand*) pas comment utiliser un CD-ROM.	❍	❍
6. Stéphane et Valérie regardent des photos sur l'ordinateur d'Amina.	❍	❍
7. Michèle est une amie de Sophie.	❍	❍
8. Stéphane n'aime pas Socrates.	❍	❍
9. Valérie pense que Rachid est un bon (*good*) étudiant.	❍	❍
10. Amina pense que préparer le bac avec Rachid est une mauvaise idée.	❍	❍

Nom ____________________ Date ____________________

Après la vidéo

5 **Corrigez** Each statement below contains one piece of false information. Underline the incorrect word(s), and write the correct one(s) in the space provided.

1. Cyberhomme est le cousin d'Amina. ____________
2. Michèle est timide. ____________
3. Stéphane a vingt-quatre ans. ____________
4. Stéphane adore ses cours. ____________
5. Stéphane a un dictionnaire espagnol-français. ____________
6. Il a aussi un cahier pour le cours de littérature. ____________
7. Henri a quarante-sept ans. ____________
8. Henri est célibataire. ____________
9. Il y a un chat sur la photo. ____________
10. Amina aime l'idée de Stéphane; elle est pessimiste. ____________

6 **Répondez** Answer these questions in complete sentences.

1. Amina mange-t-elle?
____
2. Qu'est-ce qu'Amina a besoin de faire (*do*)?
____
3. Qu'est-ce qu'il y a dans le sac à dos de Stéphane?
____
4. Quel (*Which*) cousin est-ce que Stéphane n'aime pas?
____
5. Combien d'enfants Henri et Françoise ont-ils?
____
6. Pourquoi est-ce une idée géniale de préparer le bac avec Rachid?
____

7 **À vous!** In your own words, describe the people in the family photo according to what you heard in the video episode. Include names; relationship to Valérie, Stéphane, or each other; and any other details you remember, such as age, appearance, or personality.

____
____
____
____
____
____
____
____

Nom ______________________ Date ______________________

Flash culture

LA FAMILLE ET LES COPAINS

Avant de regarder

1 **Vocabulaire supplémentaire** Look over these words and expressions before you watch the video; you will hear them in this segment.

la petite	*the little girl*	donner à manger	*to feed*
là-bas	*over there*	Vous pensez que... ?	*Do you think that... ?*
Tiens!	*Oh!*	Eh, regardez!	*Hey, look!*

2 **La famille et les copains** In this video, you will hear descriptions of people and find out about their relationships with others. In preparation, circle the statements that best describe you.

1. Je suis un garçon. / Je suis une fille.
2. J'ai 15 ans. / J'ai moins de (*less than*) 15 ans. / J'ai plus de (*more than*) 15 ans.
3. Je suis sportif/sportive. / J'ai un meilleur ami. / J'ai une meilleure amie.
4. J'ai un neveu. / J'ai une nièce. / Je n'ai pas de neveux ni (*nor*) de nièces.
5. J'ai un chat. / J'ai un chien. / J'ai un oiseau. / J'ai un poisson. / Je n'ai pas d'animaux.
6. J'ai un frère. / Je n'ai pas de frère. / J'ai une sœur. / Je n'ai pas de sœur.

3 **Les catégories** Check the appropriate column to classify these words as **une personne** or **un adjectif**.

	personne	adjectif		personne	adjectif
1. petit	________	________	**7. jeune**	________	________
2. fils	________	________	**8. célibataire**	________	________
3. marié	________	________	**9. ami**	________	________
4. copain	________	________	**10. gentil**	________	________
5. enfant	________	________	**11. fille**	________	________
6. garçon	________	________	**12. sportif**	________	________

Nom ______________________ Date ______________________

En regardant la vidéo

4 **Indiquez** Indicate which of these people or animals are mentioned in the video.

- ❑ 1. père
- ❑ 2. mère
- ❑ 3. fille
- ❑ 4. fils
- ❑ 5. femme
- ❑ 6. mari
- ❑ 7. neveu
- ❑ 8. nièce
- ❑ 9. grand-père
- ❑ 10. homme
- ❑ 11. couple
- ❑ 12. chien
- ❑ 13. chat
- ❑ 14. oiseau
- ❑ 15. poisson

5 **Complétez** Complete these sentences according to what you see and hear in the video.

1. La petite, elle a ______________ ou ______________ ans, je crois.
2. Les garçons là-bas, ce sont des ______________. Ils ont beaucoup d'énergie.
3. Et cette jeune femme, vous pensez qu'elle est ______________ ou ______________?
4. Un jeune couple. Que c'est ______________!
5. Eh, regardez! Une femme avec son ______________.
6. C'est mon ______________.

Après la vidéo

6 **À vous!** How would you describe your family and friends? Think of three friends, family members, and/or pets, and complete the descriptions of each. Include a photo or a drawing.

1. 2. 3.

1. Il/Elle s'appelle ______________________.
   C'est mon/ma ______________________.
   Il/Elle est ______________ et ______________.
2. Il/Elle s'appelle ______________________.
   C'est mon/ma ______________________.
   Il/Elle est ______________ et ______________.
3. Il/Elle s'appelle ______________________.
   C'est mon/ma ______________________.
   Il/Elle est ______________ et ______________.

Nom ____________________ Date ____________________

STRUCTURES

3A.1 Descriptive adjectives

1 **Les accords** Kim is describing her sister, Nathalie, and her cousin, Chan. Complete the sentences with the correct forms of the adjectives.

1. Ma sœur est ____________ (grand) et elle a les cheveux ____________ (roux).
2. Mon cousin Chan a les cheveux ____________ (brun) et ____________ (court).
3. Nathalie est ____________ (joli). Elle n'est pas ____________ (laid).
4. Mon cousin est ____________ (naïf). Il n'est pas ____________ (vieux).
5. Ma sœur est ____________ (fier). Son fils est ____________ (beau).
6. Le ____________ (nouveau) étudiant dans la classe de Chan est ____________ (curieux).
7. Les étudiants de l'école de Chan sont ____________ (brillant) et ____________ (sérieux).
8. Moi, j'ai les yeux ____________ (bleu). Je suis ____________ (sociable).

2 **Complétez** Complete these descriptions. Remember to make any necessary agreements.

Modèle

ma / grand / sœur / être / de taille moyenne
Ma grande sœur est de taille moyenne.

1. je / avoir / grand / famille ____________________
2. mon / nouveau / appartement / être / petit ____________________
3. grand / salle de classe / être / vieux ____________________
4. ma / jeune / voisine / être / français ____________________
5. joli / actrice / avoir / bon / rôle ____________________
6. gros / chat / avoir / yeux / vert ____________________

3 **Les contraires** Write an antonym for each adjective. Make the new adjectives agree in gender and number with the ones provided.

Modèle

petites ≠ *grandes*

1. grand ≠ ____________________
2. courtes ≠ ____________________
3. laids ≠ ____________________
4. mauvaise ≠ ____________________
5. jeune ≠ ____________________
6. bruns ≠ ____________________
7. réservées ≠ ____________________
8. malheureux ≠ ____________________

Nom ______________________ Date ______________________

4 **Une lettre** Adam is writing his first letter to his pen-pal in Guadeloupe. Help him find the right adjectives to complete his letter. Don't forget to make the necessary agreements.

Modèle

Ma sœur est _____ (≠ petit) et _____ (intellectuel).
Ma sœur est **grande** et **intellectuelle.**

Ma mère est de taille moyenne et (1) ______________ (≠ laid). Elle a les cheveux (2) ______________ (= brun) et (3) ______________ (raide). Elle a les yeux (4) ______________ (≠ noir). Mon père est (5) ______________ (≠ petit). Il a les cheveux (6) ______________ (noir) et (7) ______________ (court). Mes parents sont (8) ______________ (≠ malheureux). Nous habitons dans un (9) ______________ (≠ nouveau) appartement à Paris. J'ai un (10) ______________ (nouveau) petit chien. Il s'appelle Médor. Il est (11) ______________ (beau). Ma grand-mère habite avec nous. C'est une (12) ______________ (vieux) femme. Elle est (13) ______________ (sympathique) et (14) ______________ (bon).

5 **Les mots croisés** Read these definitions and fill in the crossword puzzle. Use the Garneau-Laval family tree in your textbook as a reference.

Across:

3. L'examen de Virginie Garneau dure (*lasts*) cinq heures. Il est...
4. Marie et Juliette Laval n'ont pas les cheveux châtains. Elles sont...
6. C'est la couleur du tee-shirt d'Isabelle Garneau.
7. Avant (*Before*) un examen, Virginie Garneau est...
9. Matthieu Laval a deux ans. Il est...
11. Bambou pèse (*weighs*) 50 kilos. C'est un... chien.

Down:

1. Les cheveux de Sophie Garneau sont...
2. Mes cousins sont heureux. Ils ne sont pas...
4. La première bande (*stripe*) du drapeau (*flag*) français est...
5. Le livre de Jean Garneau a trente pages. Il est...
8. Luc Garneau, le grand-père, est...
10. Les cheveux d'Isabelle Garneau sont...

Nom ______________________ Date ______________________

3A.1 Descriptive adjectives (audio activities)

1 **Féminin ou masculin?** Change each sentence from the masculine to the feminine or vice versa. Repeat the correct answer after the speaker. (6 *items*)

Modèle

L'oncle de Marie est français.

La tante de Marie est française.

2 **Singulier ou pluriel?** Change each sentence from singular to plural and vice versa. Repeat the correct answer after the speaker. (6 *items*)

Modèle

L'élève est jeune.

Les élèves sont jeunes.

3 **Mes camarades de classe** Describe your classmates using the cues. Repeat the correct answer after the speaker.

Modèle

You hear: Jeanne

You see: petit

You say: Jeanne est petite.

1. brun
2. roux
3. beau
4. sympathique
5. grand et gros
6. heureux et intelligent
7. bon et naïf
8. nouveau

4 **La famille Dumoulin** Look at the picture of the Dumoulin family. Listen to these statements and decide whether each statement is **vrai** or **faux.**

	Vrai	Faux
1.	❍	❍
2.	❍	❍
3.	❍	❍
4.	❍	❍
5.	❍	❍
6.	❍	❍
7.	❍	❍
8.	❍	❍

Nom ____________________ Date ____________________

3A.2 Possessive adjectives

1 **Choisissez** Mariam is introducing you to her family. Choose the correct possessive adjectives.

Modèle

Je cherche (mon, ma, mes) frère, Thomas. [mon circled]

1. Je vous présente (mon, ma, mes) amie, Catherine.
2. Elle adore (ton, leurs, vos) frère!
3. Catherine et moi parlons en français avec (notre, nos, ton) parents.
4. Voici (ma, mon, leurs) oncle, Amadou.
5. Amadou aime (sa, son, leurs) chat.
6. Amadou et son épouse aiment (son, ses, leurs) enfants.
7. Maintenant, nous cherchons (ma, notre, nos) ami Charles.
8. Charlotte est (mon, ma, leurs) cousine.

2 **Qui est-ce?** Here are some bits of conversation overheard at Georges and Elsa's wedding. Complete each sentence with the appropriate possessive adjective.

1. __________ (*My*) grand-mère est française, mais __________ (*my*) grand-père est canadien.
2. __________ (*Their*) cousins habitent en France.
3. Comment s'appelle __________ (*your, formal*) époux?
4. __________ (*Your, informal*) parents sont jeunes.
5. __________ (*My*) amie adore __________ (*her*) frère.
6. __________ (*His*) oncle est espagnol.
7. __________ (*Our*) professeurs sont intéressants.
8. __________ (*My*) enfants sont jeunes. Ils adorent __________ (*their*) chat.

3 **Complétez** Complete these sentences with the form of the possessive adjective that agrees with the subject.

Modèle

Vous avez ____vos____ livres de français?

1. J'aime __________ lycée et __________ camarades de classe.
2. Ma grand-mère adore __________ petits-enfants et __________ nièces.
3. Tu parles souvent à __________ cousins et à __________ nouvelle camarade de classe.
4. Nous aimons __________ cours et __________ professeur.
5. Ils cherchent __________ cahiers et __________ carte de restaurant universitaire.
6. Vous étudiez avec __________ ami pour __________ examens.
7. Annie a __________ sac à dos et __________ calculatrice.
8. Je ne trouve pas __________ montre. Je cherche aussi __________ feuilles de papier.

4 **Décrivez** Complete these descriptions of Hassan's family with the appropriate possessive adjectives.

Modèle

C'est le père d'Hassan. ___Son___ père s'appelle Hamed.

1. Les frères d'Hassan s'appellent Hamid et Zinédine. ____________ frères sont jeunes.
2. Ils parlent souvent avec des amis. ____________ amis sont sympathiques.
3. Hassan a des parents brillants. Il adore ____________ parents.
4. Hamid et Zinédine aiment la fac. ____________ fac est grande.
5. Hassan est marié avec Sofiane. ____________ femme est petite.
6. Zinédine et Hamid étudient l'économie. ____________ études sont importantes.
7. Les voisins de sa sœur sont étrangers. ____________ voisins sont vieux.
8. Je suis un(e) ami(e) d'Hassan. Hassan est ____________ ami.

5 **Répondez** Answer these questions in complete sentences using possessive adjectives and the clues provided.

Modèle

Est-ce que vous aimez votre chien? (aimer beaucoup)
Oui, nous aimons beaucoup notre chien.

1. Est-ce que tu aimes ton école? (adorer)
____
2. Stéphanie, comment est ton frère? (grand et brun)
____
3. Monsieur Lafarge, comment vont vos parents (*how are your parents doing*)? (très bien)
____
4. La belle-sœur de Marc est de quelle origine? (italienne)
____
5. À quelle heure est-ce que vos cousines arrivent? (à sept heures du soir)
____
6. Est-ce que tes parents aiment les chats? (aimer beaucoup)
____
7. Est-ce que les amis de Daniel sont timides? (sociables)
____
8. Comment est mon neveu? (poli et sympa)
____

Nom ____________________ Date ____________________

3A.2 Possessive adjectives (audio activities)

1 **Identifiez** Listen to each statement and mark an X in the column for the correct translation of the possessive adjective you hear.

Modèle

You hear: C'est mon professeur de français.
You mark: an **X** under *my*

	my	your (familiar)	your (formal)	his/her	our	their
Modèle	X					
1.						
2.						
3.						
4.						
5.						
6.						
7.						
8.						

2 **Choisissez** Listen to each question and choose the most logical answer.

1. a. Oui, ton appartement est grand.
   b. Non, mon appartement n'est pas grand.
2. a. Oui, nous habitons avec nos parents.
   b. Non, nous n'habitons pas avec vos parents.
3. a. Oui, c'est ton cousin.
   b. Oui, c'est son cousin.
4. a. Oui, leurs parents rentrent à 10 heures ce soir.
   b. Oui, nos parents rentrent à 10 heures ce soir.
5. a. Non, ma sœur n'étudie pas la chimie.
   b. Non, sa sœur n'étudie pas la chimie.
6. a. Oui, leur nièce est au Brésil.
   b. Oui, ma nièce est au Brésil.
7. a. Non, leurs amis ne sont pas ici.
   b. Non, nos amis ne sont pas ici.
8. a. Oui, leurs grands-parents sont italiens.
   b. Oui, nos grands-parents sont italiens.

3 **Questions** Answer each question you hear in the affirmative using the appropriate possessive adjective. Repeat the correct response after the speaker. (6 *items*)

C'est ton ami?
Oui, c'est mon ami.

Nom ______________________ Date ______________________

Unité 3

Leçon 3B

CONTEXTES

1 **Chassez l'intrus** Circle the word or expression that does not belong with the others.

1. actif, paresseux, sportif, rapide
2. doux, gentil, modeste, cruel
3. pénible, antipathique, ennuyeux, gentil
4. triste, ennuyeux, méchant, génial
5. architecte, étranger, avocat, médecin
6. faible, athlète, fort, sportif
7. fou, généreux, jaloux, antipathique
8. prêt, fatigué, inquiet, triste

2 **Les professions** What professions might these people choose?

1. Benjamin adore l'art et la sculpture. Il va être ______________________.
2. Tatiana est très rapide et elle aime le sport. Elle va être ______________________.
3. Olivier aime écrire (*to write*) des articles et voyager. Il va être ______________________.
4. Barbara aime les mathématiques et la physique. Elle va être ______________________.
5. Julien étudie l'économie et la gestion. Il va être ______________________.
6. Chakir étudie le droit. Il va être ______________________.
7. Marie étudie la biologie. Elle va être ______________________.
8. Nathalie aime étudier les styles de maison. Elle va être ______________________.

3 **Les accords** Maxine is describing the people she met while an exchange student in Montreal. Complete the sentences with the correct forms of the adjectives.

1. Mélanie est avocate. Elle est toujours ____________ (prêt) à travailler. Elle est très ____________ (actif).
2. Son mari, Jeff, est ingénieur. Il est ____________ (étranger); il est anglais. Son actrice française ____________ (favori) est Catherine Deneuve.
3. Mes camarades de classe, Jean-Philippe et Sofiane, sont ____________ (fou). C'est ____________ (pénible).
4. La femme de Jean-Philippe est très ____________ (jaloux). C'est ____________ (triste).
5. Le serveur de mon restaurant préféré n'est pas ____________ (paresseux). C'est un homme ____________ (travailleur).
6. Les chiens du voisin sont ____________ (méchant) et ____________ (cruel).
7. Mon professeur de littérature est ____________ (génial), mais ses examens sont ____________ (pénible).
8. Ma coiffeuse est très ____________ (gentil) et ____________ (modeste).

4 **Complétez** Give a synonym or an antonym for these adjectives. The new adjectives should agree in gender and number with the ones provided.

Modèle

antipathique (*fem.*) = *cruelle*

1. forte ≠ ____________________
2. méchant = ____________________
3. paresseuse ≠ ____________________
4. rapides (*masc.*) ≠ ____________________
5. modeste (*fem.*) = ____________________
6. ennuyeux (*sing.*) ≠ ____________________

5 **Comment sont-ils?** Describe each profession using the correct form of each adjective. Write complete sentences.

Modèle

(pénible, cruel)
L'ingénieur: *L'ingénieur est pénible et cruel.*

(généreux, modeste)

1. Le dentiste et le médecin: ____________________
2. L'avocate: ____________________

(étranger, sympathique)

3. L'artiste (*fem.*): ____________________
4. L'architecte (*masc.*): ____________________

(ennuyeux, antipathique)

5. La journaliste et l'homme d'affaires: ____________________
6. L'avocat: ____________________

6 **Les descriptions** Complete these descriptions with the word or expression from **CONTEXTES** that is illustrated. Don't forget to make the necessary agreements.

1. Ma sœur est très (a)  ____________________. Elle est (b) 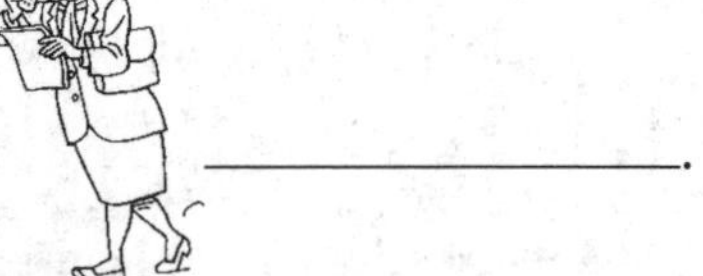 ____________________.

Son mari est (c) 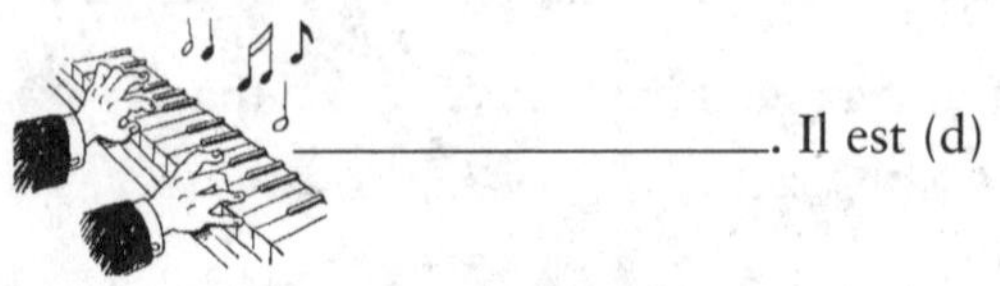 ____________________. Il est (d)  ____________________

pour sa femme. 2. Je ne suis pas (e)  ____________________ mais mon (f) 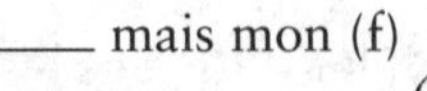

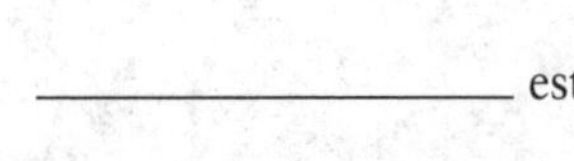 ____________________ est (g)  ____________________ et (h) 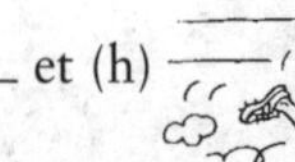 ____________________.

Nom ______________________ Date ______________________

CONTEXTES: AUDIO ACTIVITIES

1 **Logique ou illogique?** Listen to these statements and indicate whether they are **logique** or **illogique**.

	Logique	Illogique		Logique	Illogique
1.	❍	❍	5.	❍	❍
2.	❍	❍	6.	❍	❍
3.	❍	❍	7.	❍	❍
4.	❍	❍	8.	❍	❍

2 **Associez** Circle the words that are logically associated with each word you hear.

1. actif	sportif	faible
2. drôle	pénible	antipathique
3. cruel	mauvais	gentil
4. modeste	intelligent	prêt
5. favori	lent	homme d'affaires
6. architecte	fou	ennuyeux

3 **Professions** Listen to each statement and write the number of the statement below the photo it describes. There are more statements than there are photos.

a. ____________________

b. ____________________

c. ____________________

d. ____________________

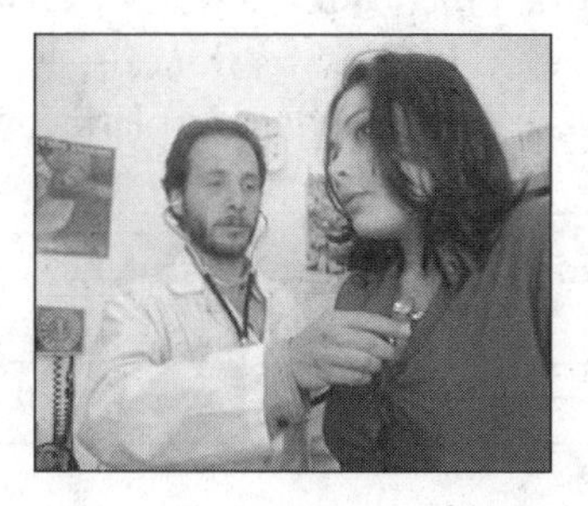

e. ____________________

Nom ______________________ Date ______________________

LES SONS ET LES LETTRES

L'accent circonflexe, la cédille, and le tréma

L'accent circonflexe (ˆ) can appear over any vowel.

pâté prêt aîné drôle croûton

L'accent circonflexe is also used to distinguish between words with similar spellings but different meanings.

mûr	**mur**	**sûr**	**sur**
ripe	*wall*	*sure*	*on*

L'accent circonflexe indicates that a letter, frequently an *s*, has been dropped from an older spelling. For this reason, **l'accent circonflexe** can be used to identify French cognates of English words.

hospital → hôpital forest → forêt

La cédille (¸) is only used with the letter **c**. A **c** with a **cédille** is pronounced with a soft **c** sound, like the *s* in the English word *yes*. Use a **cédille** to retain the soft **c** sound before an **a**, **o**, or **u**. Before an **e** or an **i**, the letter **c** is always soft, so a **cédille** is not necessary.

garçon français ça leçon

Le tréma (¨) is used to indicate that two vowel sounds are pronounced separately. It is always placed over the second vowel.

égoïste naïve Noël Haïti

1 **Prononcez** Practice saying these words aloud.

1. naïf
2. reçu
3. châtain
4. âge
5. français
6. fenêtre
7. théâtre
8. garçon
9. égoïste
10. château

2 **Articulez** Practice saying these sentences aloud.

1. Comment ça va?
2. Comme ci, comme ça.
3. Vous êtes française, Madame?
4. C'est un garçon cruel et égoïste.
5. J'ai besoin d'être reçu(e) à l'examen.
6. Caroline, ma sœur aînée, est très drôle.

3 **Dictons** Practice reading these sayings aloud.

1. Impossible n'est pas français.
2. Plus ça change, plus c'est la même chose.

4 **Dictée** You will hear six sentences. Each will be read twice. Listen carefully and write what you hear.

1. ______________________
2. ______________________
3. ______________________
4. ______________________
5. ______________________
6. ______________________

Nom ______________________ Date ______________________

Roman-photo

ON TRAVAILLE CHEZ MOI!

Avant de regarder

1 **La famille de Rachid** Look at this photo and use your imagination to write a brief description of Rachid's family. Who are the people? What do they look like? What are their personalities like? What are their professions?

____

____

____

____

____

En regardant la vidéo

2 **Qui...?** As you watch this episode, indicate which person says each statement. Write **A** for Amina, **R** for Rachid, **D** for David, **S** for Sandrine, and **St** for Stéphane.

_______ 1. Il n'est pas dans ton sac à dos?
_______ 2. Mais non! La table à côté de la porte.
_______ 3. Numéro de téléphone 06.62.70.94.87. Mais qui est-ce?
_______ 4. Tu n'es pas drôle!
_______ 5. On travaille chez moi!
_______ 6. Sandrine est tellement pénible.
_______ 7. J'ai besoin d'un bon café.
_______ 8. Allez, si x égale 83 et y égale 90, la réponse c'est...

3 **Les professions** Match the profession in the right column to the person in the left column. There are more professions than you will need.

_______ 1. Stéphane
_______ 2. Valérie
_______ 3. le père de Rachid
_______ 4. la mère de Rachid

a. coiffeur
b. propriétaire
c. avocate
d. journaliste
e. architecte
f. médecin

4 **Ce n'est pas vrai!** Place check marks beside the actions that do *not* occur in each scene.

Au café...

❑ 1. Rachid aide Sandrine à trouver son téléphone.
❑ 2. Stéphane va (*goes*) étudier chez Rachid.
❑ 3. Sandrine parle avec Pascal.
❑ 4. Sandrine demande où est David.
❑ 5. Un téléphone sonne (*rings*).

Chez David et Rachid...

❑ 6. David demande où est Sandrine.
❑ 7. David dit (*says*) qu'il a envie de manger quelque chose.
❑ 8. David va au café.
❑ 9. Rachid parle avec sa famille.
❑ 10. Stéphane donne la bonne réponse.

Nom ______________________ Date ______________________

Après la vidéo

5 **Choisissez** Select the option that best completes each statement.

1. Sandrine ne trouve pas ______________.
   a. sa montre b. son téléphone c. son sac à dos
2. Stéphane pense que Sandrine est ______________.
   a. pénible b. belle c. naïve
3. David a envie d'aller (*to go*) au café parce que ______________ y (*there*) est.
   a. Amina b. Valérie c. Sandrine
4. Rachid pense que ______________ est pénible.
   a. Stéphane b. David c. Valérie
5. Les ______________ de Rachid habitent en Algérie.
   a. parents b. sœurs c. grands-parents
6. Ses ______________ habitent à Marseille.
   a. cousins b. parents c. deux frères
7. Le père de Rachid est ______________.
   a. travailleur b. occupé c. nerveux
8. La mère de Rachid est ______________.
   a. vieille b. agréable c. active

6 **Répondez** Answer these questions in complete sentences.

1. Quand Sandrine cherche son téléphone, où est-il?

   ____

2. Qui appelle (*is calling*) Sandrine au téléphone?

   ____

3. Pourquoi est-ce que Stéphane pense que Sandrine est pénible?

   ____

4. Comment est la famille de Rachid?

   ____

5. Pourquoi est-ce que Stéphane et Rachid préparent le bac?

   ____

7 **À vous!** In your own words, write a list of the principal actions that occur in this episode in chronological order. Include as many details as you can. Your list should include at least six actions.

____

____

____

____

____

____

____

Nom ____________________ Date ____________________

STRUCTURES

3B.1 Numbers 61–100

1 **Complétez** You are babysitting a little girl from the French-American school. She needs help with her math. Help her by filling in the blanks with the missing numbers. Spell out the numbers.

Modèle

Cent moins (*minus*) trente-deux font (*makes*) *soixante-huit.*

1. Quatre-vingt-dix-neuf moins ____________________ font vingt-cinq.
2. Trente-trois plus quarante-cinq font ____________________.
3. Cinquante-sept plus quarante et un font ____________________.
4. Quatre-vingt-neuf moins ____________________ font vingt-huit.
5. Soixante-seize plus vingt-quatre font ____________________.
6. Quatorze plus ____________________ font quatre-vingt-dix-neuf.
7. Vingt-six plus cinquante-sept font ____________________.
8. Trente-deux plus soixante font ____________________.

2 **Quel est le prix?** Write out the prices of these items.

Modèle

des feuilles de papier *douze euros soixante-cinq*

1. un cahier ____________________
2. une chaise ____________________
3. des crayons ____________________
4. un sac à dos ____________________
5. une horloge ____________________
6. des stylos ____________________

3 **Les itinéraires** You are looking at a map and considering several day trips you want to take. Write complete sentences to tell how far each city is from Paris.

Modèle

Gisors (74 km) *Gisors est à soixante-quatorze kilomètres de Paris.*

1. Provins (91 km): ____________________
2. Fontainebleau (66 km): ____________________
3. Beauvais (78 km): ____________________
4. Évreux (96 km): ____________________
5. Épieds (84 km): ____________________
6. Pithiviers (94 km): ____________________
7. Chartres (88 km): ____________________
8. Soissons (100 km): ____________________

Nom ____________ Date ____________

4 **Les coordonnées** Write sentences to tell where these people live. Follow the model and spell out the numbers.

Modèle

(Jean) 75, rue Victor Hugo
Jean habite au soixante-quinze, rue Victor Hugo.

1. (Malika) 97, rue Bois des cars
____
2. (Amadou) 66, avenue du Général Leclerc
____
3. (Martine) 73, rue Vaugelas
____
4. (Jérôme) 81, rue Lamartine
____
5. (Guillaume) 100, rue Rivoli
____
6. (Nordine) 91, rue Molière
____
7. (Géraldine) 67, avenue Voltaire
____
8. (Paul) 78, rue de l'Espérance
____

5 **Les mots croisés** Complete this crossword puzzle. Run the words together without hyphens or spaces.

Across:
4. 50 + 41
6. 61 + 21
7. 49 + 14
8. 67 + 22
9. 37 + 39

Down:
1. 52 + 36
2. 19 + 51
3. 61 + 38
5. 60 + 40
6. 50 + 40

Nom ______________________ Date ______________________

3B.1 Numbers 61–100 (audio activities)

1

Numéros de téléphone You are at a party and you meet some new people. You want to see them again but you don't have their telephone numbers. Ask them what their phone numbers are and write their answers.

Modèle

You see: Julie
You say: **Quel est ton numéro de téléphone, Julie?**
You hear: C'est le zéro un, vingt-trois, trente-huit, quarante-trois, cinquante-deux.
You write: 01.23.38.43.52

1. Chloé ______________________
2. Justin ______________________
3. Ibrahim ______________________
4. Cassandre ______________________
5. Lolita ______________________
6. Yannis ______________________
7. Omar ______________________
8. Sara ______________________

2

Inventaire You and your co-worker are taking an inventory at the university bookstore. Answer your co-worker's questions using the cue. Repeat the correct response after the speaker.

Modèle

You hear: Il y a combien de livres de français?
You see: 61
You say: **Il y a soixante et un livres de français.**

1. 71
2. 92
3. 87
4. 94
5. 62
6. 96
7. 83
8. 66

3

Message Listen to this telephone conversation and complete the phone message with the correct information.

MESSAGE TÉLÉPHONIQUE

Pour: ______________________

De: ______________________

Téléphone: ______________________

Message: ______________________

____

3B.2 Prepositions of location

1

Complétez Henri is helping customers in the bookstore where he works. Complete each sentence with the appropriate preposition of location.

1. Les sacs à dos sont ____________ (*next to*) des stylos.
2. Les cahiers sont ____________ (*behind*) les livres.
3. Les cartes sont ____________ (*to the right of*) l'ordinateur.
4. La bibliothèque est ____________ (*close to*) de la maison.
5. La librairie est ____________ (*across from*) du lycée.
6. Les calculatrices sont ____________ (*on*) la table.
7. Les feuilles de papier sont ____________ (*in*) le bureau.
8. Les sacs à dos sont ____________ (*under*) la fenêtre.

2

C'est où? Choose the prepositions that logically complete this letter from a student in Dakar, Senegal.

chez	en	juste à côté	près
dans	entre	loin de	sur

(1) ____________ moi, c'est tout petit. Nous habitons (2) ____________ un appartement (3) ____________ du Café de la Place. Nous sommes heureux ici. Ma grande sœur, Adama, habite (4) ____________; nous nous voyons (*we see each other*) tous les jours. (5) ____________ Adama et moi, il y a dix ans de différence. La vie (6) ____________ Afrique est formidable! J'adore la fac de Dakar. Elle est (7) ____________ la côte (*coast*) atlantique.

3

Choisissez Barbara has sent some pictures to her cousin, Régine. She has written a short description on the back of each one. Complete each description by choosing the most logical preposition.

1. Mon chien est ______________ (sur, sous, devant, à côté) la maison.
2. Mon dictionnaire est ______________ (dans, entre, en, par) le bureau.
3. Mon ordinateur est ______________ (loin, sur, par, en) le bureau.
4. La corbeille à papier est ______________ (devant, entre, à côté, près de) du bureau.
5. La bibliothèque est ______________ (par, en, sur, près de) l'université.
6. Le lycée est ______________ (loin de, près, entre, en face) l'université.
7. La télévision est ______________ (à côté, entre, loin, près) la fenêtre et le bureau.
8. Le stylo est ______________ (en face, à côté, dans, en) mon sac à dos.

Nom ________________________ Date ________________________

4 **Le plan** Write the name of each place on the map below, according to the clues provided. Each clue is from the reader's point of view. The first item has been done for you.

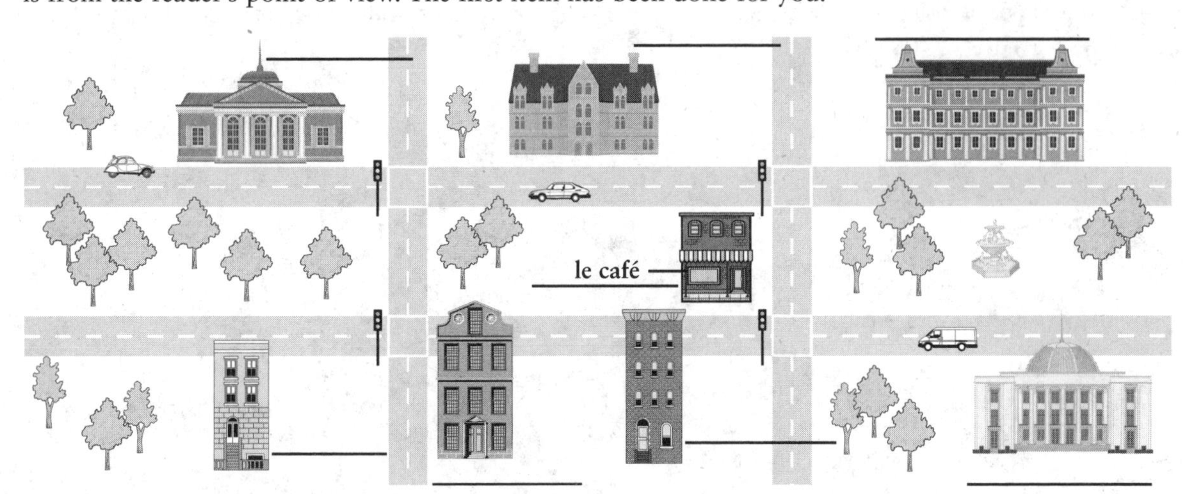

1. Le café est dans la librairie.
2. Le lycée est derrière la librairie.
3. La bibliothèque est à droite du lycée.
4. L'université est en face de la bibliothèque.
5. Chez moi, c'est en face du café, à gauche de l'université.
6. J'habite entre l'université et le restaurant «Chez Léon».
7. Le restaurant universitaire est loin de l'université, mais près du lycée.
8. Le dentiste est près du restaurant «Chez Léon».

5 **Les prépositions** Give a synonym or an antonym of these prepositions of location.

1. sur ≠ ____________
2. devant ≠ ____________
3. à droite de ≠ ____________
4. près de ≠ ____________
5. en = ____________
6. juste à côté = ____________

6 **Où est le livre?** Look at these images and tell where the book is located in relation to the desk.

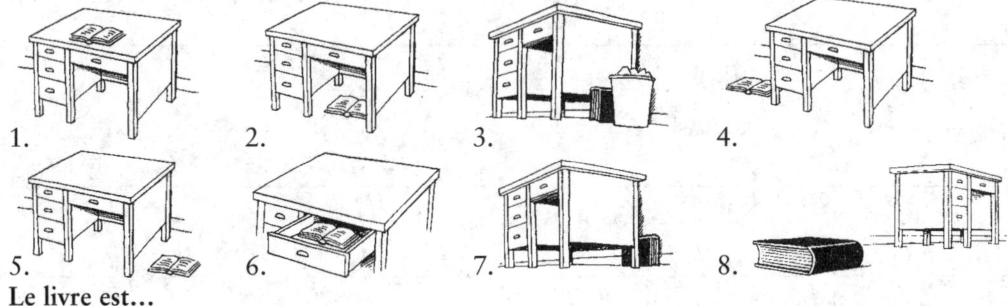

Le livre est...

1. ____________________.
2. ____________________.
3. ____________________.
4. ____________________.
5. ____________________.
6. ____________________.
7. ____________________.
8. ____________________.

3B.2 Prepositions of location (audio activities)

1

Décrivez Look at the drawing and listen to each statement. Indicate whether each statement is vrai or faux.

	Vrai	Faux
1.	❍	❍
2.	❍	❍
3.	❍	❍
4.	❍	❍
5.	❍	❍
6.	❍	❍
7.	❍	❍
8.	❍	❍

2

Où est...? Using the drawing from **Activité 1** and the cues, say where these items are located. Repeat the correct response after the speaker.

Modèle

You see: entre
You hear: le cahier
You say: **Le cahier est entre les crayons et les livres.**

1. à côté de
2. à droite de
3. en face de
4. près de
5. devant
6. sur
7. derrière
8. à gauche de

3

Complétez Listen to the conversation and correct these statements.

1. Francine habite chez ses parents.

____

2. La résidence est près des salles de classe.

____

3. Le gymnase est loin de la résidence.

____

4. La bibliothèque est derrière le café.

____

5. Le cinéma est en face du café.

____

6. Le resto U est derrière la bibliothèque.

____

Nom ______________________________ Date ______________________________

Unité 3

Savoir-faire

PANORAMA

1 **Vrai ou faux?** Indicate whether these statements are **vrai** or **faux**. Correct the false statements.

1. On peut visiter Paris très facilement à pied.

   ____

2. Paris est divisée en vingt arrondissements.

   ____

3. Il y a cent cinq musées à Paris.

   ____

4. Charles Baudelaire est un célèbre chanteur français.

   ____

5. Les catacombes sont sous les rues de Paris.

   ____

6. La tour Eiffel a été construite en 1889 pour l'Exposition universelle.

   ____

7. Paris-Plages consiste en trois kilomètres de sable et d'herbe installés sous la tour Eiffel.

   ____

8. L'architecte américain I. M. Pei a créé le musée du Louvre.

   ____

9. Des entrées du métro sont construites dans le style rococo.

   ____

10. Le métro est un système de transport très efficace.

   ____

2 **Qu'est-ce que c'est?** Label each image shown below.

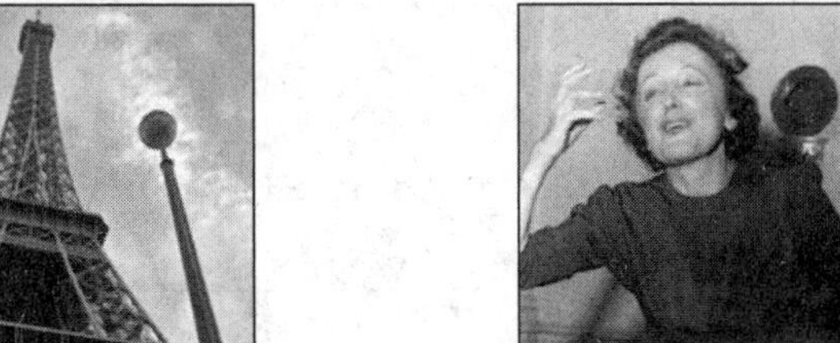

1. ______________________ 3. ______________________ 5. ______________________

2. ______________________ 4. ______________________ 6. ______________________

Nom ______________________ Date ______________________

3 **Complétez** Complete these sentences with the correct information from **Panorama** about Paris.

Paris est la (1) ______________ de la France. Sa population est de plus de (2) ______________ d'habitants. Paris est divisée en vingt (3) ______________.

Le Louvre, un des plus grands musées du monde, est un ancien palais royal. L'œuvre la plus célèbre de sa collection est (4) ______________.

Avec plus de sept millions de visiteurs par an, (5) ______________ est un autre monument célèbre. Elle attire le plus grand nombre de visiteurs en France.

(6) ______________ les rues de Paris, dans (7) ______________, il y a environ (8) ______________ de squelettes provenant d' (9) ______________ de Paris et de ses environs.

Pour visiter Paris, le métro est un système de transport efficace. Les premières entrées du métro de style Art Nouveau datent de (10) ______________. Elles sont l'œuvre de l'architecte Hector Guimard.

4 **Déchiffrez** Use what you've learned in **Panorama** about Paris to decipher the code and fill in the missing letters. Then, use the code to discover three of France's main industries.

A	B	C	D	E	F	G	H	I	J	K	L	M	N	O	P	Q	R	S	T	U	V	W	X	Y	Z
					10									1											

1. C'est le nom d'un écrivain et activiste célèbre.

   _ _ _ _ _ _   _ _ _ _
   15 8 24 13 1 12   25 23 20 1

2. Chaque arrondissement en a un (*has one*).

   _ _   _ _ _ _ _
   23 11   17 14 8 12 7

3. C'est le nom d'un fameux sculpteur.

   _ _ _ _ _
   12 1 3 8 11

4. Dans les catacombes, il y a...

   _ _ _   _ _ _ _ _ _ _ _ _ _
   3 7 2   2 26 23 7 16 7 13 13 7 2

5. La tour Eiffel a été construite (*was built*) pour cette (*this*) occasion.

   _ _ ' _ _ _ _ _ _ _ _ _   _ _ _ _ _ _ _ _ _ _ _
   16 7 22 5 1 2 8 13 8 1 11   23 11 8 15 7 12 2 7 16 16 7

6. C'est le nom du style de certaines (*some*) entrées du métro.

   _ _ _   _ _ _ _ _ _ _
   14 12 13   11 1 23 15 7 14 23

7. Voici trois des industries principales de la France:

   _ _ _   _ _ _ _ _ _ _ _
   16 7 2   10 8 11 14 11 24 7 2

   _ _   _ _ _ _ _ _ _ _ _ _ _
   16 14   13 7 24 25 11 1 16 1 20 8 7

   _ _   _ _ _ _ _ _ _ _
   16 7   13 1 23 12 8 2 17 7

Nom ______________________________ Date ______________________________

Unité 4

CONTEXTES

Leçon 4A

1 **Cherchez** In the grid, circle the words or phrases listed, looking backward, forward, vertically, horizontally, and diagonally. One of them has been done for you.

- bavarder
- bureau
- centre-ville
- déjeuner
- endroit
- épicerie
- fréquenter
- grand magasin
- gymnase
- inviter
- piscine
- terrasse de café

F	R	É	Q	U	E	N	T	E	R	E	Y	O	É	N
E	T	M	C	B	U	D	I	J	N	T	K	T	P	I
S	S	N	K	B	A	S	W	I	A	U	F	I	I	S
L	M	A	J	J	N	V	C	Q	V	A	E	O	C	A
F	Y	K	N	N	M	S	A	E	X	L	H	R	E	G
P	D	D	C	M	I	I	D	R	L	J	P	D	R	A
Q	P	L	Q	P	Y	É	S	I	D	N	K	N	I	M
Y	B	N	D	H	J	G	V	E	G	E	S	E	E	D
É	F	A	C	E	D	E	S	S	A	R	R	E	T	N
C	D	H	U	M	R	E	T	I	V	N	I	V	J	A
K	D	N	I	T	O	V	X	C	H	W	P	A	Z	R
W	E	P	N	D	B	U	R	E	A	U	K	K	W	G
R	Z	E	E	K	C	U	P	U	D	G	T	D	U	G
V	C	U	S	H	P	Z	P	O	M	O	P	U	J	N
D	B	C	F	V	X	Y	N	P	O	I	E	Y	Z	M

2 **Associez** Match the activities in the left column with the locations in the right column. Then write a complete sentence for each one to describe Marie's habits and preferences.

Modèle

travailler / un bureau *Elle travaille dans un bureau.*

____ 1. danser ______________________________

____ 2. marcher (*to walk*) ______________________________

____ 3. manger un couscous ______________________________

____ 4. regarder un film français ______________________________

____ 5. nager ______________________________

____ 6. habiter ______________________________

____ 7. acheter des fruits ______________________________

____ 8. trouver un magazine de mode ______________________________

a. un cinéma
b. une maison
c. une piscine
d. une boîte de nuit
e. un parc
f. un restaurant
g. un kiosque
h. une épicerie

3 **Chassez l'intrus** Circle the word or expression that does not belong.

1. une épicerie, un marché, un magasin, un musée
2. un parc, une piscine, un cinéma, un gymnase
3. un bureau, un magasin, un centre commercial, un grand magasin
4. un restaurant, un café, une église, une épicerie
5. un marché, une épicerie, un cinéma, un restaurant
6. une ville, une banlieue, un centre-ville, une montagne

Nom ______________________ Date ______________________

4 **L'après-midi** Marc is thinking about the errands he needs to run this afternoon. Look at the vocabulary on pages 110–111 of your textbook and complete each sentence with the most logical word or expression.

1. Il y a ______________ sur la place. C'est parfait, j'ai besoin d'un magazine.
2. Après, j'ai besoin d'aller à l' ______________ à côté du café, sur la place.
3. Je me demande (*wonder*) quels films il y a au ______________ en ce moment.
4. La ______________ de Fatima est à côté. Pourquoi ne pas ______________ elle?
5. J' ______________ Fatima au restaurant.
6. Avant, j'ai besoin de passer au ______________ pour trouver quels sports sont proposés (*offered*).
7. J'aime bien ______________, mais est-ce qu'il y a une grande piscine?
8. Ma voisine est sur la place. Pourquoi ne pas ______________ un petit peu avec elle?

5 **Complétez** To find out more about a typical day for a student in Angers, complete these sentences with the word illustrated. Be sure to make all the necessary agreements.

Le matin, je vais au (1) ______________ pour faire (*do*) du sport, ou à la (2) ______________ pour nager pendant (*for*) une heure. Après, je rentre à la (3) ______________. J'étudie l'économie et le droit pendant quatre heures. À midi, j'aime bien manger au (4) ______________ sur la place, mais je n'aime pas (5) ______________. L'après-midi, je travaille au (6) ______________ David d'Angers. Le week-end, j'aime aller au (7) ______________

LA CITÉ DU

ou bien (8) ______________ en boîte avec des amis.

Nom ______________________ Date ______________________

CONTEXTES: AUDIO ACTIVITIES

1 **Choisissez** Listen to each question and choose the most logical answer.

1. a. Non, je ne nage pas.
   b. Oui, elle mange à la piscine.
2. a. Oui, j'ai très faim.
   b. Non, il mange au restaurant.
3. a. Non, elle est au bureau.
   b. Oui, elle adore aller au centre commercial.
4. a. Non, il est absent.
   b. Non, ils sont absents.
5. a. Oui, ils ont une maison en banlieue.
   b. Non, ils sont au musée.
6. a. Oui, elle va à la montagne.
   b. Oui, elle danse beaucoup.
7. a. Oui, on va passer.
   b. Non, nous ne sommes pas chez nous ici.
8. a. Non, je n'aime pas aller en ville.
   b. Non, ils sont trop jeunes.

2 **Les lieux** You will hear six people describe what they are doing. Choose the place that corresponds to the activity.

1. ____________	a. au café
2. ____________	b. au musée
3. ____________	c. au centre commercial
4. ____________	d. à la bibliothèque
5. ____________	e. au gymnase
6. ____________	f. au restaurant

3 **Décrivez** You will hear two statements for each drawing. Choose the one that corresponds to the drawing.

1. a. b. 2. a. b. 3. a. b. 4. a. b.

Nom ______________________ Date ______________________

LES SONS ET LES LETTRES

Oral vowels

French has two basic kinds of vowel sounds: oral vowels, the subject of this discussion, and nasal vowels, presented in **Leçon 4B.** Oral vowels are produced by releasing air through the mouth. The pronunciation of French vowels is consistent and predictable.

In short words (usually two-letter words), **e** is pronounced similarly to the *a* in the English word *about.*

le	**que**	**ce**	**de**

The letter **a** alone is pronounced like the a in *father.*

la	**ça**	**ma**	**ta**

The letter **i** by itself and the letter **y** are pronounced like the vowel sound in the word *bee.*

ici	**livre**	**stylo**	**lycée**

The letter combination **ou** sounds like the vowel sound in the English word *who.*

vous	**nous**	**oublier**	**écouter**

The French **u** sound does not exist in English. To produce this sound, say *ee* with your lips rounded.

tu	**du**	**une**	**étudier**

1 **Prononcez** Répétez les mots suivants à voix haute.

1. je
2. chat
3. fou
4. ville
5. utile
6. place
7. jour
8. triste
9. mari
10. active
11. Sylvie
12. rapide
13. gymnase
14. antipathique
15. calculatrice
16. piscine

2 **Articulez** Répétez les phrases suivantes à voix haute.

1. Salut, Luc. Ça va?
2. La philosophie est difficile.
3. Brigitte est une actrice fantastique.
4. Suzanne va à son cours de physique.
5. Tu trouves le cours de maths facile?
6. Viviane a une bourse universitaire.

3 **Dictons** Répétez les dictons à voix haute.

1. Qui va à la chasse perd sa place.
2. Plus on est de fous, plus on rit.

4 **Dictée** You will hear eight sentences. Each will be read twice. Listen carefully and write what you hear.

1. ______________________________
2. ______________________________
3. ______________________________
4. ______________________________
5. ______________________________
6. ______________________________
7. ______________________________
8. ______________________________

Nom ______________________ Date ______________________

Roman-photo

STAR DU CINÉMA

Avant de regarder

1 **Examinez le titre** Look at the title of the video module. Based on the title and the video still below, what do you think Sandrine, Amina, and David are saying? Use your imagination.

____
____
____
____
____

En regardant la vidéo

2 **Qui...?** Indicate which character says each of these lines. Write **D** for David, **A** for Amina, **S** for Sandrine, or **P** for Pascal.

_______ 1. Et quand est-ce que tu vas rentrer?
_______ 2. Je vais passer chez Amina pour bavarder avec elle.
_______ 3. Bon, moi, je vais continuer à penser à toi jour et nuit.
_______ 4. Elle est là, elle est là!
_______ 5. C'est une de mes actrices préférées!
_______ 6. Mais elle est où, cette épicerie?
_______ 7. Il n'y a pas d'église en face du parc!
_______ 8. Oh, elle est belle!
_______ 9. Elle est vieille?!
_______ 10. Tu es complètement fou!

3 **Qu'est-ce qu'elle va faire?** Watch the telephone conversation between Pascal and Sandrine. Then place check marks beside the activities Sandrine mentions.

❑ 1. étudier
❑ 2. déjeuner
❑ 3. passer chez Amina
❑ 4. aller au cinéma
❑ 5. penser à Pascal jour et nuit
❑ 6. bavarder avec Amina
❑ 7. aller danser
❑ 8. dépenser de l'argent

4 **Complétez** Complete these sentences with the missing words you hear in this video segment.

1. Mais, ________________ est là?
2. ________________?!? Qui?!? Où?!?
3. Mais elle est ________________, cette épicerie?
4. Elle est à l'épicerie ________________ l'église, ________________ du parc.
5. Et ________________ d'églises est-ce qu'il y a à Aix?
6. Bon, ben, l'église ________________ la place.
7. Elle est ici au ________________ ou en ________________?
8. ________________ est-ce qu'elle ne fréquente pas le P'tit Bistrot?

Après la vidéo

5 **Une vraie star!** For items 1–7, fill in the missing letters in each word. Unscramble the letters in the boxes to find the answer to item 8.

1. Pascal adore b _ _ _ ☐ _ _ _ au téléphone.
2. Sandrine va déjeuner au c _ _ ☐ _ _-_ _ _ _ _ _.
3. Pascal est le p _ _ _ _ ☐ _ _ de Sandrine.
4. David pense que Juliette Binoche est à une é _ _ ☐ _ _ _ _ à Aix-en-Provence.
5. Il n'y a pas d'é _ _ ☐ _ _ en face du parc.
6. Amina pense que Juliette Binoche est c _ _ ☐.
7. Sandrine pense que Juliette Binoche est j _ _ _ ☐.
8. Juliette Binoche est ________________.

6 **Mettez-les dans l'ordre!** Number these events in the order in which they occur.

_____ a. David pense qu'il voit (*sees*) Juliette Binoche.
_____ b. Amina, Sandrine et David découvrent (*discover*) que la femme à l'épicerie n'est pas Juliette Binoche.
_____ c. Amina, Sandrine et David trouvent l'épicerie.
_____ d. Sandrine et Pascal parlent au téléphone.
_____ e. Amina, Sandrine et David cherchent Juliette Binoche.

7 **À vous!** Complete the chart with activities you plan to do this week. Then indicate when and where you will do each activity.

Activité	Quand?	Où?

Nom ______________________ Date ______________________

STRUCTURES

4A.1 The verb aller

1 **Conjuguez** Complete this conversation with the correct forms of the verb **aller**.

FATIMA Qu'est-ce que tu (1) ______________ faire dimanche?

ÉRIC Je (2) ______________ étudier à la bibliothèque. Il (3) ______________ y (*there*) avoir un examen demain.

FABIEN ET THUY Nous (4) ______________ explorer le parc national de la Vanoise.

FATIMA Vous (5) ______________ quitter la maison à quelle heure?

FABIEN Je (6) ______________ passer chez Thuy à 7h00. Pourquoi?

FATIMA J'aime la montagne, et mon frère aussi. Je (7) ______________ parler avec lui. Peut-être que nous pouchons (*can*) y (8) ______________ avec vous.

THUY Bonne idée!

2 **Choisissez** New students are attending orientation this week. Complete their agenda by writing the correct prepositions.

1. Vous allez rencontrer vos professeurs ______________ (sur, au, en, à la) bibliothèque du lycée.
2. Votre professeur va vous demander d'aller ______________ (à la, au, en, à) ville.
3. Vous allez déjeuner ______________ (à la, au, sur) restaurant avec d'autres élèves.
4. Le soir, vous pouvez (*can*) aller ______________ (au, à la, en) cinéma ou ______________ (à la, à l', au) piscine.
5. Lundi, vous allez ______________ (au, en, à la) kiosque.

3 **Où vont-ils?** Indicate where the students are going and an activity they might do there, using the illustrations as a guide.

Modèle

Serge et Martin
Ils vont à la librairie. Ils vont chercher des livres.

1. Nous ______________________________

2. Véronique ______________________________

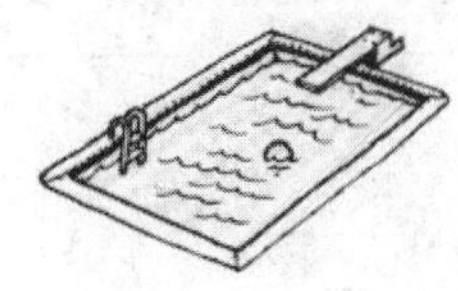

3. Hélène et Marc ______________________________

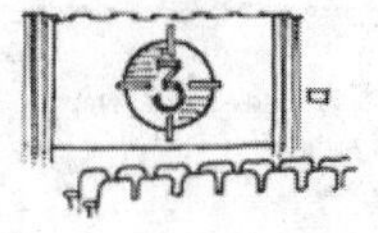

4. Annie et Sarah ______________________________

4 **Complétez** Complete this letter from your Senegalese pen-pal, Kaba, with **à**, **en**, **dans**, or **sur**. Include articles or form contractions as needed.

Je pense étudier (1) ____________ l'Université du Sénégal, (2) ____________ Dakar. L'université est (3) ____________ centre-ville. Je pense aussi habiter (4) ____________ la maison de ma sœur. Dakar, c'est loin (*far away*) de mon village. C'est une grande ville. J'aime étudier (5) ____________ la bibliothèque pour préparer mes examens.

J'aime bien passer (6) ____________ musée de Dakar. Il est intéressant. Le samedi matin, je vais (7) ____________ la piscine municipale et après, je déjeune (8) ____________ la terrasse d'un restaurant avec des amis. Je préfère le restaurant (9) ____________ la place Kermel.

5 **L'emploi du temps** Here is your schedule (**emploi du temps**) for next week. Write complete sentences to tell what you are going to do.

	lundi	mardi	mercredi	jeudi	vendredi	samedi	dimanche
matin		chercher des oranges/marché		parler/prof de français	rencontrer Théo/café	aller/ centre-ville	
après - midi	étudier/ bibliothèque		aller/cinéma			téléphoner/ mes parents	commencer/ étudier

Modèle

Lundi, je vais nager à la piscine.

1. Lundi, ____.
2. Mardi, ____.
3. Mercredi, ____.
4. Jeudi, ____.
5. Vendredi, ____.
6. Samedi, ____.
7. Samedi, ____.
8. Dimanche, ____.

Nom ______________________ Date ______________________

4A.1 The verb **aller** (audio activities)

1 **Identifiez** Listen to each statement and mark an **X** in the column of the subject of the verb you hear.

Modèle

You hear: Il ne va pas au cours de mathématiques aujourd'hui.
You mark: an **X** under **il**

	je	tu	il/elle/on	nous	vous	ils/elles
Modèle			X			
1.						
2.						
3.						
4.						
5.						
6.						
7.						
8.						

2 **Où vont-ils?** Describe where these people are going using the cue. Repeat the correct answer after the speaker.

Modèle

You hear: Samuel
You see: marché
You say: ***Samuel va au marché.***

1. épicerie
2. parc
3. magasin
4. église
5. hôpital
6. café
7. montagne
8. centre-ville

3 **Transformez** Change each sentence from the present to the immediate future. Repeat the correct answer after the speaker. (*6 items*)

Régine bavarde avec sa voisine.
Régine va bavarder avec sa voisine.

4 **Présent ou futur?** Listen to each statement and indicate if the sentence is in the present or the immediate future.

	Présent	Futur proche
1.	O	O
2.	O	O
3.	O	O
4.	O	O
5.	O	O
6.	O	O
7.	O	O
8.	O	O

Nom ____________ Date ____________

4A.2 Interrogative words

1 **Déchiffrez** Pascal just received an e-mail from a classmate in his French class. Unfortunately, his classmate is not very good at French, and the questions are all jumbled. Rewrite each question correctly.

1. vous / appelez / est-ce que / vous / comment / ?

   ____

2. est-ce que / où / habitez / vous / ?

   ____

3. ? / favori / votre / est / cours / quel

   ____

4. commencent / ? / à / est-ce que / quelle heure / les cours

   ____

5. votre restaurant / préféré / ? / chinois / quel / est

   ____

6. est-ce que / allez / marché / ? / vous / quand / au

   ____

7. vous / au / ? / le mardi soir / est-ce que / allez / pourquoi / gymnase

   ____

2 **L'entrevue** Fill in the correct interrogative words or expressions to complete this interview with Hassan, a student at a French university.

Combien	Où	Quels	Qui
Comment	Pourquoi	Qu'est-ce que	Quoi

JÉRÔME (1) ____________ vous appelez-vous?

HASSAN Je m'appelle Hassan.

JÉRÔME (2) ____________ habitez-vous?

HASSAN J'habite en ville.

JÉRÔME (3) ____________ vous étudiez?

HASSAN J'étudie l'économie.

JÉRÔME (4) ____________ étudiez-vous l'économie?

HASSAN Parce que je veux (*want*) être homme d'affaires.

JÉRÔME (5) ____________ cours aimez-vous?

HASSAN J'aime le cours de français.

JÉRÔME (6) ____________ d'étudiants y a-t-il dans la classe?

HASSAN Il y a seize étudiants dans la classe.

Nom ____________________ Date ____________________

3 **Choisissez** Complete each question with the correct form of **quel**.

1. __________ musée fréquentez-vous?
2. À __________ heure les cours commencent-ils?
3. __________ est le nom de la bibliothèque?
4. __________ sont tes restaurants favoris?
5. __________ étudiantes ont les yeux marron?
6. __________ cinéma fréquentez-vous?
7. __________ magasins sont ouverts (*open*) le dimanche?
8. __________ montagnes explorez-vous le week-end?

4 **Complétez** Complete this dialogue with logical questions.

JASMINE Bonjour Nathalie. (1) ____________________

NATHALIE Bien. Et toi?

JASMINE Bien, merci. (2) ____________________

NATHALIE Les cours commencent le 24 septembre.

JASMINE (3) ____________________

NATHALIE J'ai physique, chimie et biologie.

JASMINE (4) ____________________

NATHALIE Mon professeur de chimie est Madame Lessieur.

JASMINE Ah, oui! Et tu as déménagé (*you moved*), n'est-ce pas? (5) ____________________

NATHALIE J'habite en ville, à côté du café, sur la place. Dis, (6) ____________________

JASMINE Il est 11h30. On va bavarder au café demain, n'est-ce pas?

NATHALIE Parfait (*Perfect*). Au revoir.

5 **Les questions** Write two questions that would prompt each of these statements.

1. Laëtitia va au marché dimanche.

____

____

2. Il y a trois étudiants à la terrasse du café.

____

____

3. Mes amis vont manger au restaurant avec les nouveaux élèves.

____

____

4. Tu vas en boîte samedi soir.

____

____

4A.2 Interrogative words (audio activities)

1 **Logique ou illogique?** You will hear some questions and responses. Decide if they are **logique** or illogique.

	Logique	Illogique		Logique	Illogique
1.	❍	❍	5.	❍	❍
2.	❍	❍	6.	❍	❍
3.	❍	❍	7.	❍	❍
4.	❍	❍	8.	❍	❍

2 **Questions** Answer each question you hear using the cue. Repeat the correct response after the speaker. (6 *items*)

Modèle

You hear: Pourquoi est-ce que tu ne vas pas au café?
You see: aller travailler
You say: Parce que je vais travailler.

1. chez lui
2. avec sa cousine
3. Bertrand
4. à un journaliste
5. absent
6. sérieux

3 **Questions** Listen to each answer and ask the question that prompted the answer. Repeat the correct question after the speaker. (6 *items*)

Modèle

You hear: Grégoire va au bureau.
You say: Où va Grégoire?

4 **Conversation** Listen to the conversation and answer the questions.

1. Pourquoi est-ce que Pauline aime son nouvel appartement?

____

2. Où est cet appartement?

____

3. Comment est la propriétaire?

____

4. Combien de personnes travaillent au musée?

____

Unité 4

Leçon 4B

CONTEXTES

1 **Classez** Classify these foods in the appropriate category.

baguette	eau minérale	limonade
beurre	éclair	pain de campagne
boisson gazeuse	fromage	sandwich
café	jambon	soupe
chocolat	jus d'orange	sucre
croissant	lait	thé

Boissons	Pains/desserts	Autres
______________	______________	______________
______________	______________	______________
______________	______________	______________
______________	______________	______________
______________	**Produits laitiers** (*dairy*)	
______________	______________	
______________	______________	
	______________	

2 **Complétez** Complete each sentence with the most logical option.

1. J'aime boire (*drink*) de l'eau ______________.
   a. éclair b. minérale c. sucre
2. Avant de partir (*before leaving*), nous ______________ un pourboire.
   a. apportons b. coûtons c. laissons
3. Ma sœur est végétarienne. Elle ne mange pas de ______________.
   a. jambon b. sandwich c. frites
4. Je mets (*put*) toujours du ______________ dans mon café.
   a. beurre b. fromage c. sucre
5. Je vais demander ______________ à la serveuse.
   a. un pourboire b. l'addition c. apporter
6. J'ai ______________. Je vais manger un sandwich et une soupe.
   a. faim b. soif c. quelque chose
7. J'aime les produits laitiers (*dairy*). Je vais manger un sandwich au ______________.
   a. jambon b. fromage c. chocolat
8. Je me demande (*wonder*) quel est le ______________ du jus de pomme.
   a. addition b. coûter c. prix

Nom ______ Date ______

3 **Qu'est-ce que c'est?** Write the name of each item pictured.

1. ______ 2. ______ 3. ______

 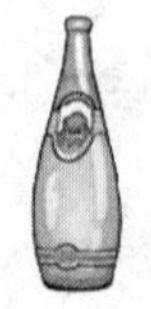 

4. ______ 5. ______ 6. ______

4 **C'est quoi?** Write the name of the item that each statement describes.

1. Il est fait (*made*) avec des pommes (*apples*) ou des oranges. C'est ______.
2. Il rend (*makes*) le thé ou le café plus doux (*sweeter*). C'est ______.
3. Le serveur/La serveuse l'apporte à la fin du dîner. C'est ______.
4. Il est au jambon ou au fromage. C'est ______.
5. On mange ça avec du ketchup. Ce sont ______.
6. C'est le pain avec lequel (*with which*) on fait (*makes*) les sandwichs. C'est ______.
7. C'est un homme qui travaille dans un restaurant. C'est ______.
8. C'est l'argent qu'on laisse pour le serveur/la serveuse. C'est ______.

5 **Choisissez** Complete this dialogue with the best phrases from the list. Make any necessary changes and do not repeat expressions.

une bouteille de	**pas assez de**	**plusieurs**	**tous les**
un morceau de	**un peu de**	**une tasse de**	**un verre de**

MAI J'ai très soif. Je vais boire (*drink*) (1) ______ eau minérale.

PAUL Vraiment? C'est trop! Tu ne veux pas (2) ______ limonade ou (3) ______ thé?

MAI D'accord, j'adore la limonade.

PAUL Moi, j'ai faim. Il y a (4) ______ types de soupe.

MAI Moi, je vais prendre (*take*) (5) ______ soupe à la tomate et (6) ______ pain.

PAUL Bonne idée, moi aussi. J'aime le thé, mais il n'y a (7) ______ sucre.

MAI Tu ne vas pas prendre (8) ______ morceaux de sucre!

PAUL Et pourquoi pas?

Nom ______________________ Date ______________________

CONTEXTES: AUDIO ACTIVITIES

1 **Associez** Circle the words that are logically associated with each word you hear.

1. frites	baguette	limonade
2. table	sandwich	pourboire
3. beurre	addition	serveur
4. morceau	coûter	soif
5. verre	tasse	sucre
6. plusieurs	soupe	apporter

2 **Logique ou illogique?** Listen to these statements and indicate whether they are **logique** or **illogique**.

	Logique	Illogique		Logique	Illogique
1.	❍	❍	5.	❍	❍
2.	❍	❍	6.	❍	❍
3.	❍	❍	7.	❍	❍
4.	❍	❍	8.	❍	❍

3 **Décrivez** Listen to each sentence and write the number of the sentence on the line pointing to the food or drink mentioned.

4 **Complétez** Listen to this story and write the missing words.

Bonjour, je m'appelle Raymond. J'aime les journées (1) ______________________ *La Rotonde*, près de chez moi. Le matin, je commence un livre avec un bon café au (2) ______________________.

Le midi, j'adore être à la terrasse. Je mange un sandwich (3) ______________________ ou jambon (4) ______________________. Quand j'ai froid, j'aime mieux (5) ______________________.

L'après-midi, je (6) ______________________ avec les (7) ______________________. Ils sont sympas, alors je laisse toujours un bon (8) ______________________.

Nom ______________________ Date ______________________

LES SONS ET LES LETTRES

Nasal vowels

When vowels are followed by an **m** or an **n** in a single syllable, they usually become nasal vowels. Nasal vowels are produced by pushing air through both the mouth and the nose.

The nasal vowel sound you hear in **français** is usually spelled **an** or **en**.

an fr**an**çais **en**ch**an**té **en**f**an**t

The nasal vowel sound you hear in **bien** may be spelled **en, in, im, ain,** or **aim**. The nasal vowel sound you hear in **brun** may be spelled **un** or **um.**

exam**en** améric**ain** l**un**di parf**um**

The nasal vowel sound you hear in **bon** is spelled **on** or **om.**

ton all**on**s **com**bien **on**cle

When **m** or **n** is followed by a vowel sound, the preceding vowel is not nasal.

image inutile ami amour

1 **Prononcez** Répétez les mots suivants à voix haute.

1. blond
2. dans
3. faim
4. entre
5. garçon
6. avant
7. maison
8. cinéma
9. quelqu'un
10. différent
11. amusant
12. télévision
13. impatient
14. rencontrer
15. informatique
16. comment

2 **Articulez** Répétez les phrases suivantes à voix haute.

1. Mes parents ont cinquante ans.
2. Tu prends une limonade, Martin?
3. Le Printemps est un grand magasin.
4. Lucien va prendre le train à Montauban.
5. Pardon, Monsieur, l'addition s'il vous plaît!
6. Jean-François a les cheveux bruns et les yeux marron.

3 **Dictons** Répétez les dictons à voix haute.

1. L'appétit vient en mangeant.
2. N'allonge pas ton bras au-delà de ta manche.

4 **Dictée** You will hear eight sentences. Each will be read twice. Listen carefully and write what you hear.

1. ______________________
2. ______________________
3. ______________________
4. ______________________
5. ______________________
6. ______________________
7. ______________________
8. ______________________

Nom ______________________ Date ______________________

Roman-photo

L'HEURE DU DÉJEUNER

Avant de regarder

1 **Au café** What kinds of things do you say and do when you have lunch in a café?

____

____

____

____

____

En regardant la vidéo

2 **Qui...?** Watch this segment and indicate who these statements describe. Write **A** for Amina, **D** for David, **R** for Rachid, and **S** for Sandrine.

1. _______ et _______ ont envie de manger un sandwich.
2. _______ a envie d'une bonne boisson.
3. _______ a envie de dessiner un peu.
4. _______ a un examen de sciences po.
5. _______ et _______ vont au café.
6. _______ et _______ rentrent.

3 **Qu'est-ce qu'elles commandent?** Watch this video segment and check the boxes to indicate whether Sandrine, Amina, or no one (**personne**) is having these foods and beverages.

	Sandrine	Amina	personne
1. la soupe de poisson			
2. un éclair			
3. de l'eau minérale			
4. un sandwich au fromage			
5. du pain			
6. un sandwich jambon-fromage			
7. une limonade			
8. des frites			

4 **Qu'est-ce qui se passe?** Match the actions in the left column with the people who do them. Some actions apply to more than one person.

______ 1. prendre un sandwich	a. Valérie
______ 2. ne pas comprendre l'addition	b. Michèle
______ 3. commander un café et des croissants	c. Sandrine
______ 4. faire (*commit*) une erreur	d. Amina
______ 5. ne pas boire de limonade	e. les clients de la table 7
______ 6. prendre du jus d'orange uniquement le matin	f. les clients de la table 8

Après la vidéo

5 **Corrigez** Each statement below contains one piece of false information. Underline the incorrect word(s), and write the correct one(s) in the space provided.

1. Amina a envie de manger un croissant. _______________
2. David et Sandrine vont au café. _______________
3. Rachid a un examen d'histoire. _______________
4. Valérie sert (*serves*) une soupe de fromage. _______________
5. Amina et Sandrine boivent du coca. _______________
6. Valérie explique l'erreur de l'addition aux clients. _______________

6 **Sélectionner** Select the expression that correctly completes each statement.

1. Sandrine a _______________.
   a. froid b. soif c. peur
2. David a envie _______________.
   a. d'étudier b. de dessiner c. d'aller au cinéma
3. Sandrine voudrait (*would like to*) apprendre à préparer _______________.
   a. des éclairs b. des frites c. des croissants
4. La boisson gazeuse de la table huit coûte _______________.
   a. 1,25 € b. 1,50 € c. 1,75 €
5. Les clients de la table sept commandent _______________.
   a. un thé b. une limonade c. une bouteille d'eau minérale

7 **À vous!** What might you order to eat and drink in a café? Complete these statements according to the situations described.

1. **Vous avez très faim:** Moi, je vais prendre _______________ et _______________.
2. **Vous avez froid:** Je vais manger _______________. Comme boisson, je vais prendre _______________.
3. **Vous n'avez pas très faim:** Je vais prendre _______________ ou peut-être _______________.
4. **Vous avez soif:** Comme boisson, je vais prendre _______________.
5. **Vous avez sommeil:** Comme boisson, je vais prendre _______________.
6. **Vous avez chaud:** Je vais boire _______________. Je ne vais pas prendre _______________.

Nom ____________________ Date ____________________

Flash culture

AU CAFÉ

Avant de regarder

1 **Vocabulaire supplémentaire** Look over these words and expressions before you watch the video.

un coca	*soft drink*
un croque-monsieur	*toasted ham and cheese sandwich*
un hot-dog	*hot dog*
une glace au chocolat	*chocolate ice cream*

2 **Qu'est-ce qu'on prend?** In this video, you are going to learn about cafés in France. Make a list of five beverages and five food items a French café might serve.

À boire	À manger
____________________	____________________
____________________	____________________
____________________	____________________
____________________	____________________
____________________	____________________

3 **Qu'est-ce que c'est?** Check the appropriate column to classify these words as a beverage (**boisson**) or food (**nourriture**).

	boisson	nourriture		boisson	nourriture
1. fromage	______	______	7. frites	______	______
2. éclair	______	______	8. eau minérale	______	______
3. jus de pomme	______	______	9. glace au chocolat	______	______
4. croissant	______	______	10. croque-monsieur	______	______
5. limonade	______	______	11. baguette	______	______
6. café au lait	______	______	12. jambon	______	______

En regardant la vidéo

4 **Qu'est-ce qu'il y a?** Check off the six foods listed below that are mentioned in the video.

❑ 1. des frites
❑ 2. un hot-dog
❑ 3. une soupe
❑ 4. une baguette
❑ 5. un croissant
❑ 6. un croque-monsieur
❑ 7. une eau minérale
❑ 8. un sandwich au jambon
❑ 9. des éclairs
❑ 10. un pain de campagne
❑ 11. une glace au chocolat
❑ 12. un fromage

Nom ______________________ Date ______________________

5 **Les boissons** What beverages are pictured below?

1. ____________

2. ____________

3. ____________

4. ____________

5. ____________

a. un café au lait
b. une limonade
c. un coca
d. un chocolat
e. un café
f. un thé

Après la vidéo

6 **Au café** Imagine you are at a café in Aix-en-Provence. Write a brief conversation in which you and a friend each order something to eat and something to drink. You should each order different things. Include what the server says, too.

Nom ______________________ Date ______________________

STRUCTURES

4B.1 The verbs prendre and boire; Partitives

1 **Le dimanche matin** Complete this paragraph with the correct forms of **boire** or **prendre**.

Le dimanche matin, nous allons au café. Pour aller au café, je (1) ____________ (prendre) toujours la ligne A du métro. Mes parents aiment mieux (2) ____________ (prendre) leur voiture. Ma sœur et moi, nous (3) ____________ (prendre) une baguette et du beurre. Mes parents (4) ____________ (boire) du café mais nous, nous ne (5) ____________ (boire) pas de café. Moi, je (6) ____________ (boire) un thé et ma sœur (7) ____________ (boire) un chocolat. Mes parents (8) ____________ (prendre) des croissants. Et vous, qu'est-ce que vous (9) ____________ (prendre) et qu'est-ce que vous (10) ____________ (boire) le matin?

2 **Et pour vous?** Reconstruct these conversations that you might hear in a café. First write a question, then answer it.

Modèle

vous / boire / café? (non)
Est-ce que vous buvez un café? Non, je ne bois pas de café.

1. tu / boire / thé? (oui)
____
2. nous / prendre / croissants? (non)
____
3. ils / prendre / soupe? (oui)
____
4. vous / boire / eau? (oui)
____
5. elle / prendre / sandwich? (non)
____
6. nous / prendre / frites? (oui)
____
7. tu / boire / chocolat chaud? (non)
____
8. Floriane et Nathalie / boire / jus d'orange? (oui)
____

3 Qu'est-ce que vous prenez?

Look at these illustrations and write a sentence describing what each person is having.

1. je ______________________

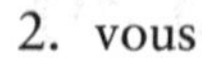

2. vous ______________________

3. elles ______________________

4. tu ______________________

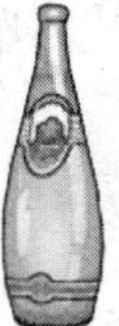

5. nous ______________________

6. il ______________________

4 Complétez

Complete this conversation with the appropriate articles.

SOPHIE Tu as (1) ____________ lait?

MARINA Désolée, non je n'ai pas (2) ____________ lait, mais j'ai (3) ____________ eau minérale et (4) ____________ jus d'orange. Tu prends (5) ____________ croissants avec (6) ____________ beurre ou bien (7) ____________ éclair?

SOPHIE Je vais simplement prendre (8) ____________ jus d'orange avec un morceau (9) ____________ pain.

MARINA Pas de problème. Tu es sûre? Tu ne prends pas un peu (10) ____________ fromage aussi?

SOPHIE Non, merci. Je n'aime pas (11) ____________ fromage. Tu as (12) ____________ pain de campagne?

MARINA Oui, voilà.

SOPHIE Merci.

Nom ____________________ Date ____________________

4B.1 The verbs **prendre** and **boire**; Partitives (audio activities)

1

Identifiez Listen to each statement and mark an **X** in the column of the verb you hear.

Modèle

You hear: Nous n'allons pas apprendre le chinois cette année.
You mark: an **X** under **apprendre**

	apprendre	prendre	comprendre	boire
Modèle	X			
1.				
2.				
3.				
4.				
5.				
6.				
7.				
8.				

2

Conjuguez Form a new sentence using the cue you hear. Repeat the correct response after the speaker.

Modèle

You hear: Elle prend un café tous les matins. (nous)
You say: **Nous prenons un café tous les matins.**

1. (vous) 2. (elles) 3. (nous) 4. (Jean-Christophe) 5. (ils) 6. (nous)

3

Choisissez Listen to each question and choose the most logical answer.

1. a. Non, elle n'a pas faim.
   b. Non, elle n'a pas soif.
2. a. Parce qu'il n'a pas de jambon.
   b. Parce que je prends aussi un chocolat.
3. a. Je ne prends pas de sucre.
   b. Oui, avec du sucre et un peu de lait.
4. a. Non, je n'aime pas le pain.
   b. Non, je prends du pain.
5. a. Oui, ils prennent ça tous les jours.
   b. Non, ils n'aiment pas le café.
6. a. Je bois un café.
   b. Je prends un éclair au café.
7. a. Quand elles ont soif.
   b. Non, elles n'ont pas soif.
8. a. Pourquoi pas.
   b. Oui, tout de suite.

Nom ______________________ Date ______________________

4B.2 Regular -ir verbs

1 **De bonnes résolutions** Decide whether each resolution is a good one (**une bonne résolution**) or a bad one (**une mauvaise résolution**).

	une bonne résolution	une mauvaise résolution
1. Je vais étudier pour réussir le bac.	❍	❍
2. Je suis déjà un peu gros et j'ai le sentiment que je vais encore grossir.	❍	❍
3. Je vais finir mes études en droit pour avoir mon diplôme.	❍	❍
4. Je vais réfléchir avant de parler quand je suis énervée (*angry*).	❍	❍
5. Je maigris trop. Je vais manger un peu plus pour grossir.	❍	❍
6. Je ne vais pas finir mes devoirs avant de sortir avec mes amis.	❍	❍
7. Mes amis du lycée ne sont pas très sympas avec moi. Je vais bien choisir mes amis à la fac.	❍	❍
8. Tous mes pantalons sont trop serrés! Je vais maigrir un peu.	❍	❍

2 **Le bon mot** Write the appropriate present tense forms of **choisir** to tell what everyone is about to order at the restaurant today.

1. Samira et moi ______________________ le sandwich au fromage. On va partager.
2. Pour mon dessert, je ______________________ l'éclair au chocolat.
3. Les Ricci ont très soif! Ils ______________________ des boissons: une limonade et deux cocas.
4. Léna, tu ______________________ quoi, déjà, comme dessert? Le gâteau aux noisettes (nuts)?
5. Vous ______________________ votre plat habituel (*usual dish*), M. Théveneau?
6. Jamel a super froid! Il ______________________ le chocolat chaud parfumé à la cannelle (*cinnamon*).

3 **Choisissez** Complete the sentences with the appropriate and most logical verb of the list.

choisir	grossir	réagir	rougir
finir	maigrir	réfléchir (à)	vieillir
grandir	obéir (à)	réussir (à)	

1. On ______________________ quand on mange trop.
2. Est-ce que les bons ______________________ derniers?
3. Je ______________________ quand je fais beaucoup d'exercice.
4. Stéphanie ______________________ comme une tomate (*tomato*).
5. ______________________ bien. Vous allez trouver la réponse.
6. Nous ______________________ la glace au chocolat pour notre dessert!
7. Tu ______________________ à travailler quand ta sœur met sa musique très fort?
8. Marc, ______________________ à ta grand-mère!

Nom ______________________ Date ______________________

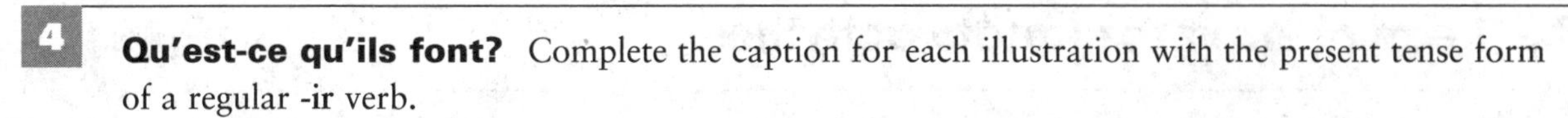

4 **Qu'est-ce qu'ils font?** Complete the caption for each illustration with the present tense form of a regular **-ir** verb.

1. Thierry, tu ________________.

2. Nathalie ________________ un dessert.

3. Louis ________________ à son voyage.

4. Jean-Yves est fatigué parce qu'il ne ________________ pas à dormir (*sleep*).

5. Thierry, tu ________________.

6. Ludo et Martin n' ________________ jamais (*never*).

5 **Question-réponse** Write a logical question including an **-ir** verb that would prompt each response.

1. ____

   Ah, oui. Je ne mange pas beaucoup en ce moment. C'est le stress!

2. ____

   Oui, je vais prendre la tarte aux pommes.

3. ____

   Oui, il fait toujours ce que sa mère demande (*he always does what his mother asks*).

4. ____

   Oui, maintenant Peter a de très bonnes notes.

5. ____

   Mais non! Ce sont mes vêtements qui rétrécissent (*shrink*)!

Nom ______________________ Date ______________________

4B.2 Regular -ir verbs (audio activities)

1 **Changez** Form a new sentence using the cue you hear as the subject. Repeat the correct answer after the speaker. (*8 items*)

Modèle

Je finis tous les devoirs de français. (nous)
Nous finissons tous les devoirs de français.

2 **Répondez** Answer each question you hear using the cue. Repeat the correct response after the speaker.

Modèle

You hear: Qui choisit le gâteau au chocolat?
You see: mes parents
You say: **Mes parents choisissent le gâteau au chocolat.**

1. dix heures
2. non
3. il fait chaud (*it's hot*)
4. oui
5. Béatrice et Julie
6. oui

3 **Logique ou illogique?** Listen to each statement and indicate if it is **logique** or **illogique**.

	Logique	Illogique
1.	❍	❍
2.	❍	❍
3.	❍	❍
4.	❍	❍
5.	❍	❍
6.	❍	❍
7.	❍	❍
8.	❍	❍

4 **Conversation** Listen to Antoine and Léa's conversation and answer the questions.

1. Pourquoi est-ce que Léa est heureuse? ______________________
2. Est-ce qu'elle va réussir ses examens? ______________________
3. Quel restaurant choisissent-ils? ______________________
4. Que prend Antoine à manger? ______________________
5. Antoine a-t-il peur de grossir? ______________________
6. Pourquoi Léa choisit-elle de prendre une salade? ______________________

Nom ______________________ Date ______________________

Unité 4

Savoir-faire

PANORAMA

1 **Où ça?** Complete these sentences with the correct information.

1. L'église du ______________________ est un centre de pèlerinage depuis 1.000 ans.
2. À ______________________, en Bretagne, il y a 3.000 menhirs et dolmens.
3. La maison de Claude Monet est à ______________________, en Normandie.
4. Les crêpes sont une spécialité culinaire de ______________________.
5. Le camembert est une spécialité culinaire de ______________________.
6. ______________________ est une station balnéaire de luxe.

2 **Qu'est-ce que c'est?** Label each image correctly.

1. ______________________

2. ______________________

3. ______________________

4. ______________________

3 **Vrai ou faux?** Indicate whether each statement is **vrai** or **faux**. Correct the false statements.

1. C'est au Mont-Saint-Michel qu'il y a les plus grandes marées du monde.
____
2. Le Mont-Saint-Michel est une presqu'île.
____
3. Le Mont-Saint-Michel est un centre de pèlerinage.
____
4. Le camembert est vendu dans une boîte ovale en papier.
____
5. Claude Monet est un maître du mouvement impressionniste.
____
6. Claude Monet est le peintre des «Nymphéas» et du «Pont chinois».
____
7. Il y a 300 menhirs et dolmens à Carnac.
____
8. Les plus anciens menhirs datent de 4.500 ans avant J.-C.
____

Nom ____________________ Date ____________________

4 **Répondez** Answer these questions in complete sentences.

1. Où est Carnac?

   ____

2. Comment sont disposés (*positioned*) les menhirs?

   ____

3. Quelle est la fonction des menhirs? Et des dolmens?

   ____

4. À quoi est associée la fonction des menhirs?

   ____

5. À quoi est associée la fonction des dolmens?

   ____

6. Pourquoi Deauville est-elle célèbre?

   ____

5 **Les mots croisés** Use the clues below to complete this crossword puzzle.

1. À Deauville, il y a un festival du...
2. C'est le nom d'un fromage.
3. On peut manger des crêpes dans une...
4. C'est le nom d'un lieu où il y a des falaises.
5. C'est la région qui a la plus grande population.
6. C'est le nom d'une célèbre femme écrivain.
7. Deauville est une station...
8. C'est un type d'énergie produite en Normandie.

Nom ______________________ Date ______________________

Unité 5

Leçon 5A

CONTEXTES

1 **Cherchez** In the grid, find the eleven other words listed. Look backward, forward, vertically, horizontally, and diagonally.

- bande dessinée
- échecs
- équipe
- joueuse
- loisir
- match
- passe-temps
- pratiquer
- skier
- spectacle
- sport
- temps libre

L O B F E C K Ô D S V T Z F U
P O B A A L V V E A E C P Q V
A L I K N V C M W M D B G A M
S V U S D D B A P P B S K M W
S B F R I T E S T É C H E C S
E M C P J R L D Q C V I P W S
T H J È I I Z A E E E L H E C
E H K U B W J G M S E P P K S
M R H R T H B A F D S I S A K
P R E U Q I T A R P U I L P I
S L W Y Z C V P M Q E L N J E
F A X B H F F F É W U W F É R
S I Y T R O P S S Z O E Q K E
Y G N K B W F E U B J S M L M
P X F D W I J W Q S T M L É R

2 **Le sport** Look at this list of sports and activities, and indicate whether people generally practice them **à l'extérieur** (*outside*), **à l'intérieur** (*inside*), or both.

aller à la pêche	le basket	le football	marcher	le tennis
le baseball	les échecs	le golf	skier	le volley-ball

à l'extérieur

____

____

____

____

____

____

à l'intérieur

____

____

à l'intérieur et à l'extérieur

____

____

3 **Chassez l'intrus** Circle the word that does not belong in each group.

1. pratiquer, le baseball, le tennis, la bande dessinée
2. indiquer, un loisir, un passe-temps, le temps libre
3. une fois, rarement, souvent, presque jamais
4. encore, souvent, parfois, jamais
5. un jeu, les cartes, skier, les échecs
6. gagner, le cinéma, un jeu, un match
7. bricoler, skier, le tennis, le volley-ball
8. jouer, gagner, aller à la pêche, pratiquer
9. rarement, maintenant, parfois, jamais
10. chanter, gagner, aider, longtemps

Nom ______________________ Date ______________________

4 **Quoi?** Complete this paragraph according to the illustrations to find out what Dalil and his friends are planning to do this weekend. Don't forget to use a preposition or an article when necessary.

Ce week-end, je vais jouer (1) ______________ avec des amis. Nous allons (2) ______________ à 15h00. Nous allons aussi jouer (3) ______________. J'aime les sports de plein air (*outdoors*), mais je n'aime pas (4) ______________. Je n'aime pas (5) ______________ non plus. Ce soir, nous allons jouer (6) ______________ (je n'aime pas (7) ______________).

5 **Les célébrités** What sports do these people play?

1. Shaquille O'Neil ______________
2. David Ortiz ______________
3. Gabrielle Reese ______________
4. Tiger Woods ______________
5. Peyton Manning ______________
6. Venus et Serena Williams ______________

6 **Les loisirs** Write a sentence indicating what these people do and how often they do it, based on the cues provided.

Modèle

Stéphane / once a month

Stéphane regarde une bande dessinée une fois par mois.

Sandrine / often

1. ______________

David and Rachid / on Tuesdays and Thursdays

2. ______________

David and Rachid / right now

3. ______________

David and Sandrine / twice a month

4. ______________

Nom ______________________ Date ______________________

CONTEXTES: AUDIO ACTIVITIES

1 **Identifiez** You will hear a series of words. Write the word that does not belong in each series.

1. ______________ 5. ______________
2. ______________ 6. ______________
3. ______________ 7. ______________
4. ______________ 8. ______________

2 **Choisissez** Listen to each question and choose the most logical answer.

1. a. Oui, le lundi et le vendredi.
   b. Non, je déteste les bandes dessinées.
2. a. Chez mes parents.
   b. Rarement.
3. a. Avec mon ami.
   b. Une fois par mois.
4. a. Nous jouons pour gagner.
   b. Nous jouons surtout le soir.
5. a. Oui, j'aime le cinéma.
   b. J'aime mieux le golf.
6. a. Non, ils ne travaillent pas.
   b. Ils bricolent beaucoup.
7. a. Oui, son équipe est numéro un.
   b. Oui, c'est son passe-temps préféré.
8. a. Oui, ils jouent aujourd'hui.
   b. Il n'y a pas de spectacle.

3 **Les lieux** You will hear a couple describing their leisure activities on a typical weekend day. Write each activity in the appropriate space.

	la femme	l'homme
le matin	______________	______________
à midi	______________	______________
l'après-midi	______________	______________
le soir	______________	______________

LES SONS ET LES LETTRES

Intonation

In short, declarative sentences, the pitch of your voice, or intonation, falls on the final word or syllable.

Nathalie est française. **Hector joue au football.**

In longer, declarative sentences, intonation rises, then falls.

À trois heures et demie, j'ai sciences politiques.

In sentences containing lists, intonation rises for each item in the list and falls on the last syllable of the last one.

Martine est jeune, blonde et jolie.

In long, declarative sentences, such as those containing clauses, intonation may rise several times, falling on the final syllable.

Le samedi, à dix heures du matin, je vais au centre commercial.

Questions that require a yes or no answer have rising intonation. Information questions have falling intonation.

C'est ta mère? **Est-ce qu'elle joue au tennis?**

Quelle heure est-il? **Quand est-ce que tu arrives?**

1 **Prononcez** Répétez les phrases suivantes à voix haute.

1. J'ai dix-neuf ans.
2. Tu fais du sport?
3. Quel jour sommes-nous?
4. Sandrine n'habite pas à Paris.
5. Quand est-ce que Marc arrive?
6. Charlotte est sérieuse et intellectuelle.

2 **Articulez** Répétez les dialogues à voix haute.

1. —Qu'est-ce que c'est?
   —C'est un ordinateur.
2. —Tu es américaine?
   —Non, je suis canadienne.
3. —Qu'est-ce que Christine étudie?
   —Elle étudie l'anglais et l'espagnol.
4. —Où est le musée?
   —Il est en face de l'église.

3 **Dictons** Répétez les dictons à voix haute.

1. Si le renard court, le poulet a des ailes.
2. Petit à petit, l'oiseau fait son nid.

4 **Dictée** You will hear eight sentences. Each will be read twice. Listen carefully and write what you hear.

1. ______
2. ______
3. ______
4. ______
5. ______
6. ______
7. ______
8. ______

Nom ______________________ Date ______________________

Roman-photo

AU PARC

Avant de regarder

1 **Les loisirs** Look at the photo and consider the title of this video episode. What do you think this episode will be about?

____

____

____

____

____

____

____

____

____

En regardant la vidéo

2 **Qui...?** Watch the first scene and indicate which character says each of these lines. Write **D** for David, **R** for Rachid, or **S** for Sandrine.

______ 1. Oh là là… On fait du sport aujourd'hui!

______ 2. Je joue au foot très souvent et j'adore!

______ 3. Mon passe-temps favori, c'est de dessiner la nature.

______ 4. Oh, quelle belle journée! Faisons une promenade!

______ 5. Je n'ai pas beaucoup de temps libre avec mes études.

______ 6. J'ai besoin d'être sérieux.

3 **Les activités** Check off the activities that are mentioned in the video.

- ❑ 1. faire du vélo
- ❑ 2. jouer au football
- ❑ 3. aller à la pêche
- ❑ 4. dessiner
- ❑ 5. jouer au volleyball
- ❑ 6. jouer aux échecs
- ❑ 7. sortir
- ❑ 8. faire du ski
- ❑ 9. jouer au baseball
- ❑ 10. jouer aux cartes
- ❑ 11. faire de la planche à voile
- ❑ 12. jouer au basket
- ❑ 13. jouer au football américain
- ❑ 14. jouer au tennis

4 **Complétez** Watch the segment with Rachid and Stéphane, and complete these sentences with the missing words.

STÉPHANE Pfft! Je n'aime pas (1) _______________.

RACHID Mais, qu'est-ce que tu aimes, à part (2) _______________?

STÉPHANE Moi? J'aime presque tous (3) _______________. Je fais (4) _______________, (5) _______________, du vélo… et j'adore (6) _______________.

5 **David et Sandrine** Watch the conversation between David and Sandrine, then choose the best answer for these questions.

1. Selon David, les sports favoris des Américains sont _______________.
   a. le baseball et le basket   b. le football et le volley-ball   c. le football et le tennis
2. Les Américains adorent regarder _______________ à la télé.
   a. le basket   b. le football américain   c. le baseball
3. Sandrine aime bien _______________ le week-end.
   a. faire du sport   b. dessiner   c. sortir
4. Sandrine aime _______________.
   a. aller au cinéma   b. aller à des concerts   c. aller au cinéma et à des concerts
5. Sandrine adore _______________.
   a. danser   b. regarder des films   c. chanter
6. David aime _______________.
   a. jouer au basket   b. dessiner   c. bricoler

Après la vidéo

6 **J'aime...** Complete the chart with the activities, pastimes, or sports that you enjoy participating in. Also, indicate when and where you do each activity.

Mes loisirs préférés	Quand?	Où?

7 **À vous!** Answer these questions in French.

1. Est-ce que vos amis sont sportifs? Quels sont leurs sports préférés?

   ____

   ____

2. Qu'est-ce que vous aimez faire avec vos amis quand vous avez du temps libre?

   ____

   ____

3. Qu'est-ce que vous allez faire ce week-end? Mentionnez au moins trois choses.

   ____

   ____

Nom ______________________ Date ______________________

Flash culture

LES LOISIRS

Avant de regarder

1 **Quels sont vos loisirs préférés?** In this video, you will learn about leisure-time activities in France. Make a list of six things you like to do in your spare time. Then make a list of six things you don't like to do in your spare time.

J'aime...	Je n'aime pas...
______________________	______________________
______________________	______________________
______________________	______________________
______________________	______________________
______________________	______________________
______________________	______________________

2 **Mes loisirs** Circle all of the statements that describe you.

1. J'aime jouer aux cartes / aux échecs.
2. Je joue du piano / de la guitare.
3. J'aime / Je n'aime pas le sport.
4. Je fais de la gym / de l'aérobic / de la danse.
5. Je joue au football / au basket / au baseball.

En regardant la vidéo

3 **Mettez-les dans l'ordre** In what order does Csilla mention these activities?

______ a. On joue au basket.

______ b. On joue à la pétanque.

______ c. On joue au football.

______ d. On joue au tennis.

______ e. On court.

______ f. On fait du jogging.

______ g. On fait de la musique.

______ h. On fait de la gym.

______ i. On fait de l'aérobic.

______ j. On fait de la danse.

4 **Écoutez** Write down five activities you see being performed indoors (**à l'intérieur**) and five you see being performed outdoors (**en plein air**). Include activities you see but Csilla doesn't mention.

À l'intérieur	En plein air

Après la vidéo

5 **Qu'est-ce que c'est?** Define these terms in English, based on what you saw and heard in the video.

1. la maison des jeunes et de la culture

2. la pétanque

6 **Les activités** How are sports and leisure activities in France different from those practiced in the United States? In what ways are they similar?

Nom ______________________ Date ______________________

STRUCTURES

5A.1 The verb faire

1 **La famille de Karine** Complete this paragraph with the correct form of the verb **faire**.

Ma famille est très active. Moi, je (1) ____________ de l'aérobic le week-end. La semaine, ma sœur et moi, nous (2) ____________ du jogging dans le parc. Mon frère n'aime pas (3) ____________ de la gym, mais il (4) ____________ la cuisine. Mes parents (5) ____________ aussi attention à leur santé (*health*). Ils (6) ____________ souvent du vélo. Et dans ta famille, qu'est-ce que vous (7) ____________? Est-ce que tu (8) ____________ du sport?

2 **Choisissez** Complete this conversation with the correct prepositions or articles.

SOPHIE Quels sont vos passe-temps préférés?

KHALED Je fais (1) ____________ aérobic tous les week-ends. Et toi, Luc?

LUC Je fais (2) ____________ cheval ou (3) ____________ planche à voile.

SOPHIE Moi, je ne fais pas beaucoup (4) ____________ sport, mais j'aime bien faire (5) ____________ camping. Maintenant, je vais faire (6) ____________ promenade dans le parc. Qui veut venir (*wants to come*) avec moi?

KHALED Moi, pourquoi pas! Il faut bien faire (7) ____________ sport.

SOPHIE Parfait. Tu vas faire (8) ____________ connaissance de ma sœur, Frédérique.

LUC Ma sœur et moi, nous y allons aussi. On va faire un pique-nique!

3 **Le mot juste** Complete this brochure with **jouer** or **faire** and the appropriate articles or prepositions.

De nombreux sports sont proposés à nos élèves. Dans notre nouveau gymnase, vous pouvez (*can*) (1) ____________ aérobic ou (2) ____________ basket ou (3) ____________ volley.

Dans notre stade, vous pouvez (4) ____________ jogging, (5) ____________ vélo ou (6) ____________ baseball.

Il y a également des clubs qui organisent des activités en dehors du (*outside of the*) lycée. Vous pouvez (7) ____________ ski ou (8) ____________ randonnée selon (*according to*) la saison. Vous pouvez également (9) ____________ échecs, (10) ____________ planche à voile ou (11) ____________ football.

Avec toutes les activités proposées, vous allez (12) ____________ connaissance de beaucoup de personnes!

4 **Que font-ils?** Look at these pictures and tell what these people are doing using the verb **faire**.

Modèle

Il fait un tour en voiture.

1. ______________________

2. ______________________

3. ______________________

4. ______________________

5. ______________________

6. ______________________

5 **Qu'est-ce qu'il faut faire?** Give these people advice about activities they might enjoy.

Modèle

J'aime les animaux. *Il faut faire du cheval.*

1. J'aime la montagne et marcher.
____
2. Je suis nouvelle à l'école.
____
3. J'aime courir (*run*).
____
4. J'adore le cyclisme (*cycling*).
____
5. J'aime dîner chez moi avec des amis.
____

Nom ______________________ Date ______________________

5A.1 The verb **faire** (audio activities)

1 **Identifiez** Listen to each statement and mark an **X** in the column of the verb form you hear.

Modèle

You hear: **François ne fait pas de sport.**
You mark: **an X under fait**

	fais	fait	faisons	faites	font
Modèle	____	X	____	____	____
1.	____	____	____	____	____
2.	____	____	____	____	____
3.	____	____	____	____	____
4.	____	____	____	____	____
5.	____	____	____	____	____
6.	____	____	____	____	____
7.	____	____	____	____	____
8.	____	____	____	____	____

2 **Conjuguez** Form a new sentence using the cue you hear as the subject. Repeat the correct response after the speaker. (*6 items*)

Modèle

You hear: Je ne fais jamais la cuisine. (vous)
You say: ***Vous ne faites jamais la cuisine.***

3 **Complétez** You will hear the subject of a sentence. Complete the sentence using a form of **faire** and the cue. Repeat the correct response after the speaker.

Modèle

You hear: Mon cousin
You see: vélo
You say: ***Mon cousin fait du vélo.***

1. baseball
2. camping
3. cuisine
4. jogging
5. randonnée
6. ski

4 **Complétez** Listen to this story and write the missing verbs.

Je m'appelle Aurélien. Ma famille et moi sommes très sportifs. Mon père (1) ______________ du ski de compétition. Il (2) ______________ aussi de la randonnée en montagne avec mon oncle. Ma mère (3) ______________ du cheval. Son frère et sa sœur (4) ______________ du foot. Mon grand frère et moi (5) ______________ du volley à l'école et de la planche à voile. Je (6) ______________ aussi du tennis. Ma sœur et notre cousine (7) ______________ du golf. Et vous, que (8) ______________-vous comme sport?

Nom ______________________ Date ______________________

5A.2 Irregular -ir verbs

1 **Les vacances** Complete this paragraph with the correct form of the verbs in parentheses to tell what Miriam does when she is on vacation.

Pendant les vacances (*vacation*), si je ne voyage pas, je (1) ______________ (dormir) toujours tard le matin, mais mes parents (2) ______________ (sortir) tôt pour aller marcher dans le parc. En général, je (3) ______________ (sortir) de la maison à 11h00 et je (4) ______________ (courir) un peu avec des amis. Ils (5) ______________ (courir) très vite. Le parc (6) ______________ (sentir) bon avec toutes les fleurs (*flowers*).

Pour les vacances d'hiver (*winter*), je vais (7) ______________ (partir) en Algérie. Nous (8) ______________ (partir) la semaine prochaine. Je (9) ______________ (sentir) que le voyage va être intéressant. J'adore un petit restaurant à Alger où on (10) ______________ (servir) un excellent couscous.

2 **Décrivez** Describe what the people in these pictures are doing. Write in complete sentences and use a dictionary if necessary.

1. 

2. 

3. 

4. 

5. 

6. 

1. ____
2. ____
3. ____
4. ____
5. ____
6. ____

Nom ______________________ Date ______________________

3 **Que font-ils?** For each sentence, choose the correct verb from those in parentheses. Then complete the sentence by writing the verb in the present.

1. Les professeurs ______________ (sortir, dormir, sentir) du lycée à 6h00 du soir.
2. Les élèves ______________ (servir, partir, sentir) pour Paris pour aller visiter les musées.
3. Maintenant, le département de français ______________ (dormir, sentir, servir) du café et du thé après les conférences.
4. Les athlètes ______________ (servir, courir, partir) dans le stade tous les matins.
5. Ton frère ne ______________ (dormir, servir, sentir) pas assez parce qu'il étudie beaucoup.
6. Je ______________ (servir, sentir, partir) que mon examen de physique va être facile.
7. Je ne ______________ (servir, sentir, sortir) plus avec Hélène.
8. Caroline ______________ (servir, partir, courir) pour la France le mois prochain.

4 **Répondez** Answer these questions in complete sentences.

1. Partez-vous pour un lieu intéressant cette année? Où allez-vous?

____

2. Combien d'heures votre frère dort-il? Et vous?

____

3. Sortez-vous souvent pendant le weekend?

____

4. Que servez-vous à vos amis?

____

5. Qui sort avec vous en boîte, le week-end?

____

6. Courez-vous dans le parc? Avec qui?

____

5A.2 Irregular -ir verbs (audio activities)

1 **Conjuguez** Form a new sentence using the cue you hear as the subject. Repeat the correct answer after the speaker.

Modèle

You hear: Vous ne dormez pas! (tu)
You say: Tu ne dors pas!

1. (nous) 2. (toi et ton frère) 3. (ils) 4. (mon chat) 5. (les sandwichs) 6. (leurs chevaux)

2 **Identifiez** Listen to each sentence and write the infinitive of the verb you hear.

Modèle

You hear: L'équipe court au stade Grandjean.
You write: courir

1. ______________________ 5. ______________________
2. ______________________ 6. ______________________
3. ______________________ 7. ______________________
4. ______________________ 8. ______________________

3 **Questions** Answer each question you hear using the cue. Repeat the correct response after the speaker.

Modèle

You hear: Avec qui tu cours aujourd'hui?
You see: Sarah
You say: Je cours avec Sarah.

1. chez ma tante 2. plus tard 3. les enfants 4. mon ami 5. le chocolat 6. une demi-heure

4 **Les activités** Listen to each statement and write the number of the statement below the drawing it describes. There are more statements than there are drawings.

a. ______________

b. ______________

c. ______________

d. 

e. ______________

f. ______________

Nom ______________________ Date ______________________

Unité 5

Leçon 5B

CONTEXTES

1 **Les saisons** Name the season that best matches each description.

1. Nous allons à la plage. ______________
2. Il neige et nous faisons du ski. ______________
3. Il fait très chaud. ______________
4. Il pleut souvent. ______________
5. Il fait frais et il fait du vent. ______________
6. C'est la fin des cours au lycée. ______________
7. Il faut utiliser un imperméable et un parapluie. ______________
8. Les cours commencent au lycée. ______________
9. C'est la fin de l'année. ______________
10. Nous célébrons la fête (*holiday*) nationale en France et aux États-Unis. ______________

2 **Le temps** Here is a weather forecast. Say what the weather is like and what the highest and lowest temperatures are.

Modèle

Il fait froid et le temps est nuageux à New York.
La température minimum est de 1 degré.
La température maximum est de 15 degrés.

New York
1°C / 15°C

1. Chambéry
2°C / 5°C

2. Abidjan
22°C / 25°C

3. Papeete
27°C / 31°C

4. Marseille
12°C / 20°C

1. ____

____

2. ____

____

3. ____

____

4. ____

____

3 **Les vacances** Farida and Thomas are going to visit Paris. Complete their conversation with the words and expressions from the list.

anniversaire	beau	degrés	imperméable	soleil
avril	date	frais	printemps	temps

FARIDA Quel (1) ______________ fait-il à Paris demain?

THOMAS Il fait beau. Il fait 17 (2) ______________.

FARIDA J'ai besoin d'un (3) ______________?

THOMAS Non, il ne va pas pleuvoir. Il va faire (4) ______________ tout le temps.

FARIDA Parfait. C'est vrai que c'est le (5) ______________.

THOMAS N'oublie pas que le matin, il fait (6) ______________. Nous sommes en (7) ______________.

FARIDA Quelle est la (8) ______________ de l' (9) ______________ de ton oncle?

THOMAS C'est le 5.

FARIDA J'espère (*hope*) qu'il va faire (10) ______________.

THOMAS Oui, moi aussi.

4 **Vrai ou faux?** Read these statements and indicate whether they are **vrai** or **faux**. Correct the false statements.

1. Quand il pleut, j'utilise un imperméable.

   ____

2. Il fait un temps épouvantable en été.

   ____

3. Quand le temps est nuageux, il fait soleil.

   ____

4. En hiver, il fait froid et il neige.

   ____

5. La Saint-Valentin est en février.

   ____

6. Avril, c'est en hiver.

   ____

7. Quand il fait 30 degrés, il fait froid.

   ____

8. Mars est ma saison préférée.

   ____

Nom ______________________ Date ______________________

CONTEXTES: AUDIO ACTIVITIES

1 **Le temps** Listen to each statement and write the number of the statement below the drawing it describes. There are more statements than there are drawings.

a. ______________

b. ______________

c. ______________

d. ______________

2 **Identifiez** You will hear a series of words. Write the word that does not belong in each series.

1. ______________
2. ______________
3. ______________
4. ______________
5. ______________
6. ______________

3 **Questions** Answer each question you hear using the cues. Repeat the correct response after the speaker.

Modèle

You hear: Qu'est-ce qu'on va faire cet été?
You see: faire du camping et une randonnée
You say: ***Cet été, on va faire du camping et une randonnée.***

1. au printemps
2. le 1er février
3. aller souvent au cinéma
4. aimer bricoler
5. aller à un spectacle
6. l'été

Nom ______________________ Date ______________________

LES SONS ET LES LETTRES

Open vs. closed vowels: Part 1

You have already learned that é is pronounced like the vowel *a* in the English word *cake*. This is a closed e sound.

étudiant	**agréable**	**nationalité**	**enchanté**

The letter combinations -er and -ez at the end of a word are pronounced the same way, as is the vowel sound in single-syllable words ending in -es.

travailler	**avez**	**mes**	**les**

The vowels spelled è and ê are pronounced like the vowel in the English word *pet*, as is an e followed by a double consonant. These are open e sounds.

répète	**première**	**pêche**	**italienne**

The vowel sound in *pet* may also be spelled et, ai, or ei.

secret	**français**	**fait**	**seize**

Compare these pairs of words. To make the vowel sound in *cake*, your mouth should be slightly more closed than when you make the vowel sound in *pet*.

mes	**mais**	**ces**	**cette**	**théâtre**	**thème**

1 **Prononcez** Répétez les mots suivants à voix haute.

1. thé
2. lait
3. belle
4. été
5. neige
6. aider
7. degrés
8. anglais
9. cassette
10. discret
11. treize
12. mauvais

2 **Articulez** Répétez les phrases suivantes à voix haute.

1. Hélène est très discrète.
2. Céleste achète un vélo laid.
3. Il neige souvent en février et en décembre.
4. Désirée est canadienne; elle n'est pas française.

3 **Dictons** Répétez les dictons à voix haute.

1. Péché avoué est à demi pardonné.
2. Qui sème le vent récolte la tempête.

4 **Dictée** You will hear eight sentences. Each will be read twice. Listen carefully and write what you hear.

1. ______________________________
2. ______________________________
3. ______________________________
4. ______________________________
5. ______________________________
6. ______________________________
7. ______________________________
8. ______________________________

Nom ______________________ Date ______________________

Roman-photo

QUEL TEMPS!

Avant de regarder

1 **Le temps** In this video episode, the characters talk about seasons, the date, and the weather. What kinds of expressions do you think they might say?

____
____
____
____
____

En regardant la vidéo

2 **Les mois de l'année** Which months are mentioned in this video episode?

- ❑ 1. janvier
- ❑ 2. février
- ❑ 3. mars
- ❑ 4. avril
- ❑ 5. mai
- ❑ 6. juin
- ❑ 7. juillet
- ❑ 8. août
- ❑ 9. septembre
- ❑ 10. octobre
- ❑ 11. novembre
- ❑ 12. décembre

3 **Quel temps fait-il?** In what order are these weather conditions mentioned in the video?

_______ a. Il fait bon.
_______ b. Il pleut.
_______ c. Il fait chaud.
_______ d. Il fait beau.
_______ e. Il neige.
_______ f. Il fait froid.

4 **Qui...?** Watch the scene in Rachid and David's apartment, and indicate which character says these lines. Write **D** for David, **R** for Rachid, or **S** for Sandrine.

_______ 1. Je sors même quand il fait très froid.
_______ 2. Je déteste la pluie. C'est pénible.
_______ 3. Cette année, je fête mes vingt et un ans.
_______ 4. Oh là là! J'ai soif.
_______ 5. C'est vrai, David, tu as vraiment du talent.
_______ 6. Mais... qu'est-ce que vous faites, tous les deux?

5 **Descriptions** Indicate which person each statement describes.

_______ 1. Il/Elle étudie Napoléon.
a. Rachid b. David c. Stéphane d. Sandrine

_______ 2. Son anniversaire, c'est le 15 janvier.
a. Rachid b. David c. Stéphane d. Sandrine

_______ 3. Il/Elle préfère l'été.
a. Rachid b. David c. Stéphane d. Sandrine

_______ 4. Il/Elle aime regarder les sports à la télé.
a. Rachid b. David c. Stéphane d. Sandrine

_______ 5. Il/Elle célèbre ses dix-huit ans samedi prochain.
a. Rachid b. David c. Stéphane d. Sandrine

Après la vidéo

6 **Vrai ou faux?** Indicate whether these statements are **vrai** or **faux**.

	Vrai	Faux
1. À Washington, il pleut souvent à l'automne et en hiver.	❍	❍
2. Stéphane a dix-neuf ans.	❍	❍
3. Le Tour de France commence au mois d'août.	❍	❍
4. L'anniversaire de Sandrine est le 20 juillet.	❍	❍
5. Sandrine va préparer une omelette pour David et Rachid.	❍	❍
6. Pour célébrer son anniversaire, Sandrine invite ses amis au restaurant.	❍	❍

7 **À vous!** Answer these questions in French.

1. C'est quand, votre anniversaire?

____

____

____

2. Quelle est votre saison préférée? Pourquoi? _______________________

____

____

____

3. Qu'est-ce que vous aimez faire quand il fait beau? _______________________

____

____

____

4. Qu'est-ce que vous aimez faire quand il pleut? _______________________

____

____

____

Nom ______________________ Date ______________________

STRUCTURES

5B.1 Numbers 101 and higher

1 **Les prix** Write out these prices in words.

1. 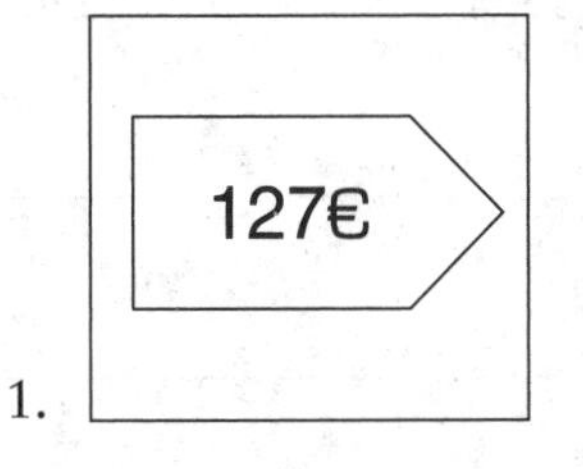

2. 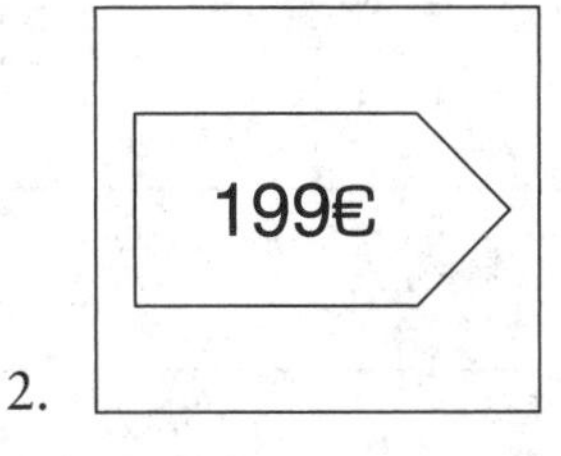

3. 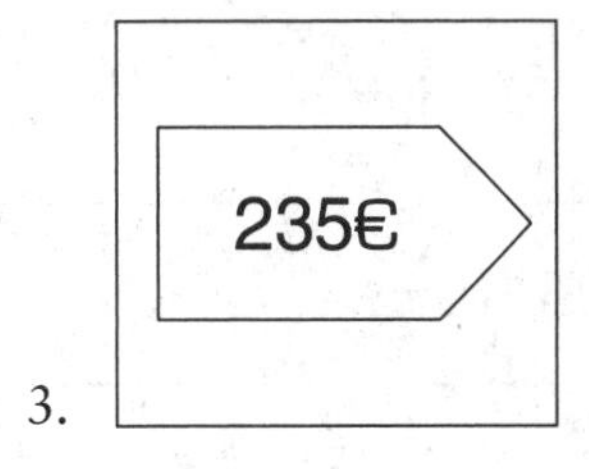

4. 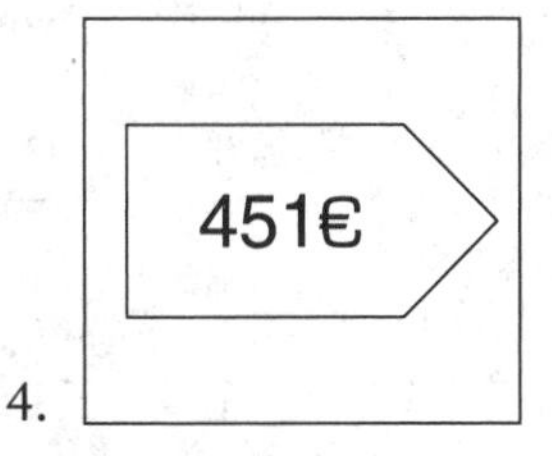

5. 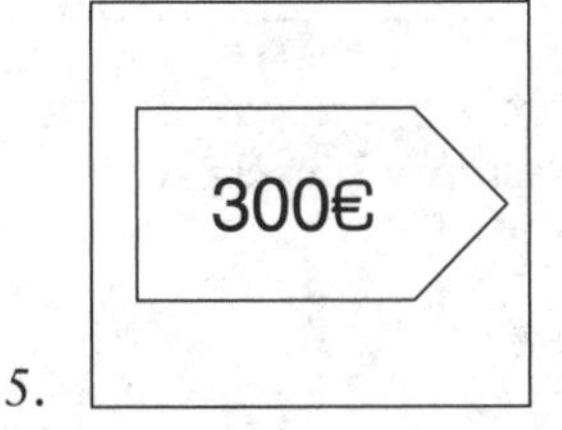

6. 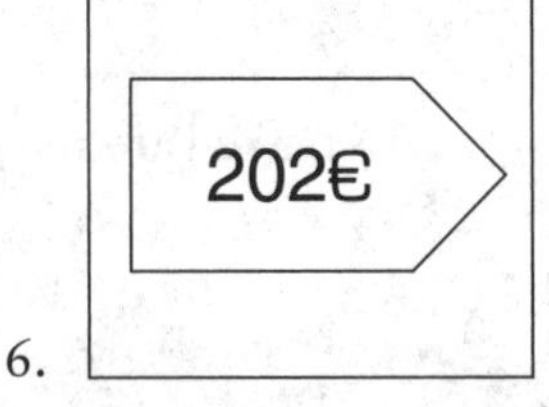

7. 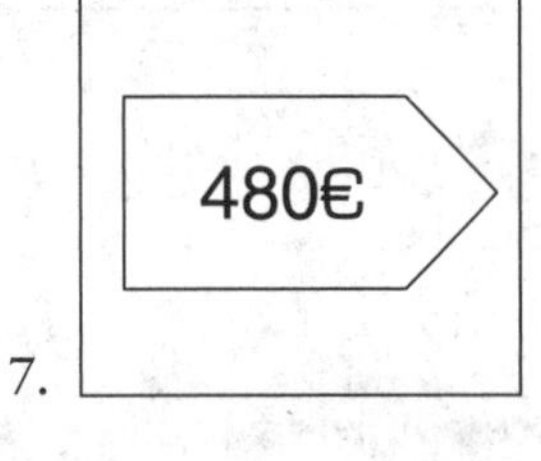

8. 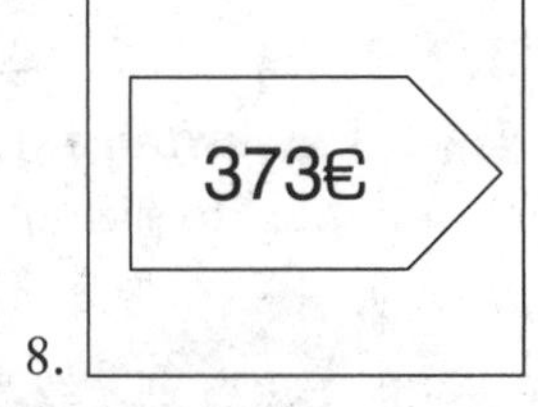

1. ______________________
2. ______________________
3. ______________________
4. ______________________
5. ______________________
6. ______________________
7. ______________________
8. ______________________

2 **Québec** Read these sentences about the French-speaking province of Quebec, Canada. Write the digits for the numbers in each sentence.

1. Jacques Cartier arrive à Gaspé en mille cinq cent trente-quatre. ________
2. La province du Québec est établie en mille sept cent quatre-vingt-onze. ________
3. La population francophone du Québec est de cinq millions huit cent mille personnes. ________
4. La population anglophone du Québec est de cinq cent quatre-vingt-onze mille personnes. ________
5. La superficie de la province du Québec est de un million cinq cent cinquante-trois mille six cent trente-sept kilomètres carrés. ________
6. La population totale du Québec est de sept millions cinq cent soixante-huit mille six cent quarante habitants. ________
7. Le Québec produit (*makes*) quatre-vingt-six millions quatre cent seize mille cinquante-sept livres (*pounds*) de sirop d'érable (*maple syrup*). ________
8. Il y a quarante et un mille cinq cent sept étudiants à l'Université du Québec, à Montréal. ________

3 **Résolvez** Solve these math problems, using the formal or the informal vocabulary.

Modèle

200 + 350 (formal) *Deux cents plus trois cent cinquante egale cinq cent cinquante.*

1. 199 + 801 (informal)
2. 28.000 – 13.000 (formal)
3. 826 x 4 (informal)
4. 1.800 ÷ 2 (formal)

4 **L'inventaire** Léo is working at the school store. To make sure the inventory is accurate, he has been asked to spell the numbers.

Modèle

Il y a cent trente-sept livres de Jules Verne.

Articles	Nombre d'articles
Livres de Jules Verne	137
Livres d'Ampâté Bâ	101
Dictionnaires français-anglais	299
Crayons	2.435
Cahiers	3.123
Stylos	6.782

1.
2.
3.
4.
5.

5 **La loterie** Imagine that you have won a million euros. List what you would like to buy and how much each item costs. Write out their prices.

Nom ______________________ Date ______________________

5B.1 Numbers 101 and higher (audio activities)

1 **Calcul** Listen carefully and choose the result that corresponds to each equation.

______	a. 1.031	______	e. 500.000
______	b. 901	______	f. 200
______	c. 4.300	______	g. 3
______	d. 459	______	h. 333

2 **Les prix** Listen to each statement and write the correct price next to each object.

1. le téléphone: ______________________ €
2. la maison: ______________________ €
3. l'équipe de baseball: ______________________ €
4. les cours de tennis: ______________________ €
5. une randonnée à cheval d'une semaine: ______________________ €
6. l'ordinateur: ______________________ €

3 **Le sport** Look at the number of members of sporting clubs in France. Listen to these statements and decide whether each statement is **vrai** or **faux**.

	Nombre de membres
basket-ball	427.000
football	2.066.000
golf	325.000
handball	319.000
judo	577.000
natation	214.000
rugby	253.000
tennis	1.068.000

	Vrai	Faux
1.	❍	❍
2.	❍	❍
3.	❍	❍
4.	❍	❍
5.	❍	❍
6.	❍	❍

4 **Questions** Answer each question you hear using the cue. Repeat the correct response after the speaker.

Modèle

You hear: Combien de personnes pratiquent la natation en France?

You see: 214.000

You say: **Deux cent quatorze mille personnes pratiquent la natation en France.**

1. 371
2. 880
3. 101
4. 412
5. 1.630
6. 129

Nom ____________________ Date ____________________

5B.2 Spelling change -er verbs

1 **Au lycée** To complete Jean's e-mail, choose the logical verb for each sentence and write its correct form in the space provided.

Salut!

Ça va? Moi, je vais bien, mais il y a beaucoup de choses à faire cette semaine. Je/J' (1) ______________ (espérer, nettoyer, acheter) beaucoup de livres pour mes cours. Bien sûr, mes professeurs (2) ______________ (envoyer, répéter, préférer) les élèves qui travaillent beaucoup, alors je suis toujours à la bibliothèque. Les élèves (3) ______________ (employer, payer, célébrer) beaucoup leur ordinateur pour étudier.

Matthieu, mon frère ne/n' (4) ______________ (acheter, emmener, nettoyer) jamais la chambre. C'est pénible! Mais il (5) ______________ (amener, espérer, protéger) avoir une bonne note en français, alors nous étudions ensemble. Je/J' (6) ______________ (envoyer, célébrer, employer) mon anniversaire la semaine prochaine avec le club de français, et je vais inviter Matthieu.

Comment allez-vous? Est-ce que vous (7) ______________ (envoyer, payer, acheter) mes CD préférés? Est-ce que vous (8) ______________ (répéter, posséder, essayer) de venir ici bientôt?

Merci et à bientôt!

Jean

2 **Que font-ils?** Write sentences to describe what the people in the photos are doing. Use a variety of words from the list.

acheter	essayer	payer
envoyer	nettoyer	répéter

1.  2.  3.  4. 

1. ______________________________
2. ______________________________
3. ______________________________
4. ______________________________

3 **La lettre** A classmate from your French class asks you to help with the letter he or she is writing to a pen-pal. Help by filling in the blanks with the appropriate verbs in the present tense.

acheter	considérer	espérer	payer	protéger
célébrer	envoyer	essayer	préférer	répéter

Bonjour!

J'étudie le français au lycée. J' (1) ____________ que tu vas comprendre la lettre que j' (2) ____________. Ici, les autres élèves (3) ____________ utiliser leur e-mail, mais je pense qu'une lettre est plus personnelle.

Moi, j'aime la musique. J'adore chanter. Mes amis et moi, nous (4) ____________ dans une salle de classe. Nous (5) ____________ de préparer un concert pour la fin de l'année. Mes parents (6) ____________ que ce n'est pas important, mais je ne suis pas d'accord. En plus, le lycée va (7) ____________ pour le concert!

J'aime aussi la nature. Est-ce que tu (8) ____________ la nature aussi? Ici, nous (9) ____________ la journée de l'environnement.

Et toi, quand est-ce que tu (10) ____________ ton billet d'avion pour venir me rendre visite?

Bon, au revoir!

4 **Répondez** Answer these questions using the cues provided.

1. À qui est-ce que vous envoyez des e-mails? (à mes amis et à mes professeurs)
____
2. Qu'est-ce que vous apportez en classe? (mon ordinateur et des crayons)
____
3. Qu'est-ce que votre professeur emploie? (des livres en français)
____
4. Qui préfère étudier à la bibliothèque? (les élèves sérieux)
____
5. Qui achète des CD de musique française? (mon cousin et moi)
____
6. Pourquoi les élèves répètent-ils les mots? (parce qu'ils / essayer d'avoir un bon accent)
____
7. Qui envoie des lettres à votre frère? (mes parents)
____
8. Qui célèbre la Révolution française? (nous)
____

5B.2 Spelling change -er verbs (audio activities)

1 **Décrivez** You will hear two statements for each drawing. Choose the one that corresponds to the drawing.

1. a. b. 2. a. b. 3. a. b. 4. a. b.

2 **Conjuguez** Form a new sentence using the cue you hear as the subject. Repeat the correct response after the speaker. (*6 items*)

Modèle

You hear: Vous ne payez pas maintenant? (tu)
You say: Tu ne payes/paies pas maintenant?

3 **Transformez** Change each sentence from the immediate future to the present. Repeat the correct answer after the speaker. (*6 items*)

Modèle

You hear: Ils vont envoyer leurs papiers.
You say: Ils envoient leurs papiers.

4 **Identifiez** Listen to each sentence and write the infinitive of the verb you hear.

Modèle

You hear: Monique promène le chien de sa sœur.
You write: promener

1. ______________________ 5. ______________________
2. ______________________ 6. ______________________
3. ______________________ 7. ______________________
4. ______________________ 8. ______________________

Nom _______________ Date _______________

Unité 5

Savoir-faire

PANORAMA

1 **Les photos** Label each photo.

1. ______________ 2. ______________ 3. ______________ 4. ______________

2 **Les Pays de la Loire** Answer these questions in complete sentences.

1. Quand le château de Chambord est-il construit (*built*)?

____

2. Combien de pièces le château de Chambord possède-t-il?

____

3. Quelle est la caractéristique des deux escaliers du logis central?

____

4. Quel est l'autre nom de la vallée de la Loire?

____

5. Qui inaugure le siècle des «rois voyageurs»?

____

6. Quel est le nom des trois châteaux les plus visités (*the most visited*)?

____

3 **Les attractions** Complete the sentences with the correct words.

1. Le Printemps de ______________________ est un festival de musique.
2. À ce festival de musique, il y a des ______________ de spectacles et des ______________ de spectateurs.
3. Les 24 heures du ______________________ est une course d'______________________.
4. Cette course existe depuis ______________________.
5. La vigne est cultivée dans la vallée de la Loire depuis l'an ______________________.
6. Les vignerons produisent ______________________ de bouteilles par an.

Nom ______________________ Date ______________________

4 **Vrai ou faux?** Indicate whether these statements are **vrai** or **faux**. Correct the false statements.

1. La viticulture est une des principales industries du Centre.
____
2. La ville des Sables-d'Olonne est située dans un département des Pays de la Loire.
____
3. George Sand est un homme. C'est un inventeur.
____
4. Louis XIV influence l'architecture du château de Chambord.
____
5. François Ier va de château en château avec sa famille.
____
6. Au Printemps de Bourges, tous les styles de musique sont représentés.
____
7. Yves Montand est un écrivain.
____
8. 75% des vins français sont produits dans la vallée de la Loire.
____

5 **Le mot mystère** Complete these definitions and fill in the corresponding spaces in the grid to find out the mystery word.

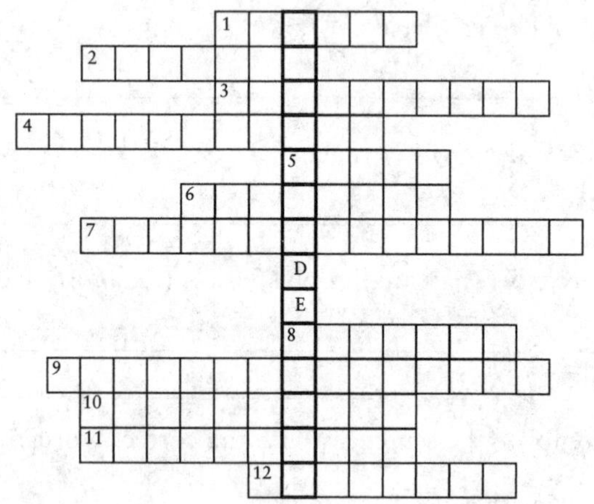

1. C'est le nom d'une dynastie de rois.
2. C'est une célèbre marque de voiture; ce n'est pas Ferrari.
3. C'est une femme écrivain du XIXe siècle.
4. C'est le style de nombreux châteaux de la vallée de la Loire.
5. C'est le mois du Printemps de Bourges.
6. C'est l'industrie principale du Centre.
7. C'est un acteur célèbre.
8. C'est une ville dans la région du Centre.
9. C'est le nom d'un chanteur au Printemps de Bourges.
10. C'est une sorte de vin.
11. C'est le nom d'un château de la Loire.
12. C'est le nom de la personne qui fait le vin.

Mot mystère: C'est le nom d'un célèbre peintre du XVIe siècle. Il a travaillé (*worked*) pour François Ier.

Nom ____________________ Date ____________________

Unité 6

Leçon 6A

CONTEXTES

1 **Trouvez des paires** List pairs of words that are related in meaning. Do not repeat the items from the model.

l'adolescence	l'enfance	marié(e)
l'âge adulte	un gâteau	la mort
un biscuit	un hôte	la vie
célibataire	des invités	la vieillesse
le divorce	le mariage	

Modèle

le mariage, le divorce

1. ____________________
2. ____________________
3. ____________________
4. ____________________
5. ____________________
6. ____________________

2 **Logique ou illogique?** Indicate whether each one of these sentences is **logique** or **illogique**.

	Logique	Illogique
1. Noémie va faire une surprise à sa sœur pour son anniversaire.	❍	❍
2. Gilles est amoureux d'une feuille de papier.	❍	❍
3. Abdel et Nora ne sont plus ensemble; ils sont divorcés.	❍	❍
4. M. Lominé va prendre rendez-vous avec sa copine pour aller au cinéma.	❍	❍
5. On prend sa retraite à l'âge de 13 ans.	❍	❍
6. Quel est votre état civil: célibataire, marié(e), veuf/veuve ou divorcé(e)?	❍	❍
7. Y a-t-il des glaçons pour le punch?	❍	❍
8. La fiancée du chat est un oiseau.	❍	❍

3 **Les étapes de la vie** Label each of these images with the appropriate stage of life.

1. ____________________

2. ____________________

3. ____________________

4. ____________________

5. ____________________

6. ____________________

4 **Une invitation** Laurent is organizing a celebration for his birthday. Complete the e-mail he wrote to his friend Marguerite making any necessary changes.

bonheur	férié	fiancé	jus de pomme
cadeau	fêter	gâteau	organiser

Marguerite,

Vendredi est un jour (1) ______ et donc, c'est l'occasion de (2) ______ mon anniversaire. C'est moi qui (3) ______, alors, est-ce que tu peux apporter des cannettes (*cans*) de Coca et des bouteilles de (4) ______? Eh, pas besoin d'apporter un (5) ______ ou un (6) ______, d'accord?

Merci d'avance et à bientôt,

Laurent

tél. 01.87.95.23.41

5 **Citations** Choose an appropriate word from the list to complete each quote.

___ 1. L'argent ne fait pas le ______.

___ 2. Le respect est le lien de l' ______.

___ 3. Une vie sans ______ est une vie sans soleil.

___ 4. Un ______ heureux est une longue conversation qui semble toujours trop brève.

___ 5. La ______ est comme on la fait.

___ 6. La ______ est le temps qu'on a devant soi (*oneself*).

___ 7. Aimer, ce n'est pas se regarder l'un l'autre, c'est regarder ______ dans la même direction.

a. jeunesse
b. amitié
c. amour
d. bonheur
e. vie
f. ensemble
g. mariage

6 **Des questions** Answer these questions in complete sentences.

1. Est-ce que vous aimez faire la fête? Pourquoi?

______

2. Est-ce que vous organisez des fêtes pour vos copains?

______

3. Comment fêtez-vous votre anniversaire?

______

4. Quel est votre jour férié préféré? Pourquoi?

______

5. Est-ce que vous avez parfois des invités chez vous? Quand?

______

6. Avez-vous déjà fait une surprise à quelqu'un? À qui?

______

Nom _______________ Date _______________

CONTEXTES: AUDIO ACTIVITIES

1 **Logique ou illogique?** You will hear some statements. Decide if each one is **logique** or **illogique**.

	Logique	Illogique		Logique	Illogique
1.	❍	❍	5.	❍	❍
2.	❍	❍	6.	❍	❍
3.	❍	❍	7.	❍	❍
4.	❍	❍	8.	❍	❍

2 **Choisissez** For each drawing you will hear three statements. Choose the one that corresponds to the drawing.

1. a. b. c.

2. a. b. c.

3. a. b. c.

4. a. b. c.

3 **L'anniversaire** Listen as Véronique talks about a party she has planned. Then answer the questions.

1. Pour qui Véronique organise-t-elle une fête?
____
2. Quand est cette fête?
____
3. Pourquoi est-ce qu'on organise cette fête?
____
4. Qui Véronique invite-t-elle?
____
5. Qui achète le cadeau?
____
6. Qui apporte de la musique?
____
7. Le gâteau est à quoi?
____
8. Qu'est-ce que les invités vont faire à la fête?
____

Nom ______________________ Date ______________________

LES SONS ET LES LETTRES

Open vs. closed vowels: Part 2

The letter combinations **au** and **eau** are pronounced like the vowel sound in the English word *coat*, but without the glide heard in English. These are closed **o** sounds.

ch**au**d   **au**ssi   b**eau**coup   tabl**eau**

When the letter **o** is followed by a consonant sound, it is usually pronounced like the vowel in the English word *raw*. This is an open **o** sound.

h**o**mme   téléph**o**ne   **o**rdinateur   **o**range

When the letter **o** occurs as the last sound of a word or is followed by a *z* sound, such as a single **s** between two vowels, it is usually pronounced with the closed **o** sound.

tr**o**p   hér**o**s   r**o**se   ch**o**se

When the letter **o** has an **accent circonflexe**, it is usually pronounced with the closed **o** sound.

dr**ô**le   bient**ô**t   p**ô**le   c**ô**té

1 **Prononcez** Répétez les mots suivants à voix haute.

1. rôle
2. porte
3. dos
4. chaud
5. prose
6. gros
7. oiseau
8. encore
9. mauvais
10. nouveau
11. restaurant
12. bibliothèque

2 **Articulez** Répétez les phrases suivantes à voix haute.

1. En automne, on n'a pas trop chaud.
2. Aurélie a une bonne note en biologie.
3. Votre colocataire est d'origine japonaise?
4. Sophie aime beaucoup l'informatique et la psychologie.
5. Nos copains mangent au restaurant marocain aujourd'hui.
6. Comme cadeau, Robert et Corinne vont préparer un gâteau.

3 **Dictons** Répétez les dictons à voix haute.

1. Tout nouveau, tout beau.
2. La fortune vient en dormant.

4 **Dictée** You will hear six sentences. Each will be read twice. Listen carefully and write what you hear.

1. ______________________
2. ______________________
3. ______________________
4. ______________________
5. ______________________
6. ______________________

Nom _______________ Date _______________

Roman-photo

LES CADEAUX

Avant de regarder

1 **Qu'est-ce qui se passe?** Look at the video still. What are the people doing? Consider the title and the photo, and guess what will happen in this episode.

____

____

____

____

____

En regardant la vidéo

2 **Les desserts** Watch the scene about Sandrine's phone call, and place a check mark next to the desserts Sandrine mentions to Pascal.

❑ 1. de la glace
❑ 2. une mousse au chocolat
❑ 3. un gâteau d'anniversaire
❑ 4. une tarte aux pommes
❑ 5. des biscuits
❑ 6. des éclairs
❑ 7. des bonbons

3 **Qui...?** Indicate which character says each of these lines. Write S for Sandrine or V for Valérie.

______ 1. On organise une fête surprise au P'tit Bistrot.

______ 2. Mais non, il n'est pas marié.

______ 3. Stéphane va bientôt arriver.

______ 4. Oh là là! Tu as fait tout ça pour Stéphane?

______ 5. Tu es un ange!

______ 6. J'adore faire la cuisine.

______ 7. Je t'aide à apporter ces desserts?

______ 8. Désolée, je n'ai pas le temps de discuter.

Nom ______________________ Date ______________________

4 **À la boutique** Choose the option that correctly completes each sentence.

1. Astrid a acheté ____________ comme cadeau pour Stéphane.
   a. un stylo b. un gâteau c. une calculatrice
2. Astrid a aussi acheté ____________ pour Stéphane.
   a. des livres b. des bonbons c. des bandes dessinées
3. Ces cadeaux sont ____________.
   a. de vrais cadeaux b. une blague (*joke*) c. très chers
4. La montre que Rachid et Astrid achètent coûte ____________.
   a. 40 € b. 50 € c. 100 €
5. La vendeuse fait ____________.
   a. un paquet cadeau b. la fête c. une erreur d'addition

Après la vidéo

5 **Vrai ou faux?** Indicate whether each of these statements is **vrai** or **faux**.

	Vrai	Faux
1. Stéphane a 18 ans.	❍	❍
2. Rachid a l'idée d'acheter une montre pour Stéphane.	❍	❍
3. Amina apporte de la glace au chocolat à la fête.	❍	❍
4. Stéphane pense qu'il va jouer au foot avec Rachid.	❍	❍
5. Astrid et Amina aident à décorer.	❍	❍
6. Stéphane va aimer tous ses cadeaux.	❍	❍

6 **Sommaire** Briefly describe the events in this episode from the perspectives of the people listed below. Write at least two sentences for each one.

Sandrine: ______________________

Valérie: ______________________

Astrid: ______________________

7 **À vous!** Make a list of things you do to throw a party. Mention at least six different activities.
Pour préparer une fête, ...

Nom ____________________ Date ____________________

Flash culture

LES FÊTES

Avant de regarder

1 **Vocabulaire supplémentaire** Look over these words and expressions before you watch the video.

carnaval	*carnival*	magnifique	*magnificent*
célèbre	*famous*	Noël	*Christmas*
chevaux	*horses*	Pâques	*Easter*
le jour de l'an	*New Year's Day*	partout	*everywhere*
la fête nationale	*national holiday*	presque toutes	*almost all*
incroyable	*incredible*		

2 **Vos fêtes préférées** In this video, you will learn about French holidays and festivals. In preparation, answer these questions about two of your favorite holidays or festivals.

Quelles sont vos fêtes préférées? Comment est-ce que vous célébrez ces fêtes chez vous?

1. fête: ____________________

   traditions: ____________________

   ____

   ____

   ____

   ____

2. fête: ____________________

   traditions: ____________________

   ____

   ____

   ____

   ____

En regardant la vidéo

3 **Dans quel ordre?** Number these items as they appear on-screen.

_____ a. des chevaux

_____ b. des danseuses

_____ c. des enfants

_____ d. des légumes

_____ e. des musiciens qui jouent

Nom ______________________ Date ______________________

4 **Les fêtes** What holiday or festival does each image represent?

1. ______
2. ______
3. ______ 
4. ______
5. ______
6. ______

a. le jour de l'an
b. la fête nationale
c. Noël
d. la fête de la Musique
e. Pâques
f. le festival de théâtre d'Avignon

5 **Répondez** Complete these sentences with words from the list according to what Benjamin says.

décembre	juillet	premier
janvier	juin	printemps

1. Le premier ____________, c'est le jour de l'an.
2. Au ____________, on célèbre Pâques.
3. Le quatorze ____________, c'est la fête nationale.
4. Le vingt-cinq ____________, c'est Noël.
5. Au mois de ____________, on célèbre la fête de la musique.

Après la vidéo

6 **Vrai ou faux?** Indicate whether these statements are **vrai** or **faux**.

	Vrai	Faux
1. On célèbre la fête de la musique seulement à Paris.	❍	❍
2. Il y a beaucoup de fêtes en France.	❍	❍
3. Le festival d'Avignon est un festival de danse.	❍	❍
4. Le festival de théâtre est à Nice.	❍	❍
5. Chaque année, Aix-en-Provence organise un carnaval.	❍	❍

7 **À vous!** Imagine that you just visited France during one of the holidays mentioned in the video. Write a short letter to a friend telling him or her about what you saw and did.

____

____

____

____

____

Nom ______________________ Date ______________________

STRUCTURES

6A.1 Demonstrative adjectives

1 **Vive la retraite!** Complete Annick and Pascal's conversation about an upcoming retirement party for their grandfather by selecting **ce**, **cet**, **cette**, or **ces**.

ANNICK Et si on fêtait la retraite de pépé avec ses amis?
PASCAL C'est génial comme idée! Il faut aussi inviter maman et papa à (1) ________ (ce/cette) fête.
ANNICK Ah, oui, bien sûr. Alors, quand? (2) ________ (Ce/Cette) week-end?
PASCAL Bon, d'accord. On va faire une surprise! Samedi après-midi, à quatre heures?
ANNICK À (3) ________ (cet/cette) heure-là, on n'a pas faim. Pourquoi pas à six heures du soir?
PASCAL Bonne idée. Si on invitait (*What if we invited*) son ami du bureau?
ANNICK (4) ________ (Cet/Ce) ami, il s'appelle Laurent Tallieu, non? Je vais téléphoner au bureau.
PASCAL Tous les invités peuvent lui donner (*can give him*) des cadeaux.
ANNICK Ah, non, tous (5) ________ (ce/ces) cadeaux! C'est trop! Tout le groupe va acheter un cadeau collectif.
PASCAL D'accord. Mais c'est toi qui va faire la collecte auprès de (*collect from*) tous (*everybody*) (6) ________ (ces/cet) invités!

2 **Impressions sur la fête** Complete what people are saying at a party with an expression using a form of **ce** and a noun. Refer to the photos for clues about which nouns to use.

Modèle

Cette fête est super! Il y a plein de monde (*lots of people*) ici.

1. Et ________________-ci, c'est pour Apolline?
2. Beurk! ________________ n'est pas bonne!
3. ________________-ci a l'air très bonne!

4. ________________ sont des caramels.
5. ________________ sont gazeuses.
6. ________________ est vraiment extraordinaire.

Nom ____________________ Date ____________________

3 **Ci et là** Complete each sentence with either ci or là.

1. Cette année-__________, on va fêter l'anniversaire de Nino au Café Cézanne.
2. Vous payez le loyer (*rent*) de ce mois- __________ ou du mois prochain?
3. Sandra, quel gâteau est-ce que tu préfères: ce gâteau-ci ou ce gâteau- __________?
4. Nous achetons cette glace-__________, au chocolat; non, cette glace-là, à la vanille.
5. Ces biscuits-ci sont bons, mais ces biscuits-__________ sont mauvais.

4 **Faites des phrases** Use the expressions in the columns to write logical sentences. Use each entry at least once.

ce	après-midi	on va fêter l'anniversaire d'Hervé
cet	cadeau	vont sur la table
cette	choses	est petit mais il est sympa
ces	glace	est parfumée (*flavored*) au chocolat
	glaçons	sont pour les boissons

1. ____________________
2. ____________________
3. ____________________
4. ____________________
5. ____________________

5 **À vous!** Respond to the questions with information about yourself. Write complete sentences.

1. Est-ce que vous allez fêter votre anniversaire cette année-ci?

____

2. Est-ce que vous allez sortir avec des copains ce week-end?

____

3. Est-ce que vous allez assister à une fête cette semaine?

____

4. Est-ce que vous allez inviter des copains chez vous ce soir?

____

5. Est-ce que vous allez suivre (*take*) des cours, travailler ou faire la fête cet été?

____

Nom ______________________ Date ______________________

6A.1 Demonstrative adjectives (audio activities)

1 **La fête** You are at a party. Listen to what the guests have to say about the party, and mark an X in the column of the demonstrative adjective you hear.

Modèle

You hear: J'adore ces petits gâteaux au chocolat.
You mark: an **X** under **ces**

	ce	cet	cette	ces
Modèle	________	________	________	X
1.	________	________	________	________
2.	________	________	________	________
3.	________	________	________	________
4.	________	________	________	________
5.	________	________	________	________
6.	________	________	________	________
7.	________	________	________	________
8.	________	________	________	________

2 **Changez** Form a sentence using the cue you hear. Repeat the correct answer after the speaker. (*6 items*)

Modèle

des biscuits
Je vais acheter *ces biscuits.*

3 **Transformez** Form a new sentence using the cue. Repeat the correct response after the speaker.

Modèle

You hear: J'aime ces bonbons.
You see: fête
You say: J'aime *cette* fête.

1. dessert
2. glace
3. hôte
4. mariage
5. eaux minérales
6. sandwich

4 **Demandez** Answer each question you hear in the negative. Repeat the correct answer after the speaker. (*6 items*)

Modèle

Tu aimes cette glace?
Non, *je n'aime pas cette glace-ci, j'aime cette glace-*là.

6A.2 The passé composé with avoir

1 **À la fête de Julie** Decide whether each sentence describes something that could have happened at Julie's party or if it is more likely to have happened elsewhere (**ailleurs**).

C'est arrivé...	à la fête de Julie	ailleurs
1. Sylvain et Cristelle ont dansé toute la nuit.	❍	❍
2. Julie a adoré ses cadeaux d'anniversaire.	❍	❍
3. Julie a passé un examen.	❍	❍
4. David a joué de la guitare et moi, j'ai chanté.	❍	❍
5. Tu as nettoyé toutes les fenêtres de la maison.	❍	❍
6. Nous avons fait du ski.	❍	❍
7. Vous avez rencontré tous les amis de Julie.	❍	❍
8. J'ai laissé un pourboire à Julie.	❍	❍
9. Augustin a pris des photos de tout le monde.	❍	❍
10. Quelle surprise! Julie n'a pas tout de suite compris que c'était (*it was*) une fête pour elle.	❍	❍

2 **À votre tour** Now tell what else happened at Julie's party, using the images as clues.

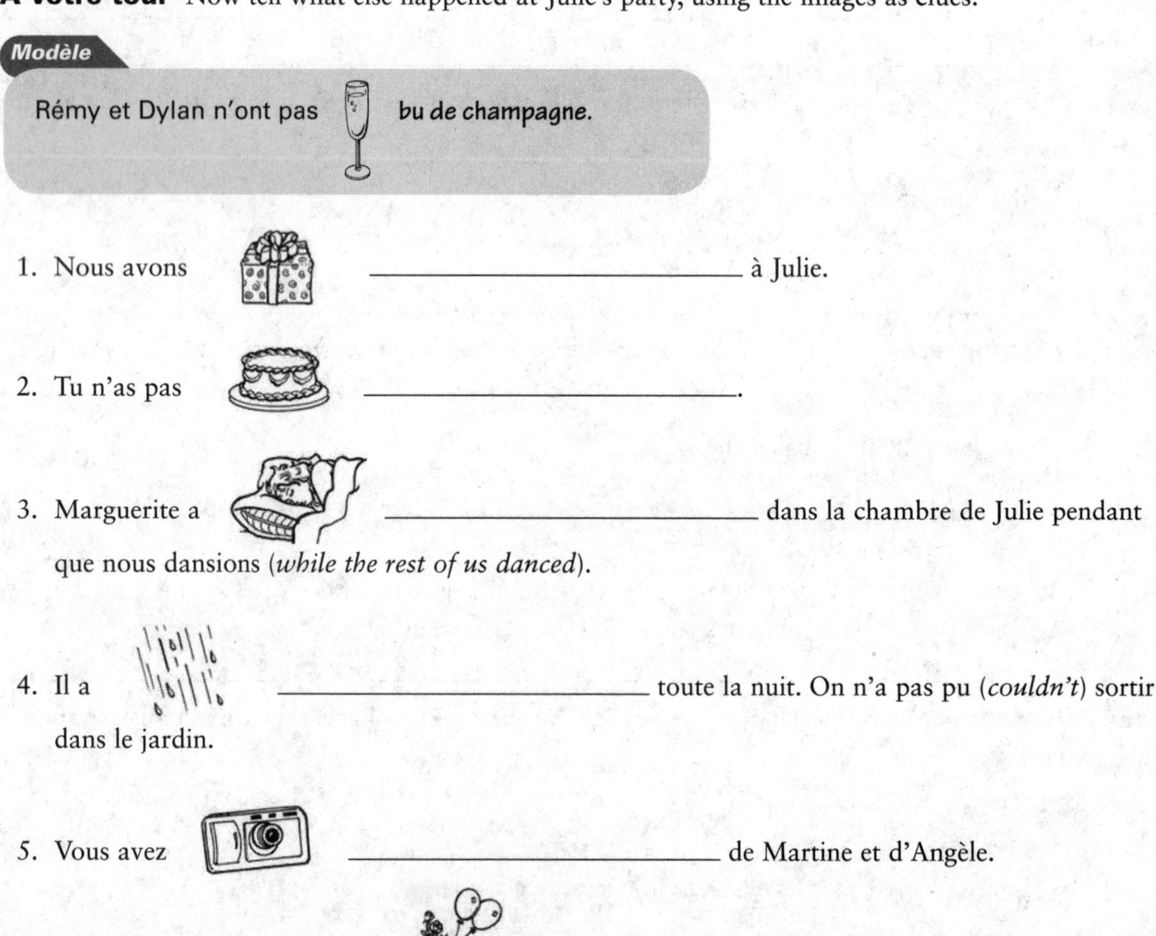

Modèle

Rémy et Dylan n'ont pas *bu de champagne.*

1. Nous avons ______________________ à Julie.
2. Tu n'as pas ______________________.
3. Marguerite a ______________________ dans la chambre de Julie pendant que nous dansions (*while the rest of us danced*).
4. Il a ______________________ toute la nuit. On n'a pas pu (*couldn't*) sortir dans le jardin.
5. Vous avez ______________________ de Martine et d'Angèle.
6. Théo et Jean-Paul ont trop ______________________.

3 **La sortie catastrophique** Complete the paragraph with appropriate past participles from the list.

cherché	été	organisé	payé
couru	fait	oublié	pris

J'ai (1) ___________ une sortie (*outing*) pour mes copains, samedi dernier. Pour commencer, Fred a (2) ___________ jusqu'au restaurant parce qu'il était en retard (*was late*). On a tous (3) ___________ des pizzas. Josiane et Simon n'ont pas aimé. Nous avons (4) ___________ une surprise à Fred avec un gâteau au chocolat pour son anniversaire. Et bien, il paraît (*it appears*) qu'il est allergique au chocolat. C'est moi qui ai (5) ___________ ce gâteau et ces pizzas. Après (*Afterwards*), Chloé a (6) ___________ son sac au restaurant et nous avons (7) ___________ ce sac pendant (*for*) une heure! Marlène n'a pas (8) ___________ très sympa avec Chloé, et puis (*then*) tout le monde est rentré (*returned*) en colère (*angry*) à la maison.

4 **Des questions** Write out a question that could elicit each response.

Modèle

Vous n'avez pas aimé la fête de l'année dernière?
Mais si! J'ai beaucoup aimé cette fête.

1. ____

   J'ai apporté du jus de pomme et des biscuits.

2. ____

   On a dîné dans un resto, et puis (*then*) on a regardé un film au ciné.

3. ____

   Ah, non, malheureusement. Et j'ai eu une mauvaise note!

4. ____

   Oui, il a fallu nettoyer toute la maison.

5. ____

   Non, j'ai pris une part (*piece*) de gâteau.

6. ____

   Oui, mais il a plu cet après-midi.

Nom ______________________ Date ______________________

6A.2 The **passé composé** with **avoir** (audio activities)

1

Identifiez Listen to each sentence and decide whether the verb is in the **présent** or the **passé composé.** Mark an **X** in the appropriate column.

Modèle

You hear: Tu as fait tout ça?
You mark: an **X** under **passé composé**

	présent	passé composé
Modèle		X
1.		
2.		
3.		
4.		
5.		
6.		
7.		
8.		

2

Changez Change each sentence from the présent to the passé composé. Repeat the correct answer after the speaker. (*8 items*)

Modèle

J'apporte la glace.
J'ai apporté la glace.

3

Questions Answer each question you hear using the cue. Repeat the correct response after the speaker.

Modèle

You hear: Où as-tu acheté ce gâteau?
You see: au marché
You say: ***J'ai acheté ce gâteau au marché.***

1. avec Élisabeth
2. Marc et Audrey
3. oui
4. non
5. non
6. oui
7. oui
8. Christine et Alain

4

C'est prêt? Listen to this conversation between Virginie and Caroline. Make a list of what is already done and a list of what still needs to be prepared.

Est déjà préparé ______________________

____

N'est pas encore préparé ______________________

____

Nom ______________________ Date ______________________

Unité 6

Leçon 6B

CONTEXTES

1

Chassez l'intrus In each set, two of the articles of clothing usually touch each other when they're being worn. Circle the item in each set that doesn't normally touch the others.

1. des baskets, un sac à main, des chaussettes
2. une ceinture, un pantalon, des lunettes de soleil
3. une casquette, un jean, un tee-shirt
4. une jupe, un chemisier, une chaussure
5. un chapeau, un sous-vêtement, une robe
6. des gants, un manteau, des chaussettes

2

En quelle saison? Name five articles of clothing that you would typically wear in the summer and five that you would typically wear in the winter.

En été, on porte...	En hiver, on porte...
1. ______________	1. ______________
2. ______________	2. ______________
3. ______________	3. ______________
4. ______________	4. ______________
5. ______________	5. ______________

3

Qu'est-ce que vous portez? Tell what items of clothing you would wear to these places. List as many articles as you can.

Modèle

au lycée: *un short, un tee-shirt, des chaussettes, des baskets, une montre et un sac à dos*

1. au bureau: ______________________________
2. à l'église: ______________________________
3. à la piscine: ______________________________
4. sur les pistes (*slopes*) de ski: ______________________________
5. à une fête: ______________________________
6. au gymnase: ______________________________
7. dans un avion (*airplane*): ______________________________
8. au parc: ______________________________

Nom ______________________ Date ______________________

4 Une personne raisonnable

Une personne raisonnable Indicate whether a reasonable person likes or doesn't like these things.

	Elle aime...	Elle n'aime pas...	
1.	❍	❍	les soldes.
2.	❍	❍	les vêtements bon marché.
3.	❍	❍	les vêtements trop chers.
4.	❍	❍	porter un pull trop large avec un blouson serré.
5.	❍	❍	les vendeurs polis.
6.	❍	❍	porter des vêtements à sa taille.

5 De quelle couleur?

De quelle couleur? Complete each description with a logical color.

1. Les ballons de basket sont ______________________.
2. Le chocolat est ______________________.
3. Les ordinateurs sont souvent ______________________.
4. Les canaris sont souvent ______________________.
5. Le lait est ______________________.
6. Les fruits sont souvent ______________________.
7. Le ciel (*sky*) est ______________________.
8. Les fleurs sont parfois ______________________.

6 Les goûts des autres

Les goûts des autres Describe what Mme Blay and M. Morande are wearing at the park today. Do you think they have good taste (**bon goût**) or bad taste (**mauvais goût**)? Justify your opinion. Write at least six complete sentences using the expressions from the list.

aller avec	court(e)	laid	large	long	porter	trop

____

____

____

____

____

____

Nom ______________________ Date ______________________

CONTEXTES: AUDIO ACTIVITIES

1 **Logique ou illogique?** Listen to each statement and indicate if it is **logique** or **illogique**.

	Logique	Illogique
1.	❍	❍
2.	❍	❍
3.	❍	❍
4.	❍	❍
5.	❍	❍
6.	❍	❍
7.	❍	❍

2 **Choisissez** Listen as each person talks about the clothing he or she needs to buy, then choose the activity for which the clothing would be appropriate.

1. a. voyager en été — b. faire du ski en hiver
2. a. marcher à la montagne — b. aller à la piscine l'été
3. a. faire de la planche à voile — b. faire du jogging
4. a. aller à l'opéra — b. jouer au golf
5. a. partir en voyage — b. faire une randonnée
6. a. faire une promenade — b. faire de l'aérobic

3 **Questions** Respond to each question saying the opposite. Repeat the correct answer after the speaker. (*6 items*)

Modèle

Cette écharpe est-elle longue?
Non, cette écharpe est courte.

4 **Quelle couleur?** Respond to each question using the cues. Repeat the correct answer after the speaker.

Modèle

You hear: De quelle couleur est cette chemise?
You see: vert
You say: ***Cette chemise est verte.***

1. gris 2. bleu 3. violet 4. marron 5. blanc 6. jaune

5 **Décrivez** You will hear some questions. Look at the drawing and write the answer to each question.

____

____

____

____

LES SONS ET LES LETTRES

Open vs. closed vowels: Part 3

The letter combination **eu** can be pronounced two different ways, open and closed. Compare the pronunciation of the vowel sounds in these words.

chev**eu**x   nev**eu**   h**eu**re   meill**eu**r

When **eu** is followed by a pronounced consonant, it has an open sound. The open **eu** sound does not exist in English. To pronounce it, say è with your lips only slightly rounded.

p**eu**r   j**eu**ne   chant**eu**r   b**eu**rre

The letter combination **œu** is usually pronounced with an open **eu** sound.

s**œu**r   b**œu**f   **œu**f   ch**œu**r

When **eu** is the last sound of a syllable, it has a closed vowel sound, similar to the vowel sound in the English word *full*. While this exact sound does not exist in English, you can make the closed **eu** sound by saying é with your lips rounded.

d**eu**x   bl**eu**   p**eu**   mi**eu**x

When **eu** is followed by a *z* sound, such as a single **s** between two vowels, it is usually pronounced with the closed **eu** sound.

chant**euse**   généreu**se**   séri**euse**   curi**euse**

1

Prononcez Répétez les mots suivants à voix haute.

1. leur
2. veuve
3. neuf
4. vieux
5. curieux
6. acteur
7. monsieur
8. coiffeuse
9. ordinateur
10. tailleur
11. vendeuse
12. couleur

2

Articulez Répétez les phrases suivantes à voix haute.

1. Le professeur Heudier a soixante-deux ans.
2. Est-ce que Matthieu est jeune ou vieux?
3. Monsieur Eustache est un chanteur fabuleux.
4. Eugène a les yeux bleus et les cheveux bruns.

3

Dictons Répétez les dictons à voix haute.

1. Qui vole un œuf, vole un bœuf.
2. Les conseilleurs ne sont pas les payeurs.

4

Dictée You will hear four sentences. Each will be read twice. Listen carefully and write what you hear.

1. ____________________
2. ____________________
3. ____________________
4. ____________________

Nom ______________________ Date ______________________

Roman-photo

L'ANNIVERSAIRE

Avant de regarder

1 **À la fête** List the kinds of things people might do and say at a birthday party.

____

____

____

____

____

En regardant la vidéo

2 **Complétez** Watch this video segment and complete these sentences with words from the list.

Aix-en-Provence	jupe	robe	soie
coton	Paris	Sandrine	Washington

1. C'est ____________ qui a presque tout préparé pour la fête.
2. David n'est pas à la fête parce qu'il visite ____________ avec ses parents.
3. Les parents de David sont de ____________.
4. Amina va emprunter la ____________ de Sandrine.
5. Sandrine va emprunter la ____________ d'Amina.
6. La jupe d'Amina est en ____________.

3 **Qui...?** Indicate which character says each of these lines. Write **A** for Amina, **As** for Astrid, **R** for Rachid, **S** for Sandrine, **St** for Stéphane, or **V** for Valérie.

_____ 1. Alors là, je suis agréablement surpris!

_____ 2. Bon anniversaire, mon chéri!

_____ 3. On a organisé cette surprise ensemble.

_____ 4. Alors cette année, tu travailles sérieusement, c'est promis?

_____ 5. Dix-huit ans, c'est une étape importante dans la vie!

_____ 6. Et en plus, vous m'avez apporté des cadeaux!

_____ 7. David est désolé de ne pas être là.

_____ 8. Cet ensemble, c'est une de tes créations, n'est-ce pas?

_____ 9. Ces gants vont très bien avec le blouson! Très à la mode!

_____ 10. La littérature, c'est important pour la culture générale!

_____ 11. Une calculatrice? Rose? Pour moi?

_____ 12. C'est pour t'aider à répondre à toutes les questions en maths.

_____ 13. Tu as aimé notre petite blague?

_____ 14. Vous deux, ce que vous êtes drôles!

4 **De quelle couleur?** What color are these objects from the video?

1. Les gants de Stéphane sont ______________.
2. Le tee-shirt d'Amina est ______________.
3. La robe de Sandrine est ______________.
4. Le blouson de Stéphane est ______________.
5. Le chemisier de Valérie est ______________.
6. La jupe d'Amina est ______________.
7. La calculatrice de Stéphane est ______________.
8. Les ballons sont ______________.

Après la vidéo

5 **Mettez-les dans l'ordre!** Number these events in the order in which they occur in the video.

_____ a. On souhaite à Stéphane un joyeux anniversaire.
_____ b. Stéphane ouvre ses cadeaux.
_____ c. Amina admire la robe de Sandrine.
_____ d. Stéphane arrive au P'tit Bistrot.
_____ e. On coupe le gâteau d'anniversaire.

6 **Que font-ils?** What do these people give to Stéphane or do for him for his birthday?

1. Sandrine: ______________________________
2. Valérie: ______________________________
3. Rachid et Astrid: ______________________________

7 **À vous!** Write a description of a birthday party you've had or that you've attended. Describe the people who were there and what they did. What foods were served? What did people wear? What gifts were given?

Nom ______________________ Date ______________________

STRUCTURES

6B.1 Indirect object pronouns

1 **Des devinettes** Solve these riddles (**devinettes**). Answers may be used more than once.

_______ 1. Vous leur envoyez des e-mails.
_______ 2. On lui pose des questions.
_______ 3. Ils vous donnent des cadeaux d'anniversaire.
_______ 4. Vous leur demandez d'apporter des vêtements.
_______ 5. Elle vous a donné le jour (*brought you into the world*).
_______ 6. Il vous donne des notes.
_______ 7. Ils vous prêtent de l'argent parfois.
_______ 8. Vous leur donnez de l'argent pour payer vos vêtements.

a. vos amis
b. des vendeurs
c. votre mère
d. le prof de français

2 **Des objets indirects** Circle the indirect objects in these sentences. If a sentence has an indirect object (not all of them do), rewrite it using the appropriate indirect object pronoun.

1. Chaque hiver, j'envoie un pull à ma sœur par la poste (*mail*).
____
2. Isabelle et moi essayons parfois des robes de mariées à la Boutique Blanche.
____
3. Nous posons des questions aux vendeurs.
____
4. Il faut payer les vêtements à la caisse (*at the register*).
____
5. Tu vas montrer ton nouveau pantalon à ta mère?
____
6. Je vais donner cette montre à mon père pour son anniversaire.
____

3 **Des extraits de conversations** Complete these conversations in a department store with appropriate indirect object pronouns.

1. **LE PÈRE** Ah, non, il n'est pas beau, ce pantalon!
KEVIN Eh bien, je ne ____________ ai pas demandé ton avis (*opinion*).
2. **VIRGINIE** Non, c'est non. Je ne vais pas te prêter de l'argent pour acheter ça!
RODRIGUE Mais tu ____________ as prêté de l'argent hier, pourquoi pas aujourd'hui?
3. **LA MÈRE** Alors, tu lui demandes de ____________ apporter une taille plus grande (*larger*).
KEVIN Mais, non, maman! Je ne vais pas lui demander de faire ça.
4. **MÉLANIE** Mais, maman! papa! Vous ne m'achetez pas la jupe? Pourquoi?
LA MÈRE Tu ____________ as parlé hier d'une jupe, non d'une micro-jupe!
5. **LA VENDEUSE** Madame, est-ce que je ____________ montre la robe en taille 40?
MME NOIRET Oui. J'aimerais (*I would like*) l'essayer.
6. **LE VENDEUR** Vous ____________ avez posé une question, Monsieur?
M. PINEAU Ah, oui. Je voulais savoir si (*I wanted to know if*) vous avez ça en 48?

4 **Méli-mélo** Unscramble each of these sentences.

1. téléphones / ne / souvent / pas / tu / très / me

____

2. va / expliquer / il / le / nous / problème

____

3. tu / parles / lui / ne / pourquoi / pas

____

4. Rodrigue / n' / prêter / de / aime / l' / pas / argent / leur

____

5. ne / laissé / pourboire / Mireille / a / pas /de / lui

____

6. quelque chose / je / montrer / te / vais

____

5 **Vos habitudes** Answer these questions about your personal habits. In each sentence, use the expression depicted by the illustration, and replace the indirect object with an indirect object pronoun.

1. Est-ce que vous _______ souvent à vos parents?

____

2. Est-ce que vous _______ à votre meilleur(e) (*best*) ami(e)?

____

3. Est-ce que vous _______ à vos amis?

____

4. Est-ce que vous _______ au prof de français quand vous êtes en classe?

____

6 **Victimes de la mode?** Carine and Lolo are talking about how they and their friends like to dress. Complete their conversation with appropriate disjunctive pronouns.

1. Tu kiffes (*like*) les blousons en jean? _______________ aussi, je kiffe!
2. Sylvain, il est vachement (*terribly*) beau dans son pantalon en cuir! Tu ne trouves pas, _______________?
3. Marie-Line? C'est bien _______________ qui porte cette jupe hyper sexy?
4. Mais leurs tee-shirts sont débiles (*lame*)! Ils n'ont aucun goût (*no taste*), _______________!
5. Sylvain a plein de trucs (*lots of things*) sympas! Il a bon goût, _______________.
6. Ouais (*Yeah*), Stéphanie et Christine ont des fringues (*gear*) géniales, _______________.

6B.1 Indirect object pronouns (audio activities)

1 **Choisissez** Listen to each question and choose the most logical response.

1. a. Oui, je lui ai montré ma robe.
   b. Oui, je leur ai montré ma robe.
2. a. Oui, je leur ai envoyé un cadeau.
   b. Oui, je vous ai envoyé un cadeau.
3. a. Non, je ne leur ai pas téléphoné.
   b. Non, je ne lui ai pas téléphoné.
4. a. Oui, nous allons leur donner cette cravate.
   b. Oui, nous allons lui donner cette cravate.
5. a. Non, il ne m'a pas prêté sa moto.
   b. Non, il ne t'a pas prêté sa moto.
6. a. Oui, ils vous ont répondu.
   b. Oui, ils nous ont répondu.

2 **Transformez** Aurore has been shopping. Say for whom she bought these items using indirect object pronouns. Repeat the correct answer after the speaker. (*6 items*)

Modèle

Aurore achète un livre à Audrey.
Aurore lui achète un livre.

3 **Questions** Answer each question you hear using the cue. Repeat the correct response after the speaker.

Modèle

You hear: Tu poses souvent des questions à tes parents?
You see: oui
You say: **Oui, je leur pose souvent des questions.**

1. non
2. une écharpe
3. des gants
4. non
5. non
6. à 8 heures

Nom ______________________ Date ______________________

6B.2 Regular and irregular -re verbs

1 **À l'arrêt de bus** Guillaume is talking to Mme Lominé at the bus stop. Decide whether these sentences could be a logical part of their conversation (**oui**) or not (**non**).

	Oui	Non
1. Ça fait 45 minutes qu'on attend ici!	❍	❍
2. Ils ne répondent pas au téléphone avant 10h00 du matin.	❍	❍
3. Vous vendez des boissons, Madame?	❍	❍
4. Mais il n'arrive pas! Nous perdons notre temps ici.	❍	❍
5. On m'a dit qu'il est souvent en retard.	❍	❍
6. Je rends souvent visite à mon grand-père qui habite au Canada.	❍	❍

2 **Le samedi d'Adama** The illustrations show what Adama did last Saturday. Complete each description with the past participle of a verb.

1. 
2. 
3. 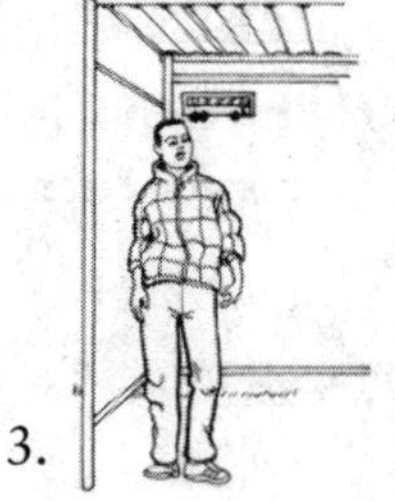
4. 

1. Il a ______________ un blouson avant de sortir.
2. Il a ______________ l'horaire (*schedule*) des bus devant sa maison.
3. Il a ______________ le bus pendant une heure mais il n'est pas venu (*didn't come*).
4. Il a ______________ jusqu'à la maison de sa tante.

3 **Qu'est-ce qu'on met?** Complete these sentences with an appropriate form of **mettre** and an article of clothing.

Modèle

Quand il neige, je **mets un manteau.**

1. Quand il fait du soleil, Nadège ______________________________.
2. Quand il pleut, Farid et moi ______________________________.
3. Quand vous sortez avec des copains, vous ______________________________.
4. Quand il fait froid, les filles ______________________________.
5. Quand tu as une mauvaise coupe de cheveux (*haircut*), tu ______________________________.
6. Quand je vais à la piscine, je ______________________________.

Nom ______________________ Date ______________________

4 **C'est fou!** Choose a verb from the list for each sentence about crazy things people do. Then give the appropriate form of the verb to complete the sentence. Each verb may be used more than once.

conduire	détruire	réduire
construire	produire	traduire

1. Ma grand-mère ne met pas ses lunettes quand elle ______________________.
2. Nous ______________________ une voiture en plastique dans notre garage.
3. Vous ______________________ un dictionnaire pour apprendre le français?
4. Ce n'est pas le mois des soldes, mais le grand magasin ______________________ ses prix.
5. Ils ______________________ leur maison dans un arbre (*tree*)?
6. Tu ______________________ ta maison pour construire un parking?
7. Marlène permet à ses enfants de ______________________ sa voiture.
8. Nous ______________________ 50 piñatas par jour dans notre maison.

5 **Qu'est-ce qui vous fait sourire?** Complete each statement about what makes people smile by filling in the appropriate present-tense form of **sourire**.

1. Nous ______________________ quand nous jouons avec notre chat, Minou.
2. Les élèves ______________________ quand ils ont de bonnes notes.
3. Le bébé ______________________ quand ses parents lui sourient.
4. Vous ______________________ quand il fait beau le samedi.
5. Je ______________________ quand je regarde des sitcoms à la télé.

6 **Forum questions-réponses** Answer these questions about yourself in complete sentences.

1. Est-ce que vous allez souvent dans les magasins avec vos copains?

   ____

2. Est-ce que vous conduisez une voiture?

   ____

3. Est-ce que vous répondez souvent aux questions du prof de français?

   ____

4. Est-ce que vous riez parfois quand vous ne devez pas (*shouldn't*) rire?

   ____

5. Est-ce que vous prenez le bus?

   ____

6. Est-ce que vous rendez visite à vos amis qui habitent dans d'autres villes (*that live in other towns*)?

   ____

Nom ____________________ Date ____________________

6B.2 Regular and irregular -re verbs (audio activities)

1 **Identifiez** Listen to each sentence and write the infinitive form of the verb you hear.

Modèle

You hear: L'enfant sourit à ses parents.
You write: **sourire**

1. ____________________
2. ____________________
3. ____________________
4. ____________________
5. ____________________
6. ____________________
7. ____________________
8. ____________________

2 **Changez** Form a new sentence using the cue you hear as the subject. Repeat the sentence after the speaker. (*6 items*)

Modèle

You hear: Elle attend le bus. (nous)
You say: **Nous attendons le bus.**

3 **Répondez** Answer each question you hear using the cue. Repeat the correct response after the speaker.

Modèle

You hear: Quel jour est-ce que tu rends visite à tes parents?
You see: le dimanche
You say: **Je rends visite à mes parents le dimanche.**

1. non
2. une robe
3. oui
4. non
5. le mois dernier
6. trois

4 **Complétez** Listen to this description and write the missing words.

Le mercredi, je (1) ____________________ à mes grands-parents. Je ne (2) ____________________ pas, je prends le train. Je (3) ____________________ à Soissons, où mes grands-parents (4) ____________________. Quand ils (5) ____________________ le train arriver, ils (6) ____________________. Nous rentrons chez eux; nous ne (7) ____________________ pas de temps et nous déjeunons tout de suite. L'après-midi passe vite et il est déjà l'heure de reprendre le train. Je (8) ____________________ à mes grands-parents de leur (9) ____________________ bientôt. Ils ne (10) ____________________ pas non plus, alors j'appelle un taxi pour aller prendre mon train.

Nom ______________________ Date ______________________

Unité 6

PANORAMA

Savoir-faire

1

Des mots associés Match each entry on the left with the one that is associated with it on the right.

______ 1. des spectacles de gladiateurs	a. une reine (*queen*) de France
______ 2. Montpellier et Nîmes	b. le Languedoc-Roussillon
______ 3. «Los cats fan pas de chins.»	c. les arènes de Nîmes
______ 4. Aliénor d'Aquitaine	d. Midi-Pyrénées
______ 5. Toulouse	e. l'occitan

2

Cherchez Find the expressions described by the clues below in the grid, looking backward, forward, vertically, horizontally, and diagonally. Circle them in the puzzle, then write the words in the blanks.

L	D	S	R	W	N	O	I	Q	L	J	B	E	I	M
J	A	L	É	F	T	R	I	H	C	O	J	U	J	D
T	A	N	Y	Y	D	T	F	E	R	N	M	Q	N	Y
N	X	C	G	X	G	C	G	D	G	Y	A	S	O	N
V	G	A	M	U	U	D	E	G	S	D	G	A	T	Y
R	C	S	A	U	E	A	M	A	M	B	V	B	S	V
W	U	S	M	S	U	D	C	Z	K	V	A	E	A	M
E	P	O	X	X	K	C	O	S	C	V	M	N	J	V
H	L	U	X	P	D	R	A	C	A	Î	Y	A	J	A
R	Z	L	O	W	K	H	F	F	N	L	R	U	B	T
A	C	E	I	Q	N	H	U	H	M	V	F	L	J	Q
S	H	T	S	A	D	I	R	R	O	C	Y	P	V	É
X	D	K	F	K	Z	D	K	B	P	W	V	F	G	R
D	I	Z	U	M	R	D	Y	Î	E	Û	C	V	L	A
Z	I	L	Q	N	D	C	V	W	M	C	Q	C	Y	O

1. C'est une grande ville d'Aquitaine.

   ____

2. On appelle cette grotte «la chapelle Sixtine préhistorique».

   ____

3. Les arènes de cette ville ressemblent au Colisée de Rome.

   ____

4. La langue d'Oc a donné son nom à cette région.

   ____

5. Le Pays ______________________ est la région qui est à la frontière entre la France et l'Espagne.

6. Ce plat populaire ressemble un peu au «*pork and beans*» américain.

   ____

7. Ces spectacles ont lieu (*take place*) aujourd'hui dans les arènes de Nîmes.

   ____

Nom ______________________ Date ______________________

3 **Qu'est-ce que c'est?** Label each photograph in French.

1. ______________

2. ______________

3. ______________

4. ______________

4 **Complétez les phrases** Supply the expression that is missing in each sentence about southwestern France.

1. ______________, c'est le nom d'un artiste connu (*famous*) de la région Midi-Pyrénées.
2. Les fresques de la grotte de Lascaux ont pour sujet des ______________.
3. On trouve le plus grand ______________ de l'ère romaine en France, à Nîmes.
4. Périgueux est une ville de la région ______________.
5. ______________ est le nom d'un homme politique de la région Midi-Pyrénées.
6. Le sud-ouest de la France se situe entre l'océan Atlantique et la mer ______________.

5 **Des fautes!** Your Canadian friend Norbert isn't good with details. Circle five mistakes in the e-mail that he wrote to you from France and correct the sentences by rewriting them on the lines that follow.

Ouaou! Je t'écris de Perpignan, une ville de la région qu'on appelle Midi-Pyrénées. Cette semaine, on va visiter des sites touristiques du sud-ouest (*southwest*) de la France. Pour commencer, jeudi, on va visiter la fameuse grotte de Lascaux, où l'on va apprécier des fresques mystérieuses qui sont vieilles de plus de 70 ans. Des adolescents ont découvert la grotte en 1940. Vendredi, on va assister à un match de rugby. (C'est un sport originaire de la région qu'on joue avec une balle en cuir et une raquette.) Samedi, on va faire un tour sur le canal du Midi et goûter (*taste*) des spécialités de la région, le pâté de luxe et le cassoulet. Et puis dimanche, on va assister à un spectacle musical aux arènes de Carcassonne. J'espère que tu vas bien.

À bientôt,
Norbert

1. ______________________________
2. ______________________________
3. ______________________________
4. ______________________________
5. ______________________________

Nom ______________________ Date ______________________

Unité 7

Leçon 7A

CONTEXTES

1 **Chassez l'intrus** Circle the item that does not belong in each set.

1. un arrêt de bus, une sortie, une station de métro, un aéroport
2. la station de ski, la mer, la plage, bronzer
3. un départ, une arrivée, un vol, un journal
4. faire les valises, bronzer, acheter un billet, prendre un train
5. la ville, la campagne, les vacances, la mer
6. le voyage, l'aéroport, la douane, l'avion
7. partir en vacances, prendre un jour de congé, travailler, faire un séjour
8. la douane, l'aéroport, le plan, le billet aller-retour

2 **Des mots brouillés** Unscramble the letters to reveal a nationality or country. Write each unscrambled name on the line after the clue.

Modèle

Au sud, le pays voisin des États-Unis, c'est le **EQMXIEU**. MEXIQUE

1. On associe les pandas et Jackie Chan à la **IHCEN**. ______________
2. Aux **TSÉAT-SUIN**, on fête le 4 juillet. ______________
3. Les habitants de l'**AILIET** mangent beaucoup de spaghettis. ______________
4. Berlin est la capitale de l'**LAEGNAMLE**. ______________
5. Au **PNAJO**, on prend des trains ultramodernes pour visiter des temples anciens. ______________
6. Madrid est la capitale de l'**EPENGSA**. ______________
7. La **ESSISU** est connue (*known*) pour ses montres, sa fondue et ses pistes (*slopes*) de ski.

   ____
8. Les **SAILARDNI** ont souvent les cheveux roux. ______________
9. L'**LNIARDE** est une île (*island*) très verte, située à l'ouest de l'Angleterre. ______________
10. La **QEBLEIGU** est un petit pays situé au nord-est (*northeast*) de la France. ______________
11. Les **GSLBEE** apprécient beaucoup le chocolat, les moules (*mussels*) et les frites.

    ____
12. Les **NSIOIHC** ont inventé l'acuponcture. ______________
13. Les **RISBNÉSLIE** fêtent leur fameux carnaval à Rio, chaque année. ______________
14. Le **LBSIÉR** est un pays d'Amérique du Sud où l'on parle portugais. ______________
15. Le **NDACAA** est situé au nord des États-Unis. ______________
16. En **EREETRNGLA**, on mange du «*fish and chips*», mais aussi du curry. ______________

Nom ____________________ Date ____________________

3 **Les moyens de transport** Write the means of transportation the Lefèvres took while on vacation. Use the images as cues.

Ils ont pris…

1. ________ 2. ________ 3. ________ 4. ________ 5. ________

4 **Une carte postale** Complete the postcard from Alexis with the logical expressions in parentheses.

Je t'écris (I'm writing you) de Cassis! On est en (1) ______________ (valises / vacances) depuis vendredi matin. On a (2) ______________ (perdu / pris) le train jusqu'à Marseille, et puis on a (3) ______________ (roulé / pris) en voiture jusqu'ici. On s'est bien perdus (We got really lost) sur l'autoroute! On a utilisé un (4) ______________ (journal / plan), mais bon… Les (5) ______________ (gens / pays) d'ici sont sympas! Il n'y a pas de métro ici et donc, on prend le (6) ______________ (bus / voiture) quand on n'a pas envie de conduire. Demain, on va visiter les fameuses calanques (inlets) et puis après-demain, on va visiter les plages de St-Tropez, en (7) ______________ (voiture / voyage). Mercredi après-midi, on va faire du (8) ______________ (shopping / séjour) à Nice.

À plus!

Alexis

5 **En vacances, que préférez-vous?** Complete each of these statements with information about your preferences.

1. J'ai envie de visiter ______________________________.
   deux pays à l'étranger
2. Quand je suis en vacances, j'aime ______________________________
   trois activités
   ______________________________.
3. Pour faire des voyages, je préfère prendre ______________________________.
   moyen de transport
4. Je n'aime pas prendre ______________________________.
   moyen de transport
5. Cette année-ci, on a une semaine de congé du ______________ au ______________.
   date / date
6. Cette semaine-là, je vais ______________________________.
   une activité

Nom ____________________ Date ____________________

CONTEXTES: AUDIO ACTIVITIES

1 **Identifiez** You will hear a series of words. Write the word that does not belong to each series.

1. ____________________
2. ____________________
3. ____________________
4. ____________________
5. ____________________
6. ____________________
7. ____________________
8. ____________________

2 **Décrivez** For each drawing you will hear two statements. Choose the one that corresponds to the drawing.

1. a. b. 2. a. b. 3. a. b.

3 **À l'agence** Listen to the conversation between Éric and a travel agent. Then read the statements and decide whether they are **vrai** or **faux**.

	Vrai	Faux
1. Éric pense partir en vacances une semaine.	❍	❍
2. Éric aime skier et jouer au golf.	❍	❍
3. Pour Éric, la campagne est une excellente idée.	❍	❍
4. Éric préfère la mer.	❍	❍
5. Il n'y a pas de plage en Corse.	❍	❍
6. Éric prend ses vacances la dernière semaine de juin.	❍	❍
7. Le vol de retour pour l'aéroport d'Ajaccio est le 9 juin.	❍	❍
8. Le billet d'avion aller-retour coûte 120 euros.	❍	❍

Nom ______________________ Date ______________________

LES SONS ET LES LETTRES

Diacriticals for meaning

Some French words with different meanings have nearly identical spellings except for a diacritical mark (**accent**). Sometimes a diacritical does not affect pronunciation at all.

ou	où	a	à
or	*where*	*has*	*to, at*

Sometimes, you can clearly hear the difference between the words.

côte	côté	sale	salé
coast	*side*	*dirty*	*salty*

Very often, two similar-looking words are different parts of speech. Many similar-looking word pairs are those with and without an -é at the end.

âge	â**gé**	entre	entr**é** (entrer)
age (n.)	*elderly* (adj.)	*between* (prep.)	*entered* (p.p.)

In such instances, context should make their meaning clear.

Tu as quel **âge**?	C'est un homme **âgé**.
How old are you? / What is your age?	*He's an elderly man.*

1 **Prononcez** Répétez les mots suivants à voix haute.

1. la (*the*) là (*there*)
2. êtes (*are*) étés (*summers*)
3. jeune (*young*) jeûne (*fasting*)
4. pêche (*peach*) pêché (*fished*)

2 **Articulez** Répétez les phrases suivantes à voix haute.

1. J'habite dans une ferme (*farm*).
   Le magasin est fermé (*closed*).
2. Les animaux mangent du maïs (*corn*).
   Je suis suisse, mais il est belge.
3. Est-ce que tu es prête?
   J'ai prêté ma voiture à Marcel.
4. La lampe est à côté de la chaise.
   J'adore la côte ouest de la France.

3 **Dictons** Répétez les dictons à voix haute.

1. À vos marques, prêts, partez!
2. C'est un prêté pour un rendu.

4 **Dictée** You will hear six sentences. Each will be said twice. Listen carefully and write what you hear.

1. ______________________
2. ______________________
3. ______________________
4. ______________________
5. ______________________
6. ______________________

Nom ______________________ Date ______________________

Roman-photo

DE RETOUR AU P'TIT BISTROT

Avant de regarder

1 **À Paris** In this video episode, David has just returned from a vacation in Paris. What do you think he might have seen and done there?

____

____

____

____

____

En regardant la vidéo

2 **Les vacances à Paris** Watch this video segment and place check marks beside the activities David says he did in Paris.

David ...

❑ 1. est allé (*went*) à la tour Eiffel.
❑ 2. a pris un bateau-mouche (*tourist boat*) sur la Seine.
❑ 3. a visité la cathédrale de Notre-Dame.
❑ 4. a pris un taxi.
❑ 5. a visité le musée du Louvre.
❑ 6. est allé à Montmartre.
❑ 7. a visité la ville en voiture.
❑ 8. est allé aux Galeries Lafayette.
❑ 9. a dîné dans une brasserie.
❑ 10. a visité le musée d'Orsay.
❑ 11. a pris le métro.
❑ 12. a visité les monuments.

3 **Vrai ou faux?** Indicate whether each of these statements is **vrai** or **faux**.

	Vrai	Faux
1. David pense que Paris est la plus belle ville du monde.	❍	❍
2. David n'a pas oublié l'anniversaire de Stéphane.	❍	❍
3. Les parents de David n'aiment pas conduire.	❍	❍
4. David a acheté des vêtements à Paris.	❍	❍
5. David n'a pas passé de bonnes vacances.	❍	❍
6. Stéphane n'a pas aimé ses cadeaux d'anniversaire.	❍	❍
7. Sandrine a l'intention de passer ses vacances d'hiver à Albertville.	❍	❍
8. David ne fait pas de ski.	❍	❍

4 **Les vacances** For items 1–5, fill in the missing letters in each word. Unscramble the letters in the boxes to find the answer to item 6.

1. David est parti pour Paris avec une v ☐ __ __ __ __.
2. Les p __ __ __ __ __ ☐ de David sont arrivés des États-Unis.
3. Ils ont pris une c __ __ __ __ ☐ __ dans un bel hôtel.
4. Ils sont venus chercher David à la gare v__ __ __ __ __ __ ☐ soir.
5. Ils aiment conduire à la c __ __ ☐ __ __ __ __, mais pas en ville.
6. Où est-ce que David aime passer ses vacances? ______________

5 **Mettez-les dans l'ordre!** Number these events in the order in which they occur.

_______ a. David raconte ses vacances à Rachid.
_______ b. David arrive à la gare d'Aix-en-Provence.
_______ c. Sandrine demande à David de revenir au café demain.
_______ d. David raconte ses vacances à Stéphane.
_______ e. David surprend Sandrine au café.
_______ f. Stéphane raconte sa fête à David.

Après la vidéo

6 **Répondez** Answer these questions in French. Use complete sentences.

1. Quand est-ce que les parents de David sont arrivés (*arrived*) des États-Unis?
____
2. Combien de temps est-ce que David a passé à Paris?
____
3. Pour Stéphane, quelles sont les vacances idéales?
____
4. Qu'est-ce que David a donné à Stéphane?
____
5. Que pense David de Sandrine?
____
6. Pourquoi est-ce que Sandrine doit (*must*) partir sans boire son café?
____

7 **À vous!** List four places you'd like to go on vacation. Then list two activities you might do in each place. Mention eight different activities.

Lieu de vacances	Activité	Activité
1. ______	______	______
2. ______	______	______
3. ______	______	______
4. ______	______	______

Nom ______________________ Date ______________________

Flash culture

LES VACANCES

Avant de regarder

1 **Qu'est-ce que vous aimez faire?** In this video, you will learn about vacations in France. Make a list of six things you like to do while on vacation. Then make a list of six things you don't like to do on vacation.

Quand je suis en vacances, j'aime...	Quand je suis en vacances, je n'aime pas...
______________________	______________________
______________________	______________________
______________________	______________________
______________________	______________________
______________________	______________________
______________________	______________________

2 **Mes vacances** Circle all of the statements that describe you.

1. J'aime voyager en avion / en train / en voiture.
2. En vacances, j'aime rester dans un hôtel / un camping / une auberge de jeunesse.
3. J'aime visiter les musées / acheter des souvenirs / manger au restaurant.
4. Dans un café, j'aime manger / prendre un verre / regarder les gens qui passent.
5. J'aime bien bronzer à la plage / rouler en voiture / skier.

En regardant la vidéo

3 **Identifiez-les!** Match these images with their captions.

1. ________

2. ________

3. ________

4. ________

5. ________

6. ________

7. ________

8. ________

a. On fait un tour en bateau.
b. Ça, c'est la gare.
c. C'est un camping.
d. Voici la plage de Cassis.
e. C'est un hôtel de luxe.
f. Voici un café.
g. On achète des souvenirs.
h. C'est un hôtel modeste.

4 **Mettez-les dans l'ordre** In what order does Csilla mention these means of transportation?

_______ a. le train

_______ b. l'autobus

_______ c. l'avion

_______ d. le taxi

_______ e. la voiture

_______ f. le car

5 **Répondez** Complete these sentences with words from the list according to what Csilla says in the video. Not all words will be used.

activités	autobus	car	manger	taxi
argent	avion	gares	région	TGV
auberges de jeunesse	bateau	gens	routière	verre

1. Pour arriver en Provence, il y a l'_______________, ou un train spécial que les Français appellent le _______________.
2. C'est une des deux _______________ d'Aix-en-Provence où il y a des trains réguliers pour visiter la _______________.
3. À la gare _______________, on prend le _______________ pour aller d'une ville à l'autre.
4. En ville, il y a l'_______________ ou le _______________.
5. Si vous n'avez pas beaucoup d'_______________, il y a toujours des _______________.
6. Il est très agréable de _______________ dans les cafés ou de prendre un _______________ à la terrasse d'un café ou d'un restaurant et de regarder les _______________ passer.

Après la vidéo

6 **En vacances** Imagine that you are on vacation in Provence. Write a postcard to a friend or relative describing your trip. Tell where you've been and how you got there. Mention at least four different things you've seen or done.

Nom ______________________ Date ______________________

STRUCTURES

7A.1 The passé composé with être

1 **Avoir ou être?** Decide whether to use **avoir** or **être** as an auxiliary for each of the verbs in Gisèle's e-mail about her spring break.

Je (1) ______________ (suis / ai) allée à Marseille, avec Micheline, pour les vacances de printemps. Samedi matin, on (2) ______________ (est / a) passé au moins trois heures dans de beaux embouteillages (*traffic jams*) sur l'autoroute! Tout le monde (3) ______________ (est / a) quitté Paris pour la province. On (4) ______________ (est / a) arrivé chez mon cousin Régis, samedi soir. Il habite au centre-ville de Marseille, donc on en a profité (*took advantage of it*) pour visiter le Vieux Port et la basilique Notre-Dame de la Garde. Le système de transports publics à Marseille est très développé et donc, on (5) ______________ (a / est) pris le métro tous les jours. On (6) ______________ (est / a) fait plusieurs sorties (*outings*) dans la région, pendant la deuxième semaine des vacances. On (7) ______________ (est / a) visité les gorges du Verdon et Saint-Paul de Vence, par exemple. On (8) ______________ (est / a) rentré dimanche soir et nous voilà de retour.

2 **Ah, les belles vacances!** Complete each sentence using the auxiliary verb **être**. Then indicate whether each statement would describe something that probably happened during vacation (**lors des vacances**) or at another time (**à un autre moment**).

	lors des vacances	à un autre moment
1. Nous ______________ parties pour la plage samedi matin.	❍	❍
2. L'auteur ______________ né à Marseille le 22 mai 1986.	❍	❍
3. Karine et Christine ______________ retournées au parc Disneyland.	❍	❍
4. Nico ______________ resté chez lui mais il a passé la semaine à dormir et à bronzer dans son jardin (*yard*).	❍	❍
5. Vous ______________ resté à l'hôtel Caron de Beaumarchais pour être près du bureau?	❍	❍
6. Je ______________ allée à Venise, où j'ai passé trois superbes journées en gondole.	❍	❍

Nom ______________________ Date ______________________

3 **Les rumeurs qui courent** Surya is not the type to gossip, but her friends sure are! She knows what's really going on, so she corrects them. For each piece of gossip, write Surya's response.

Modèle

J'ai entendu dire qu'Ahmed est allé en Tunisie pour rendre visite à sa copine!
Sa copine habite à Montpellier. Ahmed n'est pas allé en Tunisie pour lui rendre visite.

1. Le président est mort hier soir!
____
2. Jeanne est partie pour l'Espagne ce matin. Elle a quitté son mari.
____
3. Jean-Marie est tombé dans un trou (*hole*) la semaine dernière. Il est à l'hôpital maintenant.
____
4. Et tu sais (*And you know*), Vincent est le premier d'une famille de dix enfants!
____
5. L'année dernière, Samuel est sorti avec la copine de Luc.
____
6. Émilie n'est pas rentrée hier soir.
____

4 **Méli-mélo** Unscramble each of the sentences taking care to put the adverb in the correct place.

1. nous / sont / chez / Olivier / pas / encore / passés / ne / et / Joëlle
____
2. tes / tu / fait / devoirs / bien / as
____
3. rentrés / vacances / sont / de / élèves / les / déjà
____
4. sortie / Mathilde / est / pas / de / école / n' / encore / l'
____
5. Samia / vite / appris / a / leçon / la
____

5 **Que de questions!** Answer these questions in complete sentences.

1. À quelle heure êtes-vous sorti(e) de la maison aujourd'hui?
____
2. À quelle heure êtes-vous arrivé(e) à l'école?
____
3. Êtes-vous passé(e) chez un copain sur le chemin (*on the way*)?
____
4. Si oui, combien de minutes avez-vous passées là?
____
5. Êtes-vous entré(e) dans un magasin aujourd'hui?
____
6. À quelle heure êtes-vous rentré(e) chez vous hier soir?
____

Nom ______________________ Date ______________________

7A.1 The passé composé with être (audio activities)

1

Choisissez Listen to each sentence and indicate whether the verb is conjugated with **avoir** or **être**.

	avoir	être
1.	❍	❍
2.	❍	❍
3.	❍	❍
4.	❍	❍
5.	❍	❍
6.	❍	❍
7.	❍	❍
8.	❍	❍

2

Changez Change each sentence from the **présent** to the **passé composé**. Repeat the correct answer after the speaker. (*8 items*)

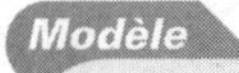

Modèle

Vous restez au Québec trois semaines.
Vous êtes resté(e)(s) au Québec trois semaines.

3

Questions Answer each question you hear using the cue. Repeat the correct response after the speaker.

Modèle

You hear: Qui est parti en vacances avec toi?
You see: Caroline
You say: ***Caroline est partie en vacances avec moi.***

1. au Canada
2. non
3. mercredi
4. par la Suisse et par l'Italie
5. trois jours
6. oui

4

Ça va? Listen to Patrick and Magali and answer the questions.

1. Est-ce que Patrick est fatigué? ______________________
2. Avec qui Magali est-elle sortie? ______________________
3. Où sont-ils allés? ______________________
4. Qui Magali a-t-elle rencontré? ______________________
5. Qu'ont-ils fait ensuite? ______________________
6. À quelle heure Magali est-elle rentrée chez elle? ______________________

Nom ____________________ Date ____________________

7A.2 Direct object pronouns

1 **Des échanges** Complete these exchanges with appropriate direct object pronouns.

1. **AMÉLIE** Nous avons faim, papa.
   LE PÈRE Je ____________ invite à partager une pizza, les filles!
2. **CAROLINE** Serge, est-ce que tu ____________ aimes?
   SERGE Je ne t'aime pas, je t'adore!
3. **LA MÈRE** Marie-Louise, je te parle!
   MARIE-LOUISE Je ____________ entends, maman.
4. **M. NOTHOMBE** Je ____________ ai rencontrée quelque part (*somewhere*), Madame?
   MME HAN Ah, non, Monsieur. Je ne pense pas.
5. **NATHALIE** Je ____________ ai attendu pendant deux heures au café, Alex.
   ALEX Désolé, j'ai oublié notre rendez-vous.
6. **M. LESAGE** C'est vous qui adorez la photographie, M. Descombes?
   M. DESCOMBES Ah oui, je ____________ adore.

2 **Des énigmes** The direct object pronouns in these sentences are underlined. Suggest an antecedent (the noun that the pronoun refers to) for each sentence. There are no set answers, so be creative.

Modèle

Sébastien, tu <u>la</u> regardes trop! *la télévision*

1. C'est Cédric qui me <u>le</u> donne, pour mon anniversaire! ____________
2. Est-ce que vous <u>les</u> faites tous les jours (*every day*)? ____________
3. Vous <u>les</u> rendez aujourd'hui? Mais la bibliothèque est fermée. ____________
4. Tu ne <u>la</u> mets pas? Mais il fait froid dehors (*outside*)! ____________
5. Où est-ce qu'il <u>les</u> achète? ____________
6. Régine <u>la</u> nettoie une fois par semaine. ____________

3 **Transformez** Rewrite these sentences with direct object pronouns in place of the direct objects.

1. Nous préférons faire les valises mercredi matin.
   ____
2. On ne va pas visiter le musée Matisse?
   ____
3. Au Café Grenoblois, on va essayer la fameuse fondue au chocolat.
   ____
4. Il faut regarder le film de Truffaut pour notre cours de français.
   ____
5. Vous aimez fréquenter ce café, Mademoiselle?
   ____

Nom ______________________ Date ______________________

4 Des énigmes (suite)

Des énigmes (suite) Match each caption with its photo. Use each answer only once.

a. 
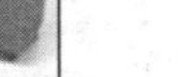

b. 

c. 

d. 

e. 

f. 

g. 

h. 

_______ 1. On l'a visitée l'année dernière.

_______ 2. Tu l'as déjà regardé?

_______ 3. On les a mangés!

_______ 4. On les a faites avant de partir.

_______ 5. Je l'ai perdue à l'école.

_______ 6. Nous l'avons pris pour aller au musée.

_______ 7. Hélène les a invités.

_______ 8. C'est Hector qui les a bues.

5 Faites l'accord

Faites l'accord Two twins, Robert and Richard, are about to leave on a trip together. Complete their conversation by writing the appropriate endings for the past participles. If no change is required, leave a blank line.

ROBERT Où sont les billets?

RICHARD Je les ai (1) oublié_______ dans mon bureau.

ROBERT Ah, non! Bon, on va passer par ton bureau sur le chemin de l'aéroport.

RICHARD Tu as fait les valises, au moins (*at least*)?

ROBERT C'est toi qui as promis de les faire.

RICHARD Mais non. C'est toi qui as promis. Ah non, tu ne les as pas (2) fait_______!

ROBERT Bon, moi, je vais mettre quelques trucs (*things*) pour nous deux dans une valise, et puis on part!

RICHARD Je vais mettre mon écharpe noire pour le voyage.

ROBERT C'est mon écharpe à moi, ça! Mais tu l'as (3) mis_______, toi? Bon, je te la donne. On part!

RICHARD Heureusement que tu as promis d'apporter le plan. Au fait, quel plan exactement (*exactly*) as-tu (4) pris_______?

ROBERT Un plan? Quel plan? Je n'ai pas de plan, moi.

RICHARD Bon, d'accord, on va trouver un plan là-bas.

ROBERT Je n'ai pas eu le temps de regarder la météo (*weather report*) avant de partir. Tu ne l'as pas (5) regardé_______ non plus?

RICHARD Mais non. Tu sais (*You know*) que je n'aime pas la télé.

ROBERT Tu n'as pas oublié ton passeport, j'espère?

RICHARD Euh…

ROBERT Mais bien sûr que tu l'as (6) oublié_______.

RICHARD Ce n'est pas possible.

ROBERT Mais je rêve! (*I must be dreaming!*)

7A.2 Direct object pronouns (audio activities)

1 **Choisissez** Listen to each question and choose the most logical answer.

1. a. Oui, je la regarde.
   b. Oui, je les regarde.
2. a. Non, je ne l'ai pas.
   b. Non, je ne les ai pas.
3. a. Non, je ne l'attends pas.
   b. Non, je ne t'attends pas.
4. a. Oui, nous vous écoutons.
   b. Oui, nous les écoutons.
5. a. Oui, je l'ai appris.
   b. Oui, je les ai appris.
6. a. Oui, ils vont te chercher.
   b. Oui, ils vont nous chercher.
7. a. Oui, je vais les acheter.
   b. Oui, je vais l'acheter.
8. a. Oui, je l'ai acheté.
   b. Oui, je les ai achetés.

2 **Changez** Restate each sentence you hear using a direct object pronoun. Repeat the correct answer after the speaker. (*8 items*)

Modèle

Nous regardons la télévision.
Nous la regardons.

3 **Répondez** Answer each question you hear using the cue. Repeat the correct response after the speaker.

Modèle

Qui va t'attendre à la gare? (mes parents)
Mes parents vont m'attendre à la gare.

1. au marché	3. oui	5. sur Internet
2. ce matin	4. midi	6. oui

4 **Questions** Answer each question you hear in the negative. Repeat the correct response after the speaker. (*6 items*)

Modèle

Est-ce que vos grands-parents vous ont attendus?
Non, ils ne nous ont pas attendus.

Nom ______________________ Date ______________________

Unité 7

Leçon 7B

CONTEXTES

1 **À l'hôtel** Label this illustration of a hotel lobby with appropriate French words.

1. ______________________
2. ______________________
3. ______________________
4. ______________________
5. ______________________
6. ______________________

2 **Vrai ou faux?** Indicate whether each statement about the illustration of the hotel lobby in Activité 1 is vrai or faux.

	Vrai	Faux
1. C'est la réception d'une auberge de jeunesse.	❍	❍
2. C'est une chambre d'hôtel.	❍	❍
3. C'est la réception d'un hôtel.	❍	❍
4. La réception est au rez-de-chaussée.	❍	❍
5. Il y a un lit au rez-de-chaussée.	❍	❍
6. Il y a des chambres au premier étage.	❍	❍
7. L'hôtelier redonne (*is giving back*) son passeport à la femme.	❍	❍
8. Un passager prend la valise du client.	❍	❍

3 **À l'agence de voyages** There are five strange details in this passage about Charles' trip to a travel agency. Rewrite the passage with corrections so that it makes sense.

Ce matin, Charles est passé par une agence de voyages pour faire des réservations. Un hôtelier très sympa l'a aidé à organiser le voyage. Pour commencer, ils ont trouvé des billets aller-retour Paris-Nice et ils les ont annulés. Puis, l'agent de police a téléphoné à des hôtels à Grenoble pour demander s'il y avait (*if there were*) des chambres complètes pour son client, et il a fait une réservation pour une chambre individuelle à l'hôtel Matisse. Après, Charles a demandé le numéro de téléphone de l'auberge de jeunesse et l'agent le lui a donné. Finalement, Charles est reparti (*left*) très content. Une semaine à Nice!

____

____

____

____

____

____

Nom ______________________ Date ______________________

4 **Une petite histoire** Complete the sentences below with appropriate expressions from the list. The words may be used more than once. Some do not have to be used at all.

alors	avant	donc	ensuite	pendant	tout à coup
après	d'abord	enfin	finalement	puis	tout de suite

(1) ____________ d'aller chez sa grand-mère, le Petit Chaperon Rouge (*Little Red Riding Hood*) fait une promenade dans le bois (*woods*). (2) ____________ qu'elle regarde de belles fleurs, un grand méchant loup (*wolf*) arrive. (3) ____________, le loup commence à lui parler. Elle trouve le loup beau et charmant. Il lui fait des compliments (il adore sa cape rouge!), et il l'invite à partir avec lui. Elle lui explique qu'elle est désolée, mais qu'elle va rendre visite à sa grand-mère cet après-midi. Le loup trouve ça intéressant et demande où habite la grand-mère. Elle lui donne l'adresse de sa grand-mère, (4) ____________ elle reprend sa route (*continues walking*). (5) ____________ sa rencontre avec le grand loup, le Petit Chaperon Rouge commence à avoir des doutes. Mais elle oublie ces sentiments (*feelings*) bizarres quand elle voit (*sees*) la maison de sa grand-mère. Elle ouvre la porte et elle laisse son panier plein de (*basket full of*) fleurs à côté du lit. Elle se met au (*gets in*) lit avec sa grand-mère qui n'a pas l'air d'aller très bien aujourd'hui. Elle ne remarque (6) ____________ pas (*doesn't notice*) que la grand-mère ressemble fort à un grand méchant loup. Elle lui parle de sa journée quand (7) ____________, elle s'aperçoit (*perceives*) qu'elle est au lit avec un loup déguisé en grand-mère! (8) ____________, le grand méchant loup la mange et met son petit chaperon (*hooded cape*) rouge pour faire une balade au bois.

5 **À quel étage?** Use the building directory as a reference to tell which floor each business is on. Write out each ordinal number in letters.

0	EUROPOSTE	19	CADORAMA	38	EUROENTREPRISE
1	ALLÔPORTABLE	20	AFSA LIMITÉE	39	CÉDÉROM.COM
2	CRÉDI-BANQUE	21	B.B. INTERNATIONAL	40	CÉDÉROM.COM
3	COGITO ERGO COM	22	NICE MULTISERVICES	41	AMNESTIE.FR
4	GIRAUD ET CIE	23	AGENCE EUROVOYAGES	42	SOCIÉTÉ FRANÇAISE
5	ACTISPORT	24	COMPTOIRS DE NICE	43	ENFANTILLAGES
6	NUTRITEL	25	NOSTALGIE ET CIE	44	FONDATION NATHAN
7	BOUVARD ET ASSOCIÉS	26	ÉDITIONS DU NORD	45	MÉDICO-TAXI
8	GROUPE ALITEL	27	SUPER-LOTO	46	GIRAUD PÈRE ET FILS
9	GALERIES DUFAYEL	28	BANQUE GÉNÉRALE	47	SERVEUR INTERNET
10	CRÉMAUX ET FILS	29	NOUVEAU MILLÉNAIRE	48	SERVEUR INTERNET

1. Crémaux et Fils est au ____________________ étage.
2. Europoste est au ____________________.
3. Le serveur Internet est au ____________________ et au ____________________ étages.
4. B.B. International est au ____________________ étage.
5. Éditions du Nord est au ____________________ étage.
6. Nostalgie et Compagnie est au ____________________ étage.
7. Cadorama est au ____________________ étage.
8. Allôportable est au ____________________ étage.
9. Comptoirs de Nice est au ____________________ étage.
10. Enfantillages est au ____________________ étage.

Nom ______________________ Date ______________________

CONTEXTES: AUDIO ACTIVITIES

1 Identifiez You will hear a series of words. Write the word that does not belong in each series.

1. ______________________
2. ______________________
3. ______________________
4. ______________________
5. ______________________
6. ______________________
7. ______________________
8. ______________________

2 La réception Look at the drawing and listen to each statement. Then decide if the statement is **vrai** or **faux**.

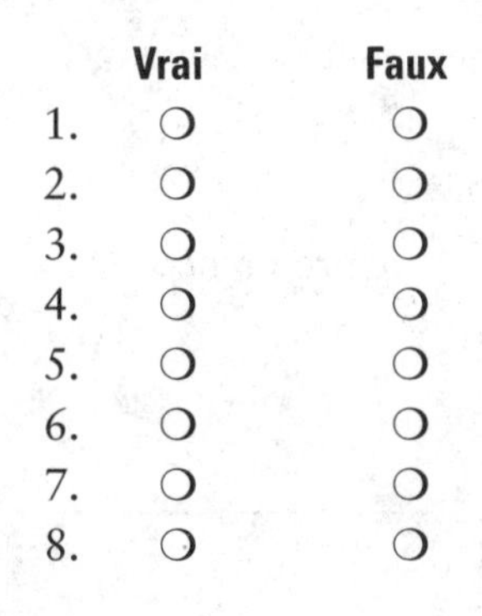

	Vrai	Faux
1.	❍	❍
2.	❍	❍
3.	❍	❍
4.	❍	❍
5.	❍	❍
6.	❍	❍
7.	❍	❍
8.	❍	❍

3 Complétez Listen to this description and write the missing words.

Pour les étudiants, les (1) ______________________ sont très bon marché quand ils ont envie de voyager. Généralement, elles ont de grandes (2) ______________________ avec trois, quatre ou cinq (3) ______________________. C'est très sympa quand vous partez (4) ______________________ avec vos amis. Les auberges sont souvent petites et il faut faire des (5) ______________________. Dans ma ville, l'auberge a une toute petite (6) ______________________, vingt chambres et trois (7) ______________________. Il n'y a pas d' (8) ______________________.

Nom ____________________ Date ____________________

LES SONS ET LES LETTRES

ti, sti, and ssi

The letters **ti** followed by a consonant are pronounced like the English word *tea*, but without the puff released in the English pronunciation.

actif petit **ti**gre u**ti**les

When the letter combination **ti** is followed by a vowel sound, it is often pronounced like the sound linking the English words *miss you*.

dic**ti**onnaire pa**ti**ent ini**ti**al addi**ti**on

Regardless of whether it is followed by a consonant or a vowel, the letter combination **sti** is pronounced *stee*, as in the English word *steep*.

ge**sti**on que**sti**on Séba**sti**en arti**sti**que

The letter combination **ssi** followed by another vowel or a consonant is usually pronounced like the sound linking the English words *miss you*.

pa**ssi**on expre**ssi**on mi**ssi**on profe**ssi**on

Words that end in **-sion** or **-tion** are often cognates with English words, but they are pronounced quite differently. In French, these words are never pronounced with a *sh* sound.

compre**ssion** na**tion** atten**tion** addi**tion**

1 **Prononcez** Répétez les mots suivants à voix haute.

1. artiste
2. mission
3. réservation
4. impatient
5. position
6. initiative
7. possession
8. nationalité
9. compassion
10. possible

2 **Articulez** Répétez les phrases suivantes à voix haute.

1. L'addition, s'il vous plaît.
2. Christine est optimiste et active.
3. Elle a fait une bonne première impression.
4. Laëtitia est impatiente parce qu'elle est fatiguée.
5. Tu cherches des expressions idiomatiques dans le dictionnaire.

3 **Dictons** Répétez les dictons à voix haute.

1. De la discussion jaillit la lumière.
2. Il n'est de règle sans exception.

4 **Dictée** You will hear six sentences. Each will be said twice. Listen carefully and write what you hear.

1. ______________________________
2. ______________________________
3. ______________________________
4. ______________________________
5. ______________________________
6. ______________________________

Nom ______________________ Date ______________________

Roman-photo

LA RÉSERVATION D'HÔTEL

Avant de regarder

1 **À l'agence de voyages** What might you say at a travel agency? When making travel arrangements, what information might a travel agent need from you?

____

____

____

____

____

En regardant la vidéo

2 **Complétez** Choose the words that complete the sentences below according to what Sandrine says in the video.

1. J'ai besoin d'une ______________ d'hôtel, s'il vous plaît.
   a. réservation   b. chambre   c. auberge
2. Nous allons ______________.
   a. en Suisse   b. à Paris   c. à Albertville
3. Il nous faut ______________ chambre(s) individuelle(s).
   a. une   b. deux   c. trois
4. Disons du ______________ décembre au 2 janvier
   a. 24   b. 25   c. 26
5. C'est vraiment trop ______________.
   a. loin   b. gentil   c. cher

3 **Les prix des hôtels** What are the prices for a single room at these hotels?

1. l'hôtel le Vieux Moulin: ______________
2. l'hôtel le Mont-Blanc: ______________
3. l'auberge de la Costaroche: ______________

4 **Qui?** Whom do these statements describe? Write **S** for Sandrine or **A** for Amina.

______ 1. Elle fête Noël en famille.

______ 2. Elle ne réussit (*succeed*) pas à faire une réservation.

______ 3. Elle correspond avec Cyberhomme.

______ 4. Elle trouve un hôtel pas cher à Albertville.

______ 5. Elle cherche un Cyberhomme.

5 **Cyberhomme** Choose the best answer for these questions.

1. Qui est Cyberhomme?
   a. le petit ami de Sandrine b. l'ami virtuel d'Amina c. un étudiant à l'université
2. Combien de messages électroniques est-ce qu'il a envoyés?
   a. 2 b. 10 c. 12
3. Pourquoi est-ce qu'Amina ne lit pas le message à Sandrine?
   a. c'est personnel b. c'est ennuyeux c. c'est trop long
4. Comment est Cyberhomme?
   a. petit, mais beau b. sympa, mais timide c. sportif, mais sérieux

Après la vidéo

6 **Répondez** Answer these questions in French. Write complete sentences.

1. Où est-ce que Sandrine a envie de passer ses vacances d'hiver?
   ____
2. Pourquoi est-ce que Sandrine ne fait pas de réservation à l'agence de voyages?
   ____
3. Après sa visite à l'agence de voyages, qu'est-ce que Sandrine a besoin de faire?
   ____
4. Qui fait une réservation pour Sandrine?
   ____
5. Qui téléphone à Sandrine? Pourquoi?
   ____
6. Pourquoi est-ce que Sandrine est fâchée (*angry*)?
   ____

7 **À vous!** In this episode, Pascal says "**Elle n'est pas très heureuse maintenant, mais quelle surprise en perspective!**" What surprise do you think he has planned? How do you think Sandrine will respond?

____
____
____
____
____
____
____
____

Nom _______________ Date _______________

STRUCTURES

7B.1 Adverbs

1 **Associez** Match the items given with a synonym or antonym from the list.

activement	discrètement	intelligemment	méchamment
dernièrement	généreusement	mal	vite

1. bien ≠ _______________
2. brillamment = _______________
3. égoïstement ≠ _______________
4. modestement = _______________
5. paresseusement ≠ _______________
6. poliment ≠ _______________
7. premièrement ≠ _______________
8. rapidement = _______________

2 **Ma nouvelle vie** Louis writes to his younger sister. Complete his e-mail by choosing the logical adverb.

Chère Nathalie,

La vie à l'université, c'est génial. Pour te parler (1) _______________ (absolument, franchement, évidemment), j'adore ma nouvelle vie ici. Dans la classe de français, nous parlons (2) _______________ (agréablement, gentiment, constamment) en français. J'espère parler (3) _______________ (fortement, couramment, activement) à la fin de l'année.

Ma chambre est (4) _______________ (joliment, indépendamment, heureusement) décorée. La vue (*view*) est (5) _______________ (faiblement, absolument, seulement) magnifique. Mes voisins sont sympas; je parle (6) _______________ (discrètement, fortement, souvent) avec eux. Ma voisine Annette m'a invité au club de randonnée, et maintenant, je participe (7) _______________ (absolument, facilement, activement) au club.

Viens (8) _______________ (heureusement, bien, vite) me voir.

Bon, @+!*
Louis

@+! *À plus tard*!

3 **Déchiffrez** Unscramble these questions and answer them with the cues provided.

1. vous / fréquemment / est-ce que / parlez / ? / français (tous les jours)
____
____
2. ? / avec / - / étudiez / vos amis / vous / à la bibliothèque (de temps en temps)
____
____
3. étudiez / pour / sérieusement / est-ce que / l'examen / vous / ? (très)
____
____
4. trouvé / un hôtel / avez / facilement / - / vous / ? (vite)
____
____
5. vous / la fête / fréquemment / faites / vos voisins / - / avec / ? (rarement)
____
____
6. toujours / à coté de / ? / vous / la chambre / l'ascenseur / prenez / - (souvent)
____
____

4 **Complétez** Complete the sentences by changing the adjective in the first sentence into an adverb in the second.

Modèle

Olivier est très lent. Il travaille **lentement**.

1. Les élèves sont nerveux. Ils attendent _______________ leur professeur en classe.
2. C'est vrai que l'hôtelière est belle. L'hôtelière est _______________ belle.
3. Elles étudient de manière indépendante. Elles étudient _______________.
4. Marilène est une mauvaise chanteuse. Marilène chante _______________.
5. C'est un bon quartier. Il est _______________ situé.
6. Les clients sont très impatients. Les clients attendent _______________ à la réception.

5 **Ma vie à Paris** Complete the sentences with the adverbs from the list. Not all adverbs will be used.

bien	difficilement	mal	modestement	récemment
couramment	fréquemment	malheureusement	rarement	vraiment

J'ai (1) _______________ fait un séjour à Paris pendant trois mois. J'ai (2) _______________ touvé un travail dans un restaurant près des Tuileries. (3) _______________, malgré ça (*inspite of that*), je n'avais pas beaucoup d'argent et mes parents m'envoyaient (4) _______________ de l'argent. Alors, je vivais (*used to live*) (5) _______________ et je ne sortais pas (6) _______________ avec mes amis. Mais la chose que j'adorais (7) _______________ faire le soir, c'était de marcher le long de la Seine. J'ai (8) _______________ aimé mon séjour à Paris.

7B.1 Adverbs (audio activities)

1 **Complétez** Listen to each statement and circle the word or phrase that best completes it.

1. a. couramment b. faiblement c. difficilement
2. a. gentiment b. fortement c. joliment
3. a. rapidement b. malheureusement c. lentement
4. a. constamment b. brillamment c. utilement
5. a. rapidement b. fréquemment c. patiemment
6. a. activement b. franchement c. nerveusement

2 **Changez** Form a new sentence by changing the adjective to an adverb. Repeat the correct answer after the speaker.

Modèle

You hear: Julie étudie.
You see: sérieux
You say: **Julie étudie sérieusement.**

1. poli
2. rapide
3. différent
4. courant
5. patient
6. prudent

3 **Répondez** Answer each question you hear in the negative, using the cue. Repeat the correct answer after the speaker.

Modèle

You hear: Ils vont très souvent au cinéma?
You see: rarement
You say: **Non, ils vont rarement au cinéma.**

1. mal
2. tard
3. rarement
4. méchamment
5. vite
6. facilement

Nom ______________________ Date ______________________

7B.2 The imparfait

1 **Quand j'étais jeune** Complete this story by conjugating the verbs in parentheses in the **imparfait**.

Quand nous (1) ______________ (être) jeunes, il n'y (2) ______________ (avoir) pas beaucoup d'étudiants à l'université. Beaucoup de personnes (3) ______________ (finir) leurs études à la fin du collège ou du lycée parce qu'elles (4) ______________ (aller) travailler. À l'université, j' (5) ______________ (étudier) tout le temps. J'ai rencontré ta maman là-bas. Elle (6) ______________ (travailler) à la bibliothèque. Elle (7) ______________ (être) sympathique. Nous (8) ______________ (parler) beaucoup ensemble. Mes parents (9) ______________ (dire) qu'il (10) ______________ (falloir) finir mes études avant d'épouser ta mère. Ils (11) ______________ (avoir) tort, mais ils (12) ______________ (penser) à mon avenir (*future*).

2 **Les vacances** Frédéric's friends are telling him what they used to do on vacation. Complete each of these sentences with the **imparfait** of a logical verb from the list.

aller à la pêche	emmener	pleuvoir
apprendre	faire une randonnée	regarder un film
bavarder	louer	skier
dormir	passer	travailler

1. Ma sœur et moi, nous ______________ en montagne tous les jours.
2. Je ______________ jusqu'à midi parce que j'étais très fatigué(e).
3. Jasmine ______________ dans un magasin du centre commercial.
4. En hiver, nous ______________ tous les jours.
5. Marc ______________, car (*because*) il aime manger du poisson frais.
6. J'______________ quelque chose de nouveau.
7. Quand il ______________, je ______________ à la télévision.
8. Je ______________ chez mes amis et nous ______________.

3 **L'enfance** Your new friend would like to know you better and has asked you to talk about your childhood. Complete this paragraph with the cues provided. Conjugate the verbs in the **imparfait**.

Quand j'étais petit(e), je (1) ____________________ beaucoup, surtout des croissants avec du beurre. Je (2) ____________________ toujours du chocolat chaud avec ça. Je n' (3) ____________________ pas beaucoup à l'école. Pendant mon temps libre, je (4) ____________________ à la piscine de mon quartier ou bien je (5) ____________________ avec des amis. Je (6) ____________________ de temps en temps. Je (7) ____________________ aussi, mais je n'étais pas très bon(ne). Et toi, qu'est-ce que tu faisais quand tu étais petit(e)?

4 **Répondez** Bénédicte wants to participate in an exchange program. Answer these questions about her past using the cues provided.

Modèle

Où habitez-vous? (Boston / New York)
Maintenant, j'habite à Boston. Avant, j'habitais à New York.

1. Qu'est-ce que vous étudiez? (le français / l'économie)
____
2. Combien de langues parlez-vous? (le français et l'espagnol / seulement le français)
____
3. Comment êtes-vous? (travailleur/travailleuse / paresseux/paresseuse)
____
4. Qu'est-ce que vous aimez faire pendant vos loisirs? (faire des randonnées / patiner)
____
5. Pourquoi souhaitez-vous (*do you wish*) partir? (avoir envie de connaître (*to know*) le Sénégal / avoir peur de voyager)
____
6. Que pensez-vous du Sénégal? (être un pays intéressant / être un pays comme les autres)
____
7. Qui paie vos études? (je / mes parents)
____
8. Quand finissez-vous les cours? (en mai / en juin)
____

7B.2 The imparfait (audio activities)

1 **Identifiez** Listen to each sentence and circle the verb tense you hear.

1. a. présent b. imparfait c. passé composé
2. a. présent b. imparfait c. passé composé
3. a. présent b. imparfait c. passé composé
4. a. présent b. imparfait c. passé composé
5. a. présent b. imparfait c. passé composé
6. a. présent b. imparfait c. passé composé
7. a. présent b. imparfait c. passé composé
8. a. présent b. imparfait c. passé composé
9. a. présent b. imparfait c. passé composé
10. a. présent b. imparfait c. passé composé

2 **Changez** Form a new sentence using the cue you hear. Repeat the correct answer after the speaker. (*6 items*)

Modèle

Je dînais à huit heures. (nous)
Nous dînions à huit heures.

3 **Répondez** Answer each question you hear using the cue. Repeat the correct response after the speaker.

Modèle

You hear: Qu'est-ce que tu faisais quand tu avais 15 ans?
You see: aller au lycée Condorcet
You say: **J'allais au lycée Condorcet.**

1. jouer au tennis avec François
2. aller à la mer près de Cannes
3. étudier à la bibliothèque de l'université
4. sortir au restaurant avec des amis
5. finir nos devoirs et regarder la télé
6. sortir le chien et jouer au foot
7. partir skier dans les Alpes
8. sortir avec des amis et aller au cinéma

Nom ______________________________ Date ______________________________

Unité 7

Savoir-faire

PANORAMA

1 **Des gens célèbres** Match each description with the name of a famous person.

_______ 1. Cet écrivain à l'imagination extraordinaire a écrit *Le Petit Prince*.
_______ 2. Cet écrivain et cinéaste de Marseille a écrit *La Gloire de mon père*.
_______ 3. Cette championne du patinage artistique (*figure skating*) est née à Nice.
_______ 4. Cet homme est surtout connu pour ses travaux d'astrologie.
_______ 5. Cette poétesse de la Renaissance a écrit des sonnets.
_______ 6. Cet écrivain a écrit *Le Rouge et le Noir*.

a. Nostradamus
b. Surya Bonaly
c. Louise Labé
d. Antoine de Saint-Exupéry
e. Stendhal
f. Marcel Pagnol

2 **Des diapos** Write a one-sentence caption in French to accompany each of these slides (**diapos**) that will be part of a presentation on southeastern France.

1. 

2. 

3. 

4.

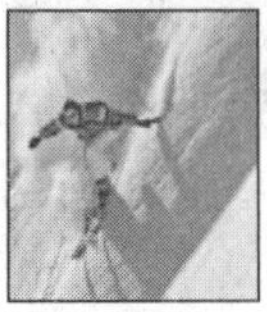

5. 

6. 

1. ____
2. ____
3. ____
4. ____
5. ____
6. ____

3 **Vrai ou faux?** Indicate whether each of these statements is **vrai** or **faux**.

	Vrai	Faux
1. Grenoble se situe dans les Pyrénées.	❍	❍
2. La raclette et la fondue sont des spécialités à base de fromage fondu.	❍	❍
3. Le synchrotron est un club à Grenoble.	❍	❍
4. La ville de Grasse donne accès à plusieurs stations de ski.	❍	❍
5. Le Festival International du Film a lieu (*takes place*) chaque année, en mai.	❍	❍
6. Des pommes de terre accompagnent le fromage de la raclette.	❍	❍
7. Chaque année, il y a vingt films en compétition au Festival International du Film.	❍	❍
8. Des vedettes (*movie stars*) assistent au Festival du Film à Grasse.	❍	❍

Nom ______________________________ Date ______________________________

4 **Des couleurs et des arômes** Complete each of these statements about the cultivation of flowers in the South of France.

1. ________________ est l'une des industries principales du sud-est de la France.
2. On cultive des fleurs à Grasse depuis le ________________.
3. Parmi les fleurs cultivées à Grasse, on compte la ________________, la ________________ et la ________________.
4. ________________ est un des grands fabricants (*makers*) de parfum du sud de la France.

5 **Les villes de la région** Write the names of the towns described by the clues.

1. C'est la ville où l'on trouve le palais des Papes. ___ V ___ ___ N ___ N
2. Cette très grande ville de la côte (*coast*) se situe entre la Camargue et Toulon.
   M ___ ___ ___ E ___ L ___ ___
3. Cette ville est la capitale mondiale de la parfumerie. G ___ ___ S ___ ___
4. Cette ville est un grand centre de recherche scientifique. ___ R E ___ ___ B ___ ___
5. De riches vacanciers anglais ont donné leur nom à la célèbre promenade de cette ville. ___ I C ___
6. Cette ville organise le festival du film le plus connu (*most famous*) du monde. ___ ___ N N ___ S

6 **Des mots cachés camarguais** First, use the clues to identify some expressions related to the Camargue. Then find the words in the puzzle.

1. On appelle les ________________ les cow-boys camarguais.
2. C'est l'un des oiseaux exotiques qu'on trouve en Camargue: le ________________.
3. En Camargue, on voit (*sees*) ces grands ________________ noirs.
4. Le meilleur (*best*) ami du cow-boy camarguais est un cheval ________________.

F A R E B C D U Î G A E J G F
X L B K T L F Y M P J S Z A W
Z P A I F F H L M U W O C R J
S N C M B Â Y J G Q J R N D B
G Z W N A E N F J Q I P A I X
A R N X S N C P T S É A L A A
T Y O A A H T A L M U O B N U
R V T Q H Z U R L B K U C S L
O C H B O R S Q O M E N P Z V
H J M E E C T C B S J F S R X
Q Z J A N C D U U U E Q P Q B
J H U K C X A I Z H U L Y X O
I X W É T A N G S V E R Z A Q
S U Y A X G Y G A W H W M O C
C D X I O I W D O S I A R A M

Nom ______________________ Date ______________________

Unité 8

Leçon 8A

CONTEXTES

1 **La maison** Label the rooms and items indicated.

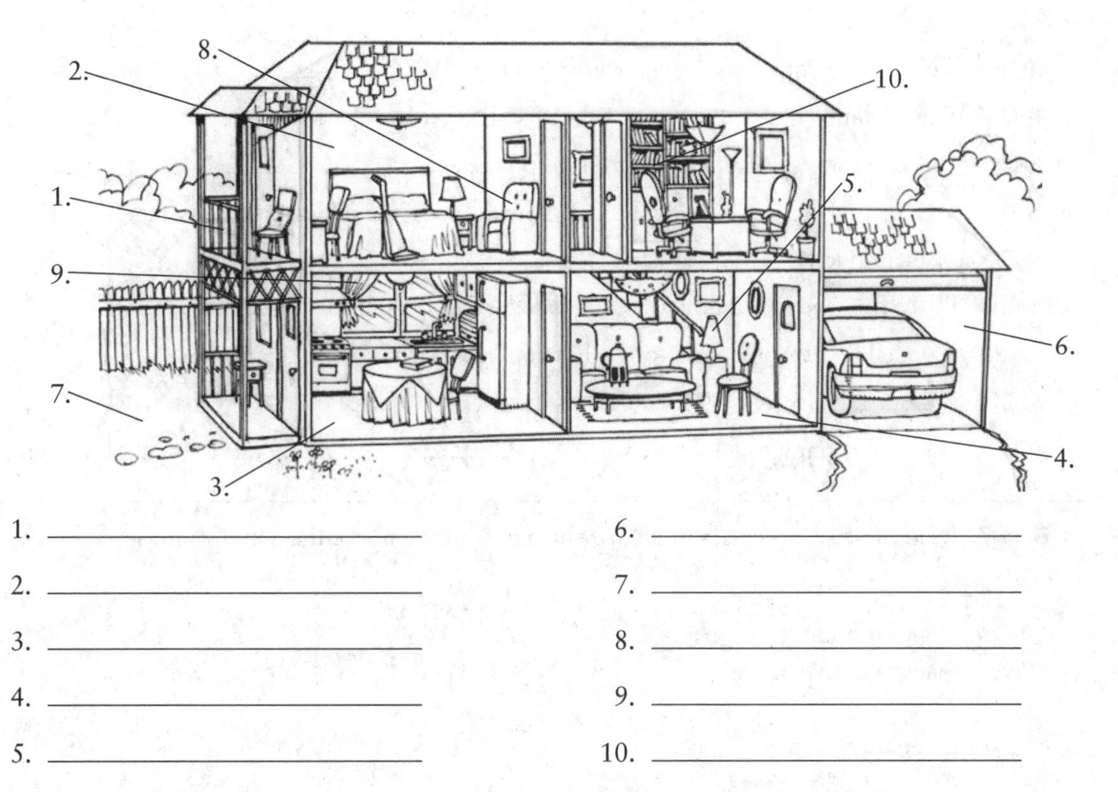

1. ______________________
2. ______________________
3. ______________________
4. ______________________
5. ______________________
6. ______________________
7. ______________________
8. ______________________
9. ______________________
10. ______________________

2 **Les règles** Complete each of these rules (**règles**) for the family residence where your parents have rented an apartment for the summer with the most appropriate option.

RÈGLES DE LA MAISON

- Les vacanciers peuvent (*The vacationers can*) (1) ______________ (emménager, déménager, louer) dans la résidence au début du mois de juillet.
- Le (2) ______________ (chambre, loyer, studio) est payé à la fin du séjour (*stay*).
- Il est demandé aux vacanciers de ne pas faire de bruit dans (3) ______________ (les appartements, les garages, les meubles) après 10h00 du soir.
- Chaque famille partage (4) ______________ (une commode, le sous-sol, une pièce) avec les autres familles.
- Il y a (5) ______________ (deux salles de bains, trois escaliers, un jardin) dans tous les appartements.
- Les vacanciers peuvent utiliser la piscine dans (6) ______________ (le garage, le jardin, le sous-sol), derrière la maison, de 8h00 à 18h00.
- Il est interdit (*forbidden*) de laisser les vélos dans le jardin. Si vous avez un vélo, il y a (7) ______________ (un quartier, un escalier, un garage) pour tous les vacanciers.
- Si vous avez d'autres questions, il y a du papier et un crayon dans (8) ______________ (le fauteuil, le tiroir, le rideau) sur votre droite.

Nom ______________________ Date ______________________

3 **La résidence** Complete this conversation with logical words or expressions.

DJAMILA Quand vas-tu (1) ______________ dans ta nouvelle maison avec tes parents?

FRÉDÉRIC La semaine prochaine, mais nous avons déjà les clés.

DJAMILA Et quand (2) ______________-tu de l'ancienne maison?

FRÉDÉRIC Demain.

DJAMILA Super! Est-ce que je peux venir voir (*see*) ta (3) ______________ maintenant?

FRÉDÉRIC Oui. Voilà.

DJAMILA Oh! Elle est grande. Il y a de la place pour des (4) ______________ pour tous tes livres.

FRÉDÉRIC Oui, et l' (5) ______________ pour mes vêtements ira près de la fenêtre. J'aime beaucoup le (6) ______________.

DJAMILA Est-ce que vous allez pouvoir tous manger dans la cuisine comme avant?

FRÉDÉRIC Non, elle est trop petite. Nous allons manger dans la (7) ______________.

DJAMILA Et pour la voiture. Qu'est-ce que tes parents vont faire?

FRÉDÉRIC Il y a deux garages, alors, ils vont (8) ______________ l'un des deux à des amis.

4 **Où ça?** Read these statements and tell in which part of the house the action is most likely taking place.

Modèle

Je prends une douche.
Je suis dans la salle de bains.

1. Sarah prépare le dîner.
____
2. Farid dort.
____
3. Catherine et Jacques lisent des romans et étudient.
____
4. Jean-Philippe sort de sa voiture.
____
5. Amadou descend chercher son vélo.
____
6. Le petit Cédric joue dans la baignoire.
____
7. Vous célébrez l'anniversaire de votre ami.
____
8. Nous nageons dans la piscine.
____

Nom ____________________ Date ____________________

CONTEXTES: AUDIO ACTIVITIES

1 **Décrivez** Listen to each sentence and write its number below the drawing of the household item mentioned.

a. ______ b. ______ c. ______

d. ______ e. ______ f. ______

2 **Identifiez** You will hear a series of words. Write the word that does not belong in each series.

1. ____________________
2. ____________________
3. ____________________
4. ____________________
5. ____________________
6. ____________________
7. ____________________
8. ____________________

3 **Logique ou illogique?** You will hear some statements. Decide if they are **logique** or **illogique**.

	Logique	Illogique
1.	O	O
2.	O	O
3.	O	O
4.	O	O
5.	O	O
6.	O	O
7.	O	O
8.	O	O

Nom ______________________ Date ______________________

LES SONS ET LES LETTRES

s and ss

You've already learned that an **s** at the end of a word is usually silent.

lavabos copains vas placards

An **s** at the beginning of a word, before a consonant, or after a pronounced consonant is pronounced like the *s* in the English word *set*.

soir salon studio absolument

A double *s* is pronounced like the *ss* in the English word *kiss*.

grosse assez intéressant rousse

An **s** at the end of a word is often pronounced when the following word begins with a vowel sound. An **s** in a liaison sounds like a *z*, like the *s* in the English word *rose*.

très élégant trois hommes

The other instance where the French **s** has a *z* sound is when there is a single **s** between two vowels within the same word. The **s** is pronounced like the *s* in the English word *music*.

musée amusant oiseau besoin

These words look alike, but have different meanings. Compare the pronunciations of each word pair.

poison poisson désert dessert

1 **Prononcez** Répétez les mots suivants à voix haute.

1. sac
2. triste
3. suisse
4. chose
5. bourse
6. passer
7. surprise
8. assister
9. magasin
10. expressions
11. sénégalaise
12. sérieusement

2 **Articulez** Répétez les phrases suivantes à voix haute.

1. Le spectacle est très amusant et la chanteuse est superbe.
2. Est-ce que vous habitez dans une résidence universitaire?
3. De temps en temps, Suzanne assiste à l'inauguration d'expositions au musée.
4. Heureusement, mes professeurs sont sympathiques, sociables et très sincères.

3 **Dictons** Répétez les dictons à voix haute.

1. Si jeunesse savait, si vieillesse pouvait.
2. Les oiseaux de même plumage s'assemblent sur le même rivage.

4 **Dictée** You will hear six sentences. Each will be said twice. Listen carefully and write what you hear.

1. ______________________
2. ______________________
3. ______________________
4. ______________________
5. ______________________
6. ______________________

Nom ______________________ Date ______________________

Roman-photo

LA VISITE SURPRISE

Avant de regarder

1 **La surprise** Look at the photo and consider the title of this video episode. Who is in this picture? How do you think Sandrine will react when she sees him? What do you think will happen in this episode?

____

____

____

____

____

En regardant la vidéo

2 **Chez Sandrine** Check off the items that Sandrine has at her place.

- ❑ 1. un escalier
- ❑ 2. une chambre
- ❑ 3. une douche
- ❑ 4. un miroir
- ❑ 5. une baignoire
- ❑ 6. une cave
- ❑ 7. une cuisine
- ❑ 8. un jardin
- ❑ 9. un salon
- ❑ 10. une salle à manger
- ❑ 11. un lavabo
- ❑ 12. un sous-sol

3 **Identifiez-les** Label the rooms that are pictured.

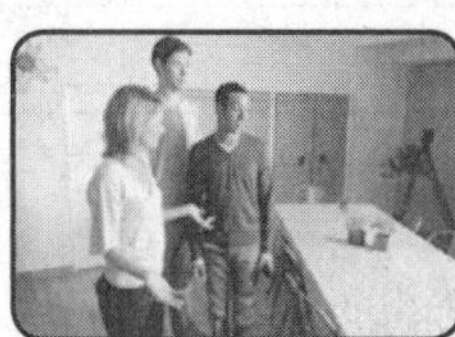

1. ______________________

2. ______________________

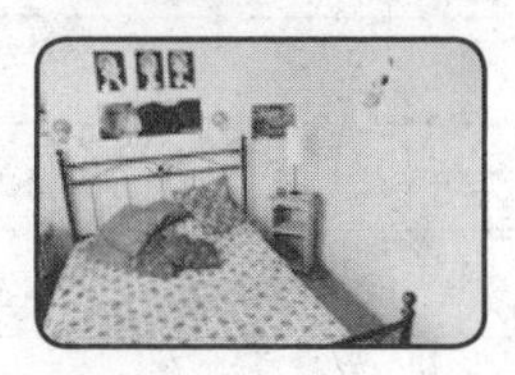

3. ______________________

4. ______________________

5. ______________________

Nom ______________________ Date ______________________

4 **Qui...?** Indicate which character says each of these lines. Write D for David or R for Rachid.

_______ 1. C'est grand chez toi!

_______ 2. Heureusement, Sandrine a décidé de rester.

_______ 3. Tu as combien de pièces?

_______ 4. Dis, c'est vrai, Sandrine, ta salle de bains est vraiment grande.

_______ 5. Chez nous, on a seulement une douche.

_______ 6. Et elle a une baignoire et un beau miroir au-dessus du lavabo!

5 **Complétez** Complete these sentences with the missing words from the video.

SANDRINE Je te fais (1) ______________________?

RACHID Oui, merci.

SANDRINE Voici la (2) ______________________.

RACHID Ça, c'est une (3) ______________________ très importante pour nous, les invités.

SANDRINE Et puis, la (4) ______________________.

RACHID Une pièce très importante pour Sandrine...

DAVID Évidemment!

SANDRINE Et voici ma (5) ______________________.

RACHID Elle est (6) ______________________!

SANDRINE Oui, j'aime le vert.

Après la vidéo

6 **Une dispute** Describe what is happening in this photo. Explain the events leading up to this moment.

____

____

____

____

____

7 **À vous!** What rooms do you have in your home? Write at least five sentences describing them.

____

____

____

____

____

____

____

Nom ______________________ Date ______________________

Flash culture

CHEZ NOUS

Avant de regarder

1

Les habitations In this video, you are going to learn about housing in France. List as many different types of places to live as you can in French.

____

____

____

____

____

____

____

2

Chez moi Complete these statements about your own home. Remember to use the correct article with each noun. Use words from the list or any other words you know.

appartement	garage	sous-sol
balcon	jardin	studio
cave	maison	terrasse
escalier	résidence universitaire	

1. J'habite dans ______________________.
2. Chez moi, il y a ______________________ et ______________________.
3. Il n'y a pas ______________________ chez moi.
4. À l'extérieur, il y a ______________________.
5. Avant, j'habitais dans ______________________.
6. Il y avait ______________________ et ______________________.
7. Il n'y avait pas ______________________.
8. À l'extérieur, il y avait ______________________.

En regardant la vidéo

3

Mettez-les dans l'ordre In what order does Benjamin mention these items?

_____ a. un balcon

_____ b. une terrasse

_____ c. un sous-sol

_____ d. un garage

_____ e. un jardin

Nom ______________________ Date ______________________

4 **Chez soi** Match these images with their captions.

1. 
2. 
3. 
4. 
5. 

_______ a. des maisons individuelles

_______ b. des appartements

_______ c. des HLM

_______ d. de grands immeubles

_______ e. des résidences pour les étudiants

5 **Complétez** Watch the video and complete the paragraphs below according to what Benjamin says.

1. Nous sommes dans la ______________ d'Aix-en-Provence. C'est un ______________ très pittoresque avec ses boutiques, ses restaurants et ses ______________. Laissez-moi vous montrer différents types de ______________.
2. Nous sommes maintenant dans la ______________ où on trouve des ______________ de toutes sortes. Par exemple, cette maison est assez ______________.

Après la vidéo

6 **La maison de mes rêves** Describe your dream home. Tell where it is and what type of residence it is. Then describe its features in detail.

____

____

____

____

____

____

____

____

Nom ______________________ Date ______________________

STRUCTURES

8A.1 The passé composé vs. the imparfait (Part 1)

1 **Souvenirs d'enfance** Sylvain and his friends are talking about some childhood memories. Complete their statements by choosing the appropriate past tense.

1. Mon ancienne maison n' ______________ pas très grande.
   a. était   b. a été
2. Nous ______________ trois garages dans notre maison.
   a. avons eu   b. avions
3. Mes sœurs ______________ toujours beaucoup d'affiches sur les murs de leurs chambres.
   a. mettaient   b. ont mis
4. Nous ______________ trois fois dans la même année.
   a. déménagions   b. avons déménagé
5. Mes parents ______________ souvent une chambre aux étudiants de l'université.
   a. louaient   b. ont loué
6. Un jour, mon frère ______________ du balcon.
   a. est tombé   b. tombait
7. Papa ______________ le vieux fauteuil de mon grand-père.
   a. a adoré   b. adorait
8. Tout à coup, je/j' ______________ un bruit (*noise*) au sous-sol.
   a. ai entendu   b. entendais
9. Quand j'avais treize ans, je/j' ______________ dans un beau quartier à Chicago.
   a. ai habité   b. habitais
10. Mes voisins ne/n' ______________ pas mon chat.
    a. ont aimé   b. aimaient

2 **Raconte!** Complete this conversation between Coralie and Sarah about what the latter did last weekend with her cousin Julie by choosing an appropriate verb from the list and putting it in the **passé composé** or the **imparfait**.

aimer	avoir	décider	faire	rentrer
aller	commencer	être	préparer	sortir

CORALIE Tu (1) ______________ avec ta cousine Julie samedi dernier?

SARAH Oui, nous (2) ______________ voir le nouveau film de Daniel Craig.

CORALIE Ah oui? Tu l' (3) ______________?

SARAH Beaucoup! Ce/C' (4) ______________ vraiment super, surtout la fin!

CORALIE Qu'est-ce que vous (5) ______________ après le film?

SARAH Julie (6) ______________ faim, alors on (7) ______________ d'aller au Café Margot. Mais il (8) ______________ à pleuvoir. Alors, nous (9) ______________ chez moi et je/j' (10) ______________ un sandwich au jambon pour elle.

Nom ______________________ Date ______________________

3 **Décrivez** Write a complete sentence in the past tense to describe each picture by choosing the phrase that matches the image. Be sure to pay attention to the cues to help you decide which past tense to use.

Modèle

Hier, Madame Boiteux *n'a pas couru.*

acheter des vêtements	beaucoup manger	ne pas courir	ne pas prendre de boisson (*drink*)
arriver en retard	commander une salade	faire de la gym	

1. Hier matin, ils ______________________.
2. Dimanche dernier, Julie ______________________.
3. Quand il était jeune, Hervé ______________________.
4. Vous ______________________ le week-end.
5. À la soirée chez Nadine samedi soir, je/j' ______________________.
6. Nous ______________________ tous les soirs.

4 **Pas de camping!** Pascal is writing an e-mail to Amadou about his camping experiences. Complete his e-mail with the **passé composé** or the **imparfait** of the verbs in parentheses.

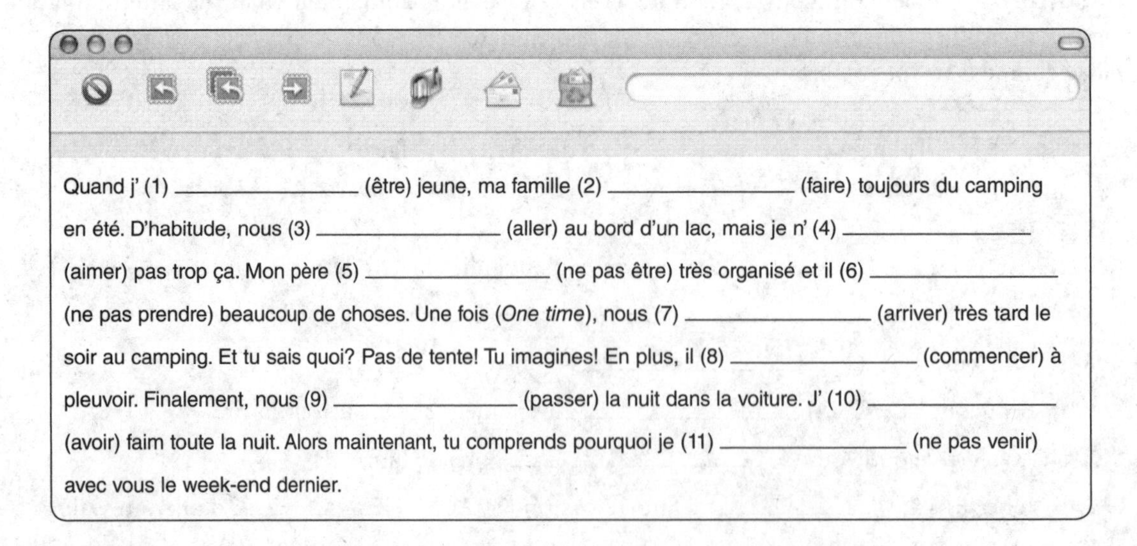

Quand j' (1) ______________ (être) jeune, ma famille (2) ______________ (faire) toujours du camping en été. D'habitude, nous (3) ______________ (aller) au bord d'un lac, mais je n' (4) ______________ (aimer) pas trop ça. Mon père (5) ______________ (ne pas être) très organisé et il (6) ______________ (ne pas prendre) beaucoup de choses. Une fois (*One time*), nous (7) ______________ (arriver) très tard le soir au camping. Et tu sais quoi? Pas de tente! Tu imagines! En plus, il (8) ______________ (commencer) à pleuvoir. Finalement, nous (9) ______________ (passer) la nuit dans la voiture. J' (10) ______________ (avoir) faim toute la nuit. Alors maintenant, tu comprends pourquoi je (11) ______________ (ne pas venir) avec vous le week-end dernier.

Nom ______________________ Date ______________________

8A.1 The passé composé vs. the imparfait (Part 1) (audio activities)

1 **Identifiez** Listen to each sentence in the past tense and indicate which category best describes it.

1. a. habitual action b. specific completed action c. description of a physical/mental state
2. a. habitual action b. specific completed action c. description of a physical/mental state
3. a. habitual action b. specific completed action c. description of a physical/mental state
4. a. habitual action b. specific completed action c. description of a physical/mental state
5. a. habitual action b. specific completed action c. description of a physical/mental state
6. a. habitual action b. specific completed action c. description of a physical/mental state
7. a. habitual action b. specific completed action c. description of a physical/mental state
8. a. habitual action b. specific completed action c. description of a physical/mental state
9. a. habitual action b. specific completed action c. description of a physical/mental state
10. a. habitual action b. specific completed action c. description of a physical/mental state

2 **Choisissez** Listen to each question and choose the most logical answer.

1. a. Il pleuvait et il faisait froid.
   b. Il a plu et il a fait froid.
2. a. J'ai joué au volley avec mes amis.
   b. Je jouais au volley avec mes amis.
3. a. Nous sommes allés au musée.
   b. Nous allions au musée.
4. a. Super! On a dansé toute la nuit.
   b. Super! On dansait toute la nuit.
5. a. Je les mettais dans ton sac.
   b. Je les ai mises dans ton sac.
6. a. Il a passé les vacances d'été en Espagne.
   b. Il passait les vacances d'été en Espagne.

3 **Complétez** Complete each sentence you hear in the **passé composé** or the **imparfait** using the cue. Repeat the correct response after the speaker.

Modèle

You hear: Ma petite amie adore danser maintenant, mais quand elle était au lycée...
You see: préférer chanter
You say: **elle préférait chanter.**

1. manger un sandwich
2. jouer au football
3. sortir tous les soirs
4. prendre un taxi
5. nettoyer le garage
6. porter des jupes

Nom ______________________ Date ______________________

8A.2 The passé composé vs. the imparfait (Part 2)

1 **C'est du passé** Change each sentence from the present tense to the past tense. Use the **passé composé** or the **imparfait** based on the adverbial expression provided.

Modèle

Je mange une pizza à midi.
Hier, *j'ai mangé une pizza à midi.*

1. Je vis en Angleterre.
   ______________________ pendant deux ans.
2. Ils font de l'aérobic.
   ______________________ tous les samedis.
3. Tu vas rarement en banlieue.
   Autrefois, ______________________.
4. Les femmes ont peur.
   Soudain, ______________________.
5. Vous buvez du café au petit-déjeuner.
   Hier, ______________________.
6. David ne paie pas le loyer à la propriétaire.
   Avant, ______________________.
7. Nous étudions dans le salon.
   Parfois, ______________________.
8. Ma tante descend au sous-sol.
   Une fois, ______________________.

2 **Une journée assez banale** Tell how these people spent their day and what the circumstances were using the correct past tense.

1. Vincent et sa sœur ______________ (aller) au Cinéma Gaumont parce qu'il y ______________ (avoir) un bon film.
2. Natasha ______________ (rester) à la maison parce qu'elle ______________ (être) fatiguée.
3. Il ______________ (neiger) quand Antoine ______________ (aller) au marché.
4. Myriam et Alisha ______________ (beaucoup manger) parce qu'elles ______________ (avoir) faim.
5. Quand maman et tante Agathe ______________ (rentrer), je ______________ (nettoyer) le tapis.
6. Mon copain et moi ______________ (attendre) devant le café quand le prof nous ______________ (parler).

3 **Qui faisait quoi?** Complete these sentences about what these people were doing using the illustrations.

1. 
2. 
3. 
4. 
5. 
6. 

1. Quand tante Élise a appelé, mon oncle _______________
2. Maxime est arrivé quand nous _______________
3. J'étais dans le jardin quand les enfants _______________
4. Elle m'a vu (*saw*) quand je _______________
5. Nous étions dans la cuisine quand vous _______________
6. Quand nous sommes partis, Karim et Delphine _______________

4 **Le départ** Lucas and Noémie are leaving for Dakar to visit their friend Saliou. Say what happened on the day of their departure by putting the verbs in the **passé composé** or the **imparfait**.

Le jour de leur départ, Lucas et Noémie (1) _______________ (prendre) tranquillement leur petit-déjeuner le matin parce que leur avion (2) _______________ (partir) seulement à 14h00. Après le petit-déjeuner, Noémie (3) _______________ (aller) au parc avec leur chien Loulou. Quand elle (4) _______________ (rentrer) à la maison, Lucas (5) _______________ (lire) le journal (*newspaper*). À 11h30, ils (6) _______________ (faire) leurs valises quand leur amie Julie (7) _______________ (venir) chercher leur chien. Ils (8) _______________ (bavarder) avec Julie quand tout à coup Lucas (9) _______________ (remarquer) (*noticed*) qu'il (10) _______________ (être) déjà 13h00! Lucas (11) _______________ (vite aller chercher) leurs bagages et Noémie (12) _______________ (appeler) un taxi. Ils n' (13) _______________ (avoir) pas beaucoup de temps! Ils (14) _______________ (arriver) à l'aéroport juste trente minutes avant le départ. Heureusement, l'avion (15) _______________ (partir) à 15h00 avec une heure de retard!

Nom ______________________ Date ______________________

8A.2 The **passé composé** vs. the **imparfait** (Part 2) (audio activities)

1 **Complétez** Listen to each phrase and complete it using the cues. Repeat the correct response after the speaker.

Modèle

You hear: Elle regardait la télé quand...
You see: son frère / sortir la poubelle
You say: **Elle regardait la télé quand son frère a sorti la poubelle.**

1. papa / rentrer
2. son petit ami / téléphoner
3. mes sœurs / dormir
4. la cafetière / tomber
5. vous / être dans le jardin
6. nous / vivre au Sénégal

2 **Changez** Change each sentence you hear in the present tense to the appropriate past tense. Repeat the correct response after the speaker. (*8 items*)

Modèle

D'habitude, je sors à huit heures du matin.
D'habitude, je sortais à huit heures du matin.

3 **Répondez** Answer each question you hear using the cue. Repeat the correct response after the speaker.

Modèle

You hear: Qu'est-ce que tu lisais quand tu avais neuf ans?
You see: des bandes dessinées
You say: **Je lisais des bandes dessinées.**

1. des frites
2. rendre visite à mes grands-parents
3. au centre commercial
4. aller au centre-ville
5. non, dans une grande maison
6. une robe noire

Nom ____________________ Date ____________________

Unité 8

Leçon 8B

CONTEXTES

1 **Chassez l'intrus** Circle the item that does not belong in each group.

1. balayer, passer l'aspirateur, un balai, salir
2. débarrasser la table, enlever la poussière, faire la vaisselle, faire la cuisine
3. faire la lessive, repasser le linge, faire le ménage, un lave-linge
4. un oreiller, une couverture, les draps, un frigo
5. un appareil électrique, une cafetière, un oreiller, un grille-pain
6. un congélateur, un frigo, une cuisinière, une tâche ménagère
7. un balai, un évier, faire la vaisselle, laver
8. une cafetière, un grille-pain, un four à micro-ondes, un sèche-linge

2 **Que font-ils?** Write a sentence describing the domestic activity in each drawing.

1. ____________________

2. ____________________

3. ____________________

4. ____________________

3 **Les tâches ménagères** Tell who does what in Farid's household by completing the sentences below.

1. Après le dîner, ma sœur ____________________.
   a. fait la poussière b. met la table c. fait la vaisselle
2. Pour faire la cuisine, ma mère n'utilise jamais de ____________________.
   a. frigo b. four à micro-ondes c. congélateur
3. Je ____________________ ma chambre une fois par semaine.
   a. salis b. range c. repasse
4. Après la lessive, mon frère ____________________ ses vêtements.
   a. lave b. repasse c. balaie
5. Ma sœur change ____________________ toutes les semaines.
   a. la couverture b. l'oreiller c. les draps
6. Mon père ____________________ avant le dîner.
   a. met la table b. sort la poubelle c. passe l'aspirateur
7. Pour faire la vaisselle, j'utilise toujours ____________________.
   a. le lave-linge b. le balai c. le lave-vaisselle
8. Quand la poubelle est pleine, mon père la ____________________.
   a. range b. sort c. débarrasse

4 **Mots croisés** Complete the crossword puzzle. Some of the words will have accents missing; write out those words with their accents in place in the spaces provided.

1. C'est l'action de nettoyer quand on n'utilise pas de balai.
2. On met sa tête dessus pour dormir.
3. Quand votre chambre est en désordre, il faut la...
4. Utiliser un balai, c'est...
5. On le fait au moins une fois par semaine quand il y a beaucoup d'ordures (*garbage*).
6. Après la lessive, on l'utilise. _______________
7. C'est le contraire de sale.
8. On l'utilise pour conserver (*keep*) longtemps la nourriture. _______________
9. On l'utilise pour faire du café. _______________
10. C'est le contraire de mettre la table. _______________
11. Quand vous avez fait la vaisselle, il faut l'...
12. Si vous n'aimez pas avoir de plis (*folds*) sur vos vêtements, vous l'utilisez. _______________

5 **Racontez** Your parents are asking you and your brother Philippe to help with the chores. Describe how you are going to divide up the housework. Suggest who should do each chore and how frequently.

____

____

____

____

____

____

____

Nom ______________________ Date ______________________

CONTEXTES: AUDIO ACTIVITIES

1 **Logique ou illogique?** Listen to these statements and indicate whether they are **logique** or **illogique**.

	Logique	Illogique
1.	❍	❍
2.	❍	❍
3.	❍	❍
4.	❍	❍
5.	❍	❍
6.	❍	❍
7.	❍	❍
8.	❍	❍

2 **Les tâches ménagères** Martin is a good housekeeper and does everything that needs to be done in the house. Listen to each statement and decide what he did. Then, repeat the correct answer after the speaker. (*6 items*)

Modèle

Les vêtements étaient sales.
Alors, il a fait la lessive.

3 **Décrivez** Julie has invited a few friends over. When her friends are gone, she goes in the kitchen. Look at the drawing and write the answer to each question you hear.

1. ______________________
2. ______________________
3. ______________________
4. ______________________

Nom ______________________ Date ______________________

LES SONS ET LES LETTRES

Semi-vowels

French has three semi-vowels. Semi-vowels are sounds that are produced in much the same way as vowels, but also have many properties in common with consonants. Semi-vowels are also sometimes referred to as *glides* because they glide from or into the vowel they accompany.

Lucien chien soif nuit

The semi-vowel that occurs in the word **bien** is very much like the *y* in the English word *yes*. It is usually spelled with an **i** or a **y** (pronounced *ee*), then glides into the following sound. This semi-vowel sound may also be spelled **ll** after an **i**.

nation balayer bien brillant

The semi-vowel that occurs in the word **soif** is like the *w* in the English word *was*. It usually begins with **o** or **ou**, then glides into the following vowel.

trois froid oui **ouistiti**

The third semi-vowel sound occurs in the word **nuit**. It is spelled with the vowel **u**, as in the French word **tu**, then glides into the following sound.

lui suis cruel intellectuel

1 **Prononcez** Répétez les mots suivants à voix haute.

1. oui	4. fille	7. minuit	10. juillet
2. taille	5. mois	8. jouer	11. échouer
3. suisse	6. cruel	9. cuisine	12. croissant

2 **Articulez** Répétez les phrases suivantes à voix haute.

1. Voici trois poissons noirs.
2. Louis et sa famille sont suisses.
3. Parfois, Grégoire fait de la cuisine chinoise.
4. Aujourd'hui, Matthieu et Damien vont travailler.
5. Françoise a besoin de faire ses devoirs d'histoire.
6. La fille de Monsieur Poirot va conduire pour la première fois.

3 **Dictons** Répétez les dictons à voix haute.

1. La nuit, tous les chats sont gris.
2. Vouloir, c'est pouvoir.

4 **Dictée** You will hear six sentences. Each will be said twice. Listen carefully and write what you hear.

1. ______________________
2. ______________________
3. ______________________
4. ______________________
5. ______________________
6. ______________________

Nom ____________________ Date ____________________

Roman-photo

LA VIE SANS PASCAL

Avant de regarder

1 **Chez moi** In this video episode, you will hear people talking about chores. In preparation, make a list of household chores in French.

____

____

____

____

____

En regardant la vidéo

2 **Les tâches ménagères** Check off the chores mentioned or seen in the video.

❑ 1. faire le lit
❑ 2. balayer
❑ 3. sortir les poubelles
❑ 4. repasser le linge
❑ 5. ranger la chambre
❑ 6. passer l'aspirateur
❑ 7. mettre la table
❑ 8. faire la vaisselle
❑ 9. faire la lessive
❑ 10. débarrasser la table
❑ 11. enlever la poussière
❑ 12. essuyer la table

3 **Sélectionnez** Watch the scenes in the café, and choose the words that complete each sentence according to what you hear.

1. Je débarrasse ______________?
   a. la poubelle b. la lessive c. la table
2. Apporte-moi ______________, s'il te plaît.
   a. l'addition b. le thé c. le balai
3. Tu dois faire ______________ avant de sortir.
   a. la lessive b. la vaisselle c. les devoirs
4. Il faut sortir ______________ ce soir!
   a. le chien b. le balai c. les poubelles
5. Il est l'heure de préparer ______________.
   a. le dîner b. les biscuits c. le petit-déjeuner
6. Est-ce que tu as rangé ______________?
   a. le lit b. la table c. ta chambre

Nom ______________________ Date ______________________

4 **Les réponses** Watch the scene in Sandrine's apartment, and choose the response to each statement or question you hear in the video.

_______ 1. Mmmm. Qu'est-ce qui sent bon?
_______ 2. Tu as soif?
_______ 3. Tu vas le rencontrer un de ces jours?
_______ 4. Ne t'en fais pas, je comprends.
_______ 5. Je ne le connais pas vraiment, tu sais.

a. Un peu, oui.
b. Toi, tu as de la chance.
c. Il y a des biscuits au chocolat dans le four.
d. Oh... Je ne sais pas si c'est une bonne idée.
e. Comme d'habitude, tu as raison.

Après la vidéo

5 **Qui?** Who did these chores? Write **M** for Michèle, **St** for Stéphane, **V** for Valérie, or **X** if no one did it.

_______ 1. faire le lit
_______ 2. ranger sa chambre
_______ 3. faire la lessive
_______ 4. débarrasser la table
_______ 5. passer l'aspirateur
_______ 6. repasser le linge
_______ 7. sortir les poubelles
_______ 8. essuyer la table

6 **Expliquez** Answer these questions in French. Write complete sentences.

1. Pourquoi est-ce que Sandrine est de mauvaise humeur?

____

____

2. Pourquoi est-ce que Sandrine pense qu'Amina a de la chance?

____

____

3. Quand Sandrine parle d'un petit ami artistique, charmant et beau, à qui pense-t-elle? Comment est-ce que vous le savez?

____

____

7 **À vous!** Imagine that you are dividing household chores with your sibling. Write a conversation in which you discuss which chores you will each do. Talk about at least six different things.

____

____

____

____

____

____

____

____

Nom ______________________________ Date ______________________________

STRUCTURES

8B.1 The passé composé vs. the imparfait: Summary

1 **Comme d'habitude?** Your big sister explains there have been some changes in the organization of the chores in her dorm. Complete each pair of sentences by using the **imparfait** or the **passé composé** of the verb in parentheses.

1. D'habitude, je/j' ______________________ le couloir. (balayer)
2. Hier, Serge ______________________ le couloir avant moi.
3. Je/J' ______________________ de temps en temps. (faire le ménage)
4. Mardi, Hassan ______________________.
5. La nouvelle étudiante ______________________ deux fois. (mettre la table)
6. Deux étudiantes ______________________ tous les jours.
7. Je/J' ______________________ toujours ma chambre avant de partir. (ranger)
8. Ce matin, Sylvain ______________________ la chambre.
9. Ils ______________________ ce matin, à 6h00. (sortir la poubelle)
10. Autrefois, mon camarade de chambre ______________________.

2 **Que faisaient-ils?** Complete these descriptions of what the people in the photos were doing yesterday afternoon and where each activity took place.

1. 

2. 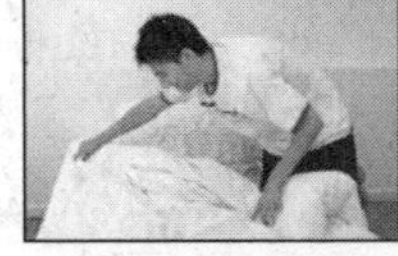

3. 

4.

5. 

6. 

1. Hier, avant de venir me voir (*to see*), il ____
____.
2. Tous les après-midi, il ____
____.
3. Quand je l'ai appelé, il ____
____.
4. Elle ____ pour la première fois.
5. Quand je l'ai vu, il ____
____.
6. Comme elle fêtait l'anniversaire de ses parents, elle ____
____.

Nom ______________________ Date ______________________

3 **Quoi de neuf?** Complete Marc's letter to his parents by selecting the appropriate form of each verb in parentheses.

La semaine dernière, quand je (1) ____________ (rentrais / suis rentré) à la résidence universitaire, il (2) ____________ (faisait / a fait) très froid. Il (3) ____________ (neigeait / a neigé). Ma chambre (4) ____________ (était / a été) sale et en désordre, et mon camarade de chambre (5) ____________ (passait / a passé) l'aspirateur. Je lui (6) ____________ (demandais / ai demandé) ce qui s'était passé (*had happened*). Il me/m' (7) ____________ (disait / a dit) que nos voisins avaient fait la fête dans notre chambre. J' (8) ____________ (étais / ai été) très inquiet car (*because*) il (9) ____________ (fallait / a fallu) tout ranger rapidement avant la nuit. Les voisins nous (10) ____________ (aidaient / ont aidés) quand même un peu. Quelle histoire!

4 **Racontez** There was a burglary in your building and the police is asking people what they were doing when it happened. Write questions and answers based on the cues provided. Ask where these people were or what they were doing that night.

Modèle

Mlle Hu   M. Jouan / téléphoner // dans sa chambre / faire le ménage
Que faisait Mlle Hu quand M. Jouan (lui) a téléphoné?
Elle était dans sa chambre. Elle faisait le ménage.

1. M. Ibrahim   M. Dupont / sortir la poubelle à 9h00 // dans la cuisine / nettoyer l'évier
   ____
2. vous   votre sœur / sortir avec ses amis // dans le salon / repasser le linge
   ____
3. M. Dubois   M. Traoré / aller au cinéma // dans la bibliothèque / lire
   ____
4. Mlle Christophe   Mlle Mojon / partir pour le gymnase // dans sa chambre / faire la poussière
   ____
5. Mme Rodier   M. Rodier / balayer le garage pour la première fois // dans le salon / ranger les magazines
   ____
6. Mme Fossier   sa fille / essuyer rapidement la table // dans le garage / faire la lessive
   ____
7. M. Ardan   son fils / rentrer // dans la cuisine / balayer
   ____
8. M. Hassan   sa femme / quitter la résidence // dans la salle de bains / laver la baignoire
   ____

5 **Une aventure** Here is the account of what happened to Cédric during his stay in Yamoussoukro in **Côte d'Ivoire.** Complete his story by conjugating the verbs in parentheses in the **imparfait** or the **passé composé.**

L'été dernier, je/j' (1) ____________ (être) en Côte d'Ivoire. Je/J' (2) ____________ (rendre) visite à mon ami Amadou. Le jour de mon arrivée, je/j' (3) ____________ (passer) sept heures dans l'avion. Comme il (4) ____________ (faire) très chaud à Yamoussoukro, nous (5) ____________ (décider) de visiter la basilique. C'est la plus grande du monde! Ça/C'(6) ____________ (être) formidable. Malheureusement, nous (7) ____________ (ne pas tout visiter) parce que nous (8) ____________ (ne pas avoir) assez de temps. Ensuite, nous (9) ____________ (aller) au café, et puis nous (10) ____________ (rentrer) à la maison.

Nom ______________________ Date ______________________

8B.1 The passé composé vs. the imparfait: Summary (audio activities)

1 **Identifiez** Listen to each statement and identify the verbs in the **imparfait** and the **passé composé**. Write them in the appropriate column.

Modèle

You hear: Quand je suis entrée dans la cuisine, maman faisait la vaisselle.
You write: *suis entrée* under **passé composé** and *faisait* under **imparfait**

	Imparfait	Passé composé
Modèle	faisait	suis entrée
1.		
2.		
3.		
4.		
5.		
6.		
7.		
8.		

2 **Répondez** Answer the questions using cues. Substitute direct object pronouns for the direct object nouns when appropriate. Repeat the correct response after the speaker.

Modèle

You hear: Pourquoi as-tu passé l'aspirateur?
You see: la cuisine / être sale
You say: *Je l'ai passé parce que la cuisine était sale.*

1. avoir des invités
2. pleuvoir
3. être fatigué
4. avoir soif
5. ranger l'appartement
6. faire beau
7. pendant que Myriam / préparer le repas
8. être malade

3 **Vrai ou faux?** Listen as Coralie tells you about her childhood. Then read the statements and decide whether they are **vrai** or **faux**.

	Vrai	Faux
1. Quand elle était petite, Coralie habitait à Paris avec sa famille.	❍	❍
2. Son père était architecte.	❍	❍
3. Coralie a des frères et une sœur.	❍	❍
4. Tous les soirs, Coralie mettait la table.	❍	❍
5. Sa mère sortait le chien après dîner.	❍	❍
6. Un jour, ses parents ont tout vendu.	❍	❍
7. Coralie aime beaucoup habiter près de la mer.	❍	❍

Nom ______________________ Date ______________________

8B.2 The verbs savoir and connaître

1 **Savoir ou connaître?** Describe what these people know using the verbs **savoir** and **connaître**.

1. Il ______________.

2. Il ______________.

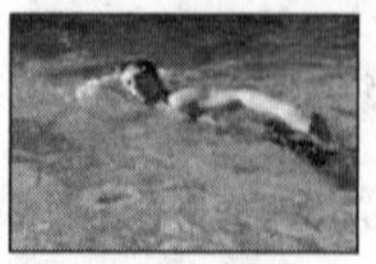

3. Il ______________.

4. Rachid ______________.

5. Elle ______________.

6. Ils ______________.

2 **Choisissez** Complete these sentences using the present tense of **savoir** or **connaître**.

1. Ma mère ______________ où sont les draps.
2. Hassan ______________ quand il faut sortir la poubelle.
3. Je ______________ comment fonctionne le congélateur.
4. Vous ______________ les élèves des autres classes.
5. Ils ______________ comment repasser le linge.
6. Elle ______________ conduire.
7. Tu ______________ le propriétaire de la maison.
8. Nous ______________ bien le quartier et le supermarché.

3 **Écrivez** Write sentences with **savoir** or **connaître** based on the cues provided.

1. Chuyên / mon copain, Marc
____
2. mon frère / conduire
____
3. je / le garage où il gare (*parks*) sa voiture
____
4. Marc / le propriétaire du garage
____
5. le propriétaire du garage / parler français et vietnamien
____
6. Chuyên / le centre franco-vietnamien
____
7. je / nager
____
8. nous / Tûan
____

Nom ______________________ Date ______________________

4 **Mon correspondant** Complete this paragraph by selecting the appropriate verbs in parentheses.

Quand je suis arrivé(e) en France, je (1) ________________ (savais, connaissais) un peu Paris, mais je ne (2) ________________ (savais, connaissais) pas bien parler français et je ne (3) ________________ (savais, connaissais) pas non plus mon correspondant. Je (4) ________________ (savais, connaissais) seulement qu'il était grand et brun et que nous avions le même âge. Les premiers jours, j'ai visité les grands monuments. Mon correspondant (5) ________________ (savait, connaissait) où aller. Je (6) ________________ (savais, connaissais) déjà les monuments, mais je ne (7) ________________ (savais, connaissais) pas qu'il y aurait (*would be*) des centaines de touristes là-bas. Heureusement que mon correspondant était avec moi parce que je ne (8) ________________ (savais, connaissais) pas le quartier et je ne (9) ________________ (savais, connaissais) pas qu'il était difficile de trouver certains endroits. Maintenant, je (10) ________________ (sais, connais) bien Paris et mon correspondant.

5 **Un accident** Séverine and Malika run into their friend, Bénédicte. Complete their conversation with the correct form of the verb **savoir, connaître,** or **reconnaître** in the present, the **imparfait,** or the **passé composé.**

BÉNÉDICTE Est-ce que vous (1) ________________ ce qui s'est passé?

SÉVERINE Non, raconte.

BÉNÉDICTE Eh bien, vous (2) ________________ Yannick, n'est-ce pas?

SÉVERINE Oui, je le/l' (3) ________________ en cours de français l'année dernière. Et toi, Malika, tu le/l' (4) ________________?

MALIKA Non, je ne pense pas.

BÉNÉDICTE Il a eu un accident et il ne (5) ________________ plus personne. Il a perdu la mémoire!

MALIKA Je ne/n' (6) ________________ pas que ça arrivait comme ça.

SÉVERINE Tu (7) ________________ dans quel hôpital il est?

BÉNÉDICTE Oui, mais je ne/n' (8) ________________ pas les heures de visite.

SÉVERINE et MALIKA Appelons l'hôpital.

8B.2 The verbs savoir and connaître (audio activities)

1

Connaître ou savoir You will hear some sentences with a beep in place of the verb. Decide which form of **connaître** or **savoir** should complete each sentence and circle it.

1.	a. sais	b. connais
2.	a. sait	b. connaît
3.	a. savons	b. connaissons
4.	a. connaissent	b. savent
5.	a. connaissez	b. savez
6.	a. connaissons	b. savons

2

Changez Listen to the following statements and say that you do the same activities. Repeat the correct answer after the speaker. (*6 items*)

Modèle

Alexandre sait parler chinois.

Moi aussi, je sais parler chinois.

3

Répondez Answer each question using the cue that you hear. Repeat the correct response after the speaker. (*6 items*)

Modèle

Est-ce que tes parents connaissent tes amis? (oui)

Oui, mes parents connaissent mes amis.

4

Mon amie Listen as Salomé describes her roommate Then read the statements and decide whether they are **vrai** or **faux**.

	Vrai	Faux
1. Salomé a connu Christine au bureau.	❍	❍
2. Christine sait parler russe.	❍	❍
3. Christine sait danser.	❍	❍
4. Salomé connaît maintenant des recettes.	❍	❍
5. Christine sait passer l'aspirateur.	❍	❍
6. Christine ne sait pas repasser.	❍	❍

Nom ______________________ Date ______________________

Unité 8

PANORAMA

Savoir-faire

1 **Photos d'Alsace-Lorraine** Label each photo.

1. ______________________

3. ______________________

2. ______________________

4. ______________________

2 **Dates importantes** Complete these sentences with dates based on **Panorama**.

1. Jeanne d'Arc est née en __________ et a été exécutée en __________.
2. L'Église catholique a canonisé Jeanne d'Arc en __________.
3. Jeanne d'Arc est partie au combat pour libérer la France en __________.
4. Strasbourg est le siège du Conseil de l'Europe depuis __________.
5. Strasbourg est le siège du Parlement européen depuis __________.
6. L'Alsace et le département de la Moselle ont été français pour la première fois en __________.
7. Albert Schweitzer a reçu le prix Nobel de la paix en __________.
8. Les Alsaciens bénéficient des lois sociales allemandes depuis __________.

3 **Un peu d'histoire** Complete these sentences by conjugating the verbs in parentheses in the **imparfait** or the **passé composé.**

En 1429, alors qu'elle (1) ______________ (avoir) 17 ans, Jeanne d'Arc (2) ______________ (décider) de libérer son pays. Elle (3) ______________ (prendre) la tête d'une armée et elle (4) ______________ (libérer) Orléans des Anglais. Plus tard, ses ennemis (5) ______________ (vendre) Jeanne d'Arc aux Anglais. Quand elle (6) ______________ (être) leur prisonnière, ils la/l' (7) ______________ (condamner) à mort pour hérésie.

L'Alsace et la Lorraine (8) ______________ (être) françaises depuis 1678. Elles sont devenues (*became*) allemandes en 1871. Le traité de Versailles (9) ______________ (rendre) les deux régions à la France.

4 **Répondez** Answer these questions in complete sentences.

1. Quelle(s) boisson(s) l'Alsace produit-elle?
2. Quel est le nom du sculpteur de la statue de la Liberté? De quelle région est-il originaire?
3. Quel est le nom de la grande place pittoresque de Nancy?
4. Quelle est la particularité de l'Alsace et du département de la Moselle?
5. Quel est le nom d'un plat typiquement alsacien? De quel mot vient-il?
6. Pourquoi ce plat typiquement alsacien se conserve-t-il longtemps?
7. D'où vient la langue alsacienne?
8. À quoi contribue le Parlement européen?

5 **Vrai ou faux?** Indicate whether these statements are **vrai** or **faux**. Correct the false statements.

1. L'Alsace et la Lorraine sont situées dans le nord-est de la France.
2. Georges de La Tour est un dessinateur du dix-huitième siècle.
3. Patricia Kaas est une chanteuse originaire d'Alsace.
4. L'Alsace et la Lorraine ont été influencées par la culture allemande.
5. La choucroute est cuite avec du gros sel et des baies de genièvre.
6. On mange la choucroute avec de la charcuterie et des pommes de terre.
7. Les membres du Parlement européen sont élus dans chaque pays de l'Union européenne.
8. La langue alsacienne n'est plus parlée aujourd'hui.

Photography and Art Credits
All images © Vista Higher Learning unless otherwise noted.

27 (l) © Hulton-Deutsch Collection/Corbis; (ml) © Eddy Lemaistre/For Picture/Corbis; (mr) © Caroline Penn/Corbis; (r) © Allstar Picture Library/Alamy; **67** Martín Bernetti; **73** (tl) Ventus Pictures; (tm, tr, bl, br) Martín Bernetti; **83** (tl) © Benjamin Herzoq/Fotolia.com; (tm) Tom Delano; (tr) © Keystone Pictures USA/Alamy; (bl) © Jeremy Reddington/Shutterstock.com; (bm) © Images of France/Alamy; (br) © abadesign/Shutterstock.com; **111** (tl) © Christophe Boisvieux/Corbis; (tr) © Daniel Brechwoldt/iStockphoto; (bl) © Leslie Garland Picture Library/Alamy; (br) © Chris Hellier/Corbis; **139** (l) © Bettmann/Corbis; (ml) © Hulton-Deutsch Collection/Corbis; (mr) © Dianne Maire/iStockphoto; (r) © Edyta Pawlowska/iStockphoto; **149** (t) Martín Bernetti; (ml) Pascal Pernix; (mm) © photolibrary.com/Index Open; (mr) © Larry Lilac/Alamy; (bm) © Tetra Images/Alamy; **168** (tl) © Mikhail Lavrenov/123RF; (tr) © Philip Lange/iStockphoto; (bl) © Bettmann/Corbis; (br) © Peter Leyden/iStockphoto; **181** (tr) © Ingram Publishing/Photolibrary; (bl) © Greg Vote/2005 VStock L LC; (bml) © Tetra Images/Alamy; **195** (tl) © Andreas Karelias/iStockphoto; (tm) © Larry Dale Gordon/zefa/Corbis; (tr) © John Schults/Reuters/Corbis; (bl) © Beyond Fotomedia GmbH/Alamy; (bm) © Tom Brakefield/Corbis; (br) © Ferdericb/Dreamstime.com; **223** (tl) © Bettmann/Corbis; (tr) *Entry of Joan of Arc Into Orleans* by J.J. Scherrer. Photo credit: © Gianni Dagli Orti/Corbis; (bl) © Chromacome/Stockbyte/Getty Images; (br) © Bogdan Lazar/iStockphoto.